Forensic Focus 18

VIOLENCE

*Reflections on
Our Deadliest Epidemic*

JAMES GILLIGAN, M.D.

Jessica Kingsley Publishers
London

Excerpt from Life Sentences: Rage and Survival Behind Bars by Wilbert Rideau
and Ron Wikberg, © Wilbert Rideau and Ron Wikberg, published in 1992 by Times
Books, a division of Random House, Inc.

The right of James Gilligan to be identified as author of this work has been asserted by
him in accordance with the Copyright, Designs and Patents Act 1988.

First published in the United States in 1996 by G.P. Putnam's Sons, New York.

This edition published in the United Kingdom in 2000 by
Jessica Kingsley Publishers Ltd
116 Pentonville Road,
London N1 9JB, England
and
325 Chestnut Street,
Philadelphia, PA19106, USA

www.jkp.com

Copyright © 2000 James Gilligan

Library of Congress Cataloging in Publication Data
A CIP catalog record for this book is available from the Library of Congress

British Library Cataloguing in Publication Data
A CIP catalogue record for this book is available from the British Library

ISBN 1 85302 842 8

Printed and Bound in Great Britain by
Athenaeum Press, Gateshead, Tyne and Wear

C O N T E N T S

Prologue: Violence as Tragedy   1

PART I
THE PATHOLOGY OF VIOLENCE

CHAPTER 1   Visits to Hell: Entering the World
             of the Prison   29

CHAPTER 2   Dead Souls   45

CHAPTER 3   Violent Action as Symbolic Language:
             Myth, Ritual, and Tragedy   57

PART II
THE "GERM THEORY" OF VIOLENCE

CHAPTER 4   How to Think About Violence   89

CHAPTER 5   Shame: The Emotions and Morality
             of Violence   103

PART III
THE EPIDEMIOLOGY OF VIOLENCE

CHAPTER 6   The Symbolism of Punishment   139

CHAPTER 7   How to Increase the Rate of Violence—and
             Why   163

C O N T E N T S

CHAPTER 8   The Deadliest Form of Violence
Is Poverty   191

CHAPTER 9   The Biology of Violence   209

CHAPTER 10   Culture, Gender, and Violence:
"We Are Not Women"   225

Epilogue   Civilization and Its Malcontents   241

Notes   269

Acknowledgments   295

Index   299

To all the victims of violence:
past, present, and future

The invention of nuclear weapons has changed everything—except the way we think. . . . We shall require a substantially new manner of thinking if mankind is to survive.

—ALBERT EINSTEIN

War, to sane men at the present day, begins to look like an epidemic insanity, breaking out here and there like the cholera or influenza, infecting men's brains instead of their bowels.

—RALPH WALDO EMERSON, *MISCELLANIES* (1884)

When a man is suffering from an infectious disease, he is a danger to the community, and it is necessary to restrict his liberty of movement. But no one associates any idea of guilt with such a situation. On the contrary, he is an object of commiseration to his friends. Such steps as science recommends are taken to cure him of his disease, and he submits as a rule without reluctance to the curtailment of liberty involved meanwhile. The same method in spirit ought to be shown in the treatment of what is called "crime."

—BERTRAND RUSSELL, *ROADS TO FREEDOM* (1918)

Violence is every bit as much a public health issue for me and my successors in this century as smallpox, tuberculosis, and syphilis were for my predecessors in the last two centuries.

—C. EVERETT KOOP, M.D.,
SURGEON GENERAL OF THE UNITED STATES *(1984)*

The deadliest form of violence is poverty.

—GANDHI

Of human beings: "None are good but all are sacred."

—GLENN TINDER, *THE POLITICAL MEANING OF CHRISTIANITY: AN INTERPRETATION* (1989)

I have set before you life and death, blessing and curse; therefore choose life.

—DEUTERONOMY 30:19

P R O L O G U E

Violence as

Tragedy

THE LAND OUT THERE IS SO VAST AND FLAT YOU COULD SEE THEM COMING all day, visible first as a single black speck suddenly appearing over the horizon, then differentiating into three figures silhouetted against the gunmetal-gray sky: Man, woman, and child slowly making their way, like ants crossing the Sahara, over the immense unbroken Nebraska/Dakota plain called for good reason the Badlands. No markers to orient them, no boundaries to limit their wandering—nothing visible but grass and sky. A land before time and outside law—on they came across that millennial dreamscape, that ancient sandy sea bottom for a hundred million years that was still an ocean extending uninterrupted across the continent from the Rocky Mountains to the Alleghenies. Its boundless sandy floor was now covered by grass, not water, and they were adrift in the middle of that sea of grass until they spotted the first sign of human life—a thin spiral of smoke drifting tentatively toward the empty heavens from the ranchhouse, like a signal of distress sent up without much hope of rescue. A wisp of smoke curling like a question mark into the void where the only surprise would be getting an answer back, as if

1

marooned, shipwrecked sailors had tossed a message in a bottle into the ocean without really expecting anyone to find it and then discover to their astonishment and chagrin that the only people who found it were just as lost and shipwrecked as they: a bearded French-Canadian fur trapper, his squaw from one of the tribes he had traded with, and their fourteen-year-old daughter who was forever after known not by her name but simply as the halfbreed. When they got there, they were fed and offered a bed for the night, as all travelers have been since the time of Odysseus, by the rancher. He was an immigrant who had not fled Ireland, that mockery of Eden, simply to starve in another famine. So his life was consumed by the battle of turning a continent of unwilling, unwelcoming sandy soil into a working ranch, figuring that if that sparse grass could support the tidal wave of buffalo who still flowed across the open prairie when he first arrived—covering it as the Milky Way blankets the night sky—then it could now feed as many beef cattle as he could breed in a lifetime of struggle, not so much with the cattle themselves as with the ragtag band of hired hands who only worked because he dominated them with his fists—a war against man and God so all-absorbing that it had simply not occurred to him yet to take a wife and start a family. But when the halfbreed arrived, he remembered what he had forgotten, and whenever he did make up his mind to do something he was too impatient to wait any longer than it took to get the thing done. So the next morning the furtrapper and his squaw went on their way over the opposite horizon leaving their daughter behind to be the Irish rancher's wife and bear his children—no family, no friends, no tribe—and over the years they had a child every year. But one—a five-year-old son—was her favorite, the child she cherished over everyone else on that unfriendly godforsaken earth.

"Perhaps love (is anything more dangerous?) is the mother of tragedy," the boy thought when he heard this story two generations later, *"love in an unloving world of pain, loneliness and confusion."*

———

For the rancher only knew how to talk with his fists, even with his children. And the halfbreed did not know how to protect her favorite child except with threats, warning the rancher that if he hit him again he would regret it to the end of his life. But he hit him again, anyway, and then the son disappeared and so did the sun as far as the mother was concerned. But the Irishman who never stopped fighting was frantic with grief, so he organized his band of wildmen into search parties, even sending one of them to fetch his only relative, a doctor who lived in the nearest town three counties away. When the son was found, he was at the bottom of a well, so they thought at first he had fallen in and drowned. But the rancher's relative the doctor saw at once that the youngster had been dead before he arrived at the bottom of the well, there being no water in his lungs. A half-eaten pie in the kitchen was full of rat poison, as was the dead son's body when they thought to examine that, too. So had the halfbreed poisoned her own son? But before a sheriff could be summoned to question her, she too disappeared—vanished as completely as her son had, as her own parents had when they left her alone on the ranch, and were never seen or heard from again. It is not known to this day what happened to her, whether she simply ran away or (as seems more likely given how mothers from time immemorial have behaved after sacrificing their children) had she followed one death with another, this time by walking into the nearby river from which her body might never surface. The third and equal possibility was that the rancher had killed her himself, so maybe no one will ever know what happened to her.

"Or is too much already known about what happened to her," the boy wondered, *"more than anyone wants to know or think about, since even if they can see why she did what she did they still don't know what to do about it?"*

———

This is the story as the boy, the doctor's grandson, saw it in his mind's eye, when as a child he overheard the adults talking after dinner in front of the fireplace, describing events to each other that they considered unsuitable to tell a child even half a century after the events had occurred (especially to one who was his own mother's favorite son). I know this story. I am the doctor's grandson. This is a family story.

Listening to these endless tellings and retellings of family tragedies, one can hear the interminable reworking of disasters too painful to let go, yet too scandalous to acknowledge. So generation after generation tells the same story over and over again, in hushed tones, with this variation or that of one detail or another, but always with the same horrifying denouement. Why keep telling the story? In the effort to make sense of a "senseless" tragedy? To follow the old formula and see if there might finally be a catharsis of the pity and fear this story arouses? To reach the end of a collective mourning for a lost mother and child and the amputated family they left behind? In the hope that in the latest retelling the story will, by some magic, end differently, that the act of telling and retelling might undo the past and make it not have happened? Or in the hope that even if the story does remain the same, the process of telling it might change what happened from reality to fiction, to "nothing but" a story, a "myth"? But, of course, that never occurs, since nothing reflects reality more pitilessly and relentlessly than so-called myth and fiction. So our stories go on and on, as they have since we humans first began sitting around fires, in caves, acquiring the language with which to tell our stories. For it is in telling stories that we originally acquired our humanness; and we are not so much rational animals, as Aristotle said, or tool-making ones, as Benjamin Franklin[1] put it, but first and foremost story-telling ones.

———

I have chosen to begin with a story I know—and know deeply—in part, because this family story raises so many of the issues I will be discussing in this book: the themes of family violence; of relations between different nations and races; women and men, young and old; questions about justice and morality, crime and punishment, guilt and innocence, shame and pride, victims and perpetrators, and—overshadowing all these themes—the sheer human tragedy that violence always is.

For a psychiatrist to begin a book on violence by telling a story of violence from his own family's history is to say, as plainly as I can, that violence, like charity, begins at home. The use of violence as a means of resolving conflict between persons, groups, and nations is a strategy we learn first at home. All of our basic problem-solving, problem-exacerbating, and problem-creating strategies, for living and dying, are learned first at home.

The more I learn about other peoples' lives, the more I realize that I have yet to hear the history of any family in which there has not been at least one family member who has been overtaken by fatal or life-threatening violence, as the perpetrator or the victim—whether the violence takes the form of suicide or homicide, death in combat, death from a drunken or reckless driver, or any other of the many nonnatural forms of death.

Human violence is much more complicated, ambiguous and, most of all, tragic, than is commonly realized or acknowledged. Much of what has been written about violence, even by those experts who study it—criminologists, criminal lawyers, forensic psychiatrists, moral philosophers, political scientists, and historians—comes only from the point of view of their own specialties, which tend to preclude the tragic dimensions of violence. But those who deal with individual violence on a daily basis, judges and lawyers, criminologists and forensic psychiatrists, law-enforcement professionals and prison administrators, are fully aware of how tragic violence is, not only for the victims but also for the perpetrators. Yet the conventions of professional discourse leave little room for the articulation of the tragic point of view, even for those who see the phenomenon itself most clearly.

If we limit ourselves to the mode of discourse of the criminal legal process in the courtroom, only two questions about violence are admissible: how to distinguish the innocent from the guilty (the "good guys" from the "bad guys"); and the guilty from the criminally insane (the "bad guys" from the "mad guys"). The problem with this discourse is that it limits our capacity both to understand violence and to prevent it. This moral, legal framework, which is the existing arena of jurisprudence, judgment, and punishment, often leads to the aggravation of violence and its perpetuation, rather than deterring it. And perhaps no one realizes this more clearly than those very judges and lawyers whose thinking about the problem of violence is confined by necessity to the narrow and limited range of conventional legal discourse.

After spending much of my professional career working with violent offenders and with the judges, lawyers, and correctional professionals who are called upon to deal with them, I have come to see the necessity of bringing the discussion of violence into the interpretive arena of tragedy, in the realization that just as tragic drama is always violent, violence itself is always tragic. But what does it mean for a psychiatrist to begin a serious psychoanalytic study of violence by using the human category of tragedy as an interpretive framework for understanding violence? What do I mean by "tragedy"?

First, I distinguish it from pathos, those natural disasters or "acts of Nature"—sometimes called "acts of God"—over which we have no human agency or control. When faced with the great malignancies of fate, our only range of choice may be the manner in which we respond. Are we tempted to despair? Can we mobilize the courage to go on? What are the limits of our strength to endure the unendurable? It is in the effort we each make to find our own answers to such painful questions that we still read such ancient sources as the Book of Job, which deals with the undeniable fact that life is inherently, inescapably, unfair. Job teaches that it is not only futile to expect life to be just or fair, it is absurd and meaningless even to think about it in that way. The rain falls on the just and the unjust alike; bad things—terrible things—happen to good people. The language and lessons of pathos have their place in our lives.

And some people are victims of violence purely by accident, or because of circumstances which they did not cause, could not have foreseen or prevented, and cannot by any reasonable criterion be held responsible for. If we think in terms of the victim alone—such as the child who was beaten by his father and poisoned by his mother, as in the family story I recounted—would such a victim's suffering and death best be described in terms of pathos? I think not, because there is a major difference between pathos and tragedy. Because of that difference, violence—even for the wholly "innocent" victim—cannot be reduced to pathos. For the tragedy of violence involves not just victims, but also victimizers. What we need to see—if we are to understand violence and to prevent it—is that human agency or action is not only individual; it is also, unavoidably, familial, societal, and institutional. Each of us is inextricably bound to others—in relationship. All human action (even the act of a single individual) is relational. Understanding that point is essential to understanding the origins of violent acts, and the strategies that might be helpful in preventing them. The whole story of violence includes, inescapably, the lives of the victimizers, and the moment we realize that, we are in the territory of tragedy.

To approach the study of violence as the study of tragedy is to see that tragic dramas are all about violence; that violence is what they have been re-enacting and embodying, meditating and pondering· on, and eliciting grief and compassion about, from the time they first evolved from religious rituals two and a half millennia ago.

A morality play, by contrast, differs from both pathos and tragedy.

Morality plays reduce the question to that of "innocence" versus "guilt" (the "good guys" vs. the "bad guys"). This is a simplification of human complexity into the ready moral categories of "good" and "bad." These three modes, pathos, tragedy, and morality play, appear at different times in our discussion, as attitudes toward violence and as ways to approach solutions.

When I was first subpoenaed into court to testify as a psychiatric "expert witness" as to what the mental state of the violent men I was treating had been at the time they committed their acts of illegal violence, it was clear that the principal purpose of the criminal trial was to distinguish the innocent from the guilty and the guilty from the "insane," those found not guilty of a criminal act by reason of "insanity," meaning that they were mentally incapable of forming a criminal intent. My role was to assist the court in deciding if a particular defendant belonged in the latter group. There were days when I felt that participating in the criminal trial process was tantamount to being in the midst of a morality play or in the dramatic realm of pathos. Of course the work of the legal system was necessary, and the role of psychiatry integral to that process, but to judge someone "guilty" requires the judge to make the moral value judgment that the defendant has an "evil mind," a *mens rea*. And this does not help us to understand the defendant psychologically; it does not help us to understand the *cause* of a violent act—nor is it intended to.

A similar point could be made about the legal concept of "insanity." If our goal is to attain a psychological understanding of the causes of a violent person's behavior, all that the legal concept of "insanity" does is effectively to reduce the violent person to a status of (non)personhood incapable of moral, "personal" judgment and responsibility. In effect, an "insane" person in the legal arena amounts to a passive victim of brain disease, whose behavior is beyond his control and is therefore essentially meaningless, unintelligible, senseless, and incomprehensible.

Neither distinction leads to a psychological understanding of the meaning of a violent act—that is, its cause—to the person who committed it.

Given the degree to which our society (and our legal system) is
confined in its thinking about violence to the two alternative interpretive frames of the morality play and of pathos, we have tended as a
society to respond to the violence that surrounds us with a mixture of
fatalism, apathy, frustration, and punitiveness. Limited by these ways of
thinking about violence, our societal response has been focused on
punishing violent offenders after the violence has happened—or to hos-
pitalizing those who have committed acts of violence after their illness
has brought about someone else's death.

But even the most apparently "insane" violence has a rational meaning to the person who commits it, and to prevent this violence, we need
to learn to understand what that meaning is. And even the most apparently rational, self-interested, selfish, or "evil" violence is caused by
motives that are utterly irrational and ultimately self-destructive. We
cannot prevent this violence, either, until we can recognize what those
motives are. Psychoanalytically, all behavior, including violent behavior,
whether it is labeled as "bad" or "mad," is psychologically meaningful.
But until it is understood, it cannot be prevented—that is, brought
under individual and societal self-control. The psychological understanding of violence requires recognizing how much method there is in
violent madness, and how much psychopathology there is in the violence of everyday life. But such a psychological understanding requires
that we see violence as tragedy.

And in the legend from my own family, it seems clear that the mother's
motive was not to do something evil; rather, it was to do something
good, namely to protect the son from his father's violence. The detail
that is unclear is how she intended to do this. The poison, for example,
could have been intended for the father, in which case the son's being
killed by it accidentally would have been an even more horrifying

tragedy, from the point of view of both the mother and the son. But in either case, the ultimate purpose of her behavior would have been to attain a goal that she saw as morally good and even morally obligatory.

And if she died, too—and I say if, because I will never know—then she, too, was a victim, whether of herself, her husband, or both. But this is where words fail us, and I feel we virtually need to invent a new language with which to talk about violence. For to speak of both the parents and the son as "victims" is to use one word to refer to three quite different realities, because the sense in which they were each victims is so different and the context and meanings of their respective "victimizations" was so different.

For example, weren't both of this child's parents also victims of multiple injuries? For the mother, of the racial stereotypes and prejudices that led to her having been deprived of the common dignity of being known as a person, by being referred to by means of a demeaning label, "the halfbreed," which was not even an accurate label since it only acknowledged one half of her parentage. She was not a "halfbreed": She was, like everyone else, "whole bred," a whole human being. And did she not also suffer the injury of being uprooted from a culture, a family, and a community? Had not her own mother's people and their traditional way of life been so uprooted, overwhelmed, and disintegrated by the European invasion of America that it might better be described as a dying culture whose population itself was dying? Would it be so surprising, then, if in the midst of that pain the mother would have held on desperately to one rule from her mother's people that was still capable of giving moral structure to her life: that the beating of a child is unthinkable? What then would have been the pain of seeing her favorite child beaten repeatedly, feeling that she was powerless to prevent this violence—except by the drastic, destructive, and self-destructive means to which she finally resorted in desperation?

But wasn't the rancher a victim also? He had barely escaped from a mass disaster that ranks among the worst in modern history, the Irish famine, making his way as "a stranger in a strange land," armed with no money, little education, and only his two fists, surrounded by men as desperate as he. That he lacked gentleness was perhaps neither the most surprising nor the most reprehensible quality about him; could he have survived otherwise? Even if we could answer yes to that question, the fact remains that he may not have known that he could have survived if he had been more gentle and patient. In fact, he may well have seen his whole life as an attempt to reach the point where he could finally support a family and start a new life, in which case it would be no exaggeration to say that he was also fighting for his life, and that of his family.

The inadequacy of reducing violence to the level of the morality play becomes apparent the moment we begin to ask such questions as, Who was to blame for the death of the son? Who should have been punished for it? Was the father not as guilty as the mother? Was not his battering of the child just as lethal as the mother's act, since she presumably would not have done what she did if he had not done what he did?

From the tragic point of view, all violence is tragic—in fact it is more tragic, the more inescapable and necessary it appears to be. The most tragic of dilemmas is to be forced (as the "halfbreed" saw herself) into the choice between committing one form of violence (physical murder) in order to prevent another form of it (soul murder), versus acquiescing passively in the other form of violence (letting her child be beaten) and thus permitting it to occur.

The first lesson that tragedy teaches (and that morality plays miss) is that *all violence is an attempt to achieve justice,* or what the violent person perceives as justice, for himself or for whomever it is on whose behalf he is being violent, so as to receive whatever retribution or compensation the violent person feels is "due" him or "owed" to him, or to those on whose behalf he is acting, whatever he or they are "entitled" to or have a "right" to; or so as to prevent those whom one loves or identi-

fies with from being subjected to injustice. Thus, *the attempt to achieve
and maintain justice, or to undo or prevent injustice, is the one and only
universal cause of violence.*

My father's father was the doctor in the family myth recounted above,
and since he was also the mayor of his town and then became a state
senator as well, he divided much of his time between the pursuit of
justice, and the attempt to heal or prevent the injuries caused by other
people who were also pursuing justice. And since he was there when
there was little of what we would call "civilization" (the culture of
cities), the institutions supporting what we equally hopefully call "justice" and "law" were still in the process of being formed. The history of
his time, like most history at most times, was largely a history of violence and the pursuit of justice, and specifically, of the violence that is
caused by the pursuit of justice.

My father grew up in a world shaped by physical violence. Following
the death of the child and the disappearance of the "halfbreed," the
surviving children came to live with my grandparents, so my father and
his siblings grew up with the surviving siblings of a son who, according
to family legend, had been beaten by his own father and then killed by
his own mother.

My grandmother never spoke to me of this family tragedy, but she
did read to me from the tragedies of Shakespeare, giving me a language
and a way to think about these things. My grandmother was a remarkable woman. Before she married my grandfather, she worked as a re-
porter on the local newspaper. Some of her pioneering spirit is captured
in the family story that accounts for what she did after my grandfather
was expelled from the Roman Catholic church. My grandfather, a man
of science, was at odds with the priest in a small town of Irish Catholic
immigrants that was not large enough for two patriarchs. Grandmother,
the only non-Catholic in town, decided to convert an old barn into a

mission church, which the townspeople promptly christened "Mrs. Gilligan's Church." There she raised my father and his siblings in her own Scottish Anglican faith. From time to time, Bishop Beecher, the Episcopal bishop for several western states, would come riding in on his horse over the prairies to confirm the faithful in this small but devoted congregation. Grandmother knew Bishop Beecher well. A man of strong character, he would later become the model for the bishop in Willa Cather's *Death Comes for the Archbishop*.

Church or no church, and regardless of what was taught on Sundays, violence had been so pervasive a part of the atmosphere in which my father grew up that it may come as no surprise that some of my earliest memories are of violence at home. My father, like his father, was a surgeon, and an extremely conscientious one whose extraordinary dedication to his patients was something I always admired about him; it was that side of his character that inspired me to go into medicine myself. But there was another side to his character as well. My father was given to violent outbursts of temper, especially when he felt my two brothers needed discipline.

On one occasion, when I could not have been much older than five or six, my father struck my older brother—who was five years older than I—so hard that he was hurled across a good-sized living room into a table, knocking it over and breaking the lamp that had stood on it. I remember being terrified that my father might accidentally kill my brother, that if my brother's head had hit the door jamb in the wrong way he might have fractured his skull. It was a violent scene: I remember the tears, my mother trying to restrain my father, my father's rage, my brother's fear, and the injuries that became the unspeakable secrets we were never to utter.

Why could my mother not keep my father from hitting my brothers? Why didn't she leave him and take us, her children, with her? That was, of course, the question I later asked about the "halfbreed." It is also the complicated question being asked today about so many women who live with violent men, although the question itself is complicated by the fact that it is often in the act of leaving that these women and their children are most at risk.

Later in life, I heard more of my family story. I learned that my mother did leave my father. When she was pregnant with my older brother, apparently my father struck her because he was so angered by the fact that my mother had gone on an outing for an hour or two with a woman friend, instead of staying at home to answer the phone in case any of his patients were trying to reach him. My mother responded to my father's violence by leaving him, returning to her own family to live with one of her sisters. It was only after he promised never to hit her again that she agreed to return. And, as far as I know, my father kept his word.

But when it came to my brothers, my father's word did not apply. During the Second World War, while all my father's partners were away in the Medical Corps, my father was the only physician in town, seeing as many as a hundred patients a day, working to the point of exhaustion. I remember one Fourth of July, when I was about eight, my older brother, who was thirteen, experimented with a firecracker, putting it in the keyhole of a bedroom door. When he lit it, to his surprise, the firecracker damaged the keyhole so badly that it was going to have to be replaced. My father did not return home from the hospital until several hours after my brother had gone to sleep. When my father saw what my brother had done, he lost his temper, took off his belt, pulled back the sheets on my brother's bed, and started lashing him with the belt. My brother, who had been sound asleep, awoke in terror. By the time my mother could restrain my father, my brother's back and buttocks were covered with bruises and welts.

My mother was a woman of artistic sensibilities, devoted to her children and their education, but she had no financial resources of her own. She had no career or paid work. She had left college without a degree to marry my father, and had no parents who could take her in. Like many women of her generation and class, she saw herself as having no reasonable or realistic means of supporting her children on her own, or of providing for them in the way that my father could. It is a story, of course, known to many mothers and children caught in the web of domestic violence. My father was caught in a cycle of generations of violence that played itself out in our family as it had, indeed, in the very land on which we were living, a land purchased with the blood of the natives whom we displaced. The violence in my family was only a smaller version of the violence that is writ large across the whole landscape of American history. This is why I think the microcosm of any one family's violence can only be understood fully when it is seen as part of the macrocosm, the culture and history of violence, in which it occurs.

Probably no American novel speaks more powerfully to the tragic flaw of violence in the American character than does Herman Melville's masterpiece, *Moby-Dick*. In the novel, Captain Ahab, who embodies the purest, most extreme example of one strain in our national character, becomes convinced that Moby-Dick, the great white whale, is the embodiment of evil. Ahab pursues Moby-Dick in the mad conviction that if only he can find him and kill him, he will have attained justice and destroyed evil. The voyage of Ahab and his men, aboard the *Pequod,* is the story of that tragic quest which ends in the destruction of Ahab and his entire crew, except for Ishmael; it is he alone who returns to bear witness.

Perhaps in every family where there is violence, there is an Ishmael, the bearer of the tale, the one who tells the story. I write not because my background is unique or extraordinary, but because it is not. Like many in this country, I am "typical" of someone who grew up in the American West, less than a hundred years after the frontier. In the attic of the house I grew up in, the oldest of my grandmother's family photographs is an old tintype dating from the 1830s or '40s of a very old man dressed in fringed buckskin leggings and a coonskin cap, grasping a musket and glaring fiercely into the camera. His name was John Colvin, and I was told he had been one of Daniel Boone's scouts as a young man. Staring back into this man's eyes, I could not help but think that I was surely looking into the eyes of an Indian-killer. No American family can be untouched by the moral and tragic dilemmas that run like a blood-stained thread through the whole tapestry of our national—and, indeed, our human—heritage.

In the same attic there is a detailed drawing, a long "epic" poem, and a scale model made of matchsticks and glue, all recalling Andersonville, the notorious Confederate prisoner-of-war camp known today as the spiritual prototype and forerunner of the German concentration camps of the following century, in which Yankee soldiers died like flies under appalling conditions. Two of my great-grandfathers were imprisoned there, and were among the few who survived physically; their continuing attempts to survive mentally as well were memorialized in the surviving artifacts in our attic.

Since I was a child, I have tried to make sense of the stories I heard and the things I saw. Did the "halfbreed" deliberately kill her son? Or was the poisoned pie intended for the rancher? Why did my father beat my mother and my brothers? Why was I spared? Why did the settlers kill the Indians? What did it mean to grow up on a new land so vast, so fertile and beautiful in parts, so desolate and awe-inspiring in others, where everywhere there were reminders, remnants, of my ancestors' massacre of the natives from whom we seized the land? What does it mean, I ask myself, to be the "carrier," the bearer, of all these tales? Why am I the family Ishmael? Was it because I was not beaten by my father? And was that because he thought I was my mother's favorite son, and my father knew the story of the rancher and his wife's favorite son—not so much as a cautionary tale but as a deeply tragic and traumatic story that may have stayed his hand against me at the same time that it forced him to tempt fate by striking my brothers?

All this violence—against the son, against the native peoples of this land, against my brothers—was part of a larger pattern—that statistically, most lethal violence is committed by men against other men.[2] Violence is primarily men's work; it is carried out more frequently against men; and it is about the maintenance of "manhood." To say that is not to minimize men's violence against women; it is, rather, to take the first step toward understanding the etiology of all violence, against both men and women. When a woman is beaten or killed by a man, the result is a tragedy, not a statistic; and it is no less tragic merely because it is far less frequent than the beatings and killings to which men subject other men (and themselves, as in suicide). The role of women has often been that of trying to restrain all this violence of males against males (although in the case of the "halfbreed," her desperation, and despair, reached the point where it provoked her to engage in violence of her own—although even with her the target of her violence was male, whether it was intended for the son or his father). All of this raises a larger question, which I think goes to the heart of most of the lethal and life-threatening violence that is committed on this earth: for most of that violence, in every nation, every culture, and every continent in which it has been studied, and in every period of history, has always been violence by men against other men. I did not know these facts about violence as a child, of course.

Any realistic notion of tragic drama must start from the fact of catastrophe. Tragedies end badly. The tragic personage is broken . . . Tragedy is irreparable. It cannot lead to just and material compensation for past suffering.

—GEORGE STEINER, THE DEATH OF TRAGEDY[3]

I work as a psychiatrist. My approach to the problem of violent behavior is bio-medical, or to be more precise, bio-psycho-social: I view violence as a problem in public health and preventive and social psychiatry. My purpose is to arrive at an understanding of the causes of the various forms of violent behavior, in the hope that understanding will help to clarify how we can most effectively and efficiently prevent such behavior. In arriving at that understanding, however, I have been led by my experience in working with violent men to question and even reject many assumptions that I, at least, had been taught and simply taken for granted about the psychology of violent behavior. I am aware that my repudiation of certain commonly held assumptions about the psychology of violent behavior might at first seem to subvert conventional notions of law and morality. But I believe that the insights and points of view expressed here can help to accomplish the goals of our legal system, and of the most widely agreed upon moral value systems, far more effectively than some of the more conventional moral and legal beliefs we now hold. For example, the point of the most basic moral commandments, such as "Thou shalt not kill," and of criminal laws declaring murder to be a crime and setting penalties for it, is to deter people from killing each other (or for that matter, from killing themselves); thus, any insight into the motives that cause people to kill others and themselves can help us to advance the goals of law and morality. In order to arrive at a position from which we can improve our ability to attain those goals, we will first have to question and perhaps even reject some of the assumptions that may seem to be essential parts of the foundations of law and morality—such as the notion that the solution to the problem of violence is to teach violent people (called "criminals") to "learn the difference between right and wrong."

When I speak of the motives that cause people to pursue justice by means of revenge, punishment, and violence, I am not speaking exclusively about the motives that underlie the traditional criminal justice and penal systems. I am speaking also of the motives that give rise to criminal violence itself—that is to say, the motives that cause those whom we have come to think of as "criminals" to commit their acts of violence, in the hope of attaining justice by punishing those whom they feel have punished them, unjustly. In other words, the motives and goals that underlie crime are the same as those that underlie punishment—namely, the pursuit of what the violent person considers "justice." What is conventionally called "crime" is the kind of violence that the legal system calls illegal, and "punishment" is the kind that it calls

legal. But the motives and the goals that underlie both are identical—
they both aim to attain justice or revenge for past injuries and injustices. Crime and punishment are conventionally spoken of as if they
were opposites, yet both are committed in the name of morality and
justice, and both use violence as the means by which to attain those
ends. So not only are their ends identical, so are their means.

It is for this reason that I approach violence as a medical, biological
problem. For what I mean by "violence" is the creation of a medical
problem, namely, the infliction of physical injury on a person by a
person, especially lethal injury, but also including those injuries that are
serious enough to be life-threatening, mutilating, or disabling. From
that standpoint, we would see violence as a problem in public health
and preventive medicine, including social and preventive psychiatry;
and finally, as a problem in evolutionary biology, since the ultimate
question with respect to human violence is: Will we be the first species
to render ourselves extinct (victims of our own tragedy), rather than
simply being the passive victims of natural processes beyond our control (pathos)? That approach to violence would lead us to ask more
modest (and perhaps more answerable) questions about violence,
rather than the metaphysical ones generated by the moral point of view.

If we want to gain the knowledge we need in order to achieve the
age-old dream of learning how to prevent violence, I am suggesting that
instead of asking the unanswerable moral and legal question, "How
should we live?" it would be more productive of knowledge to ask an
empirical question instead: namely, "How can we live?" That is, what
biological, psychological, and social forces and processes protect, sustain, and preserve life, and which ones lead to death (and under what
circumstances)? Not "How can we attain justice?" or "What is good and
evil, moral and immoral, just and unjust?" but rather, "What are the
causes of homicide and suicide and assault; how do they vary from one
context to another; and how can we use that knowledge to reduce the
frequency with which people inflict those kinds of injuries on themselves and others?"—questions that can be answered, because they can

be investigated, and their answers can be tested, empirically. Not "How much pain and anguish does this criminal or war-criminal 'deserve' as his punishment?" but "How can we help these violent offenders to survive, without further violence, when they are drowning in their own self-righteous hate and despair, feeling justified in exterminating others, and feeling that they have to take others down with them?"

In my own life, as I grew older and became familiar with some of the great collective myths of family life, I wondered at first if the unfortunate mother referred to as the "halfbreed" was not another Medea; like the latter, the "halfbreed," too, was seen as a "barbarian" by the (none too civilized) people among whom she had come to live, and was isolated from her parental home and her native culture. Did the "halfbreed's" murderous act, in analogy to Medea's, express and discharge in a final, fatal catharsis her hopeless, impotent rage at her son's father, by displacing that fury onto their son, hurting the father in the only place where he too might be vulnerable beneath his mask of machismo, and thus finally succeeding in getting him to listen, to hear, to feel the pain she herself had felt over the outrages to which he repeatedly exposed their son?

I think not. I think the story of *Beloved* is actually a closer, more faithful rendering into literature of events that had occurred in my own family. It seems to me that just as in Toni Morrison's great novel, Sethe kills her daughter to prevent her from being taken into slavery, so the halfbreed had killed her own best-beloved child not out of hatred for him, nor simply out of hatred displaced from his father, but out of despairing love: as a desperate means—the only means she saw as available to her—to protect her son from the violence of his father by ending it once and for all with ultimate violence of her own—by killing the child's body before his spirit died as well.

But if I am saying that we can best understand violence if we approach it from the point of view of tragic drama, then how can I also be suggesting that we can best understand violence if we conceptualize it in psychiatric and psychoanalytic terms—which is the set of terms in which I will cast the theory of violence in this book? What can an approach that has one leg in medicine and the other in the human sciences have in common with tragic drama?

I can only answer that by expressing two viewpoints that are basic to this book: the psychoanalytic view of violence, and the tragic view of psychoanalysis. For psychoanalysis, in my view, is the transfer or application of the tragic point of view from the stage and the library to the consulting room and, for that matter, to the living room and the bedroom—to what Freud called "the psychopathology of everyday life" (and to what we might in this context call the violence of everyday life).

The reason I see psychoanalysis as compatible with tragedy is because the core of the process by which analysis attempts to fulfill the oracle's ancient commandment to "Know thyself" consists of coming to see oneself as the tragic protagonist of one's own life. That, in turn, means coming to recognize the extent to which one's character is one's fate; and vice versa—that, to a greater extent than one realized, one's fate is being determined by one's character, rather than by outside forces over which one has no control. Of course it is true that one's fate is never completely determined by one's character, since one is also always subjected to forces over which one has no control. Those forces constitute the range of problems that are not amenable to being solved by self-knowledge, though some of them might be solvable by other means, such as medical research or political action.

The tragic sense of life carries with it the awareness that there is no guarantee as to how far any given society will succeed in transcending moralism and thus preventing violence. I say *will* succeed, not *can*. For it is really quite clear that we can prevent violence, and it is also clear how we can do so, if we want to. For example, the enormous differences between different societies around the earth in their rates of both individual violence and of collective violence constitute repeated empirical demonstrations that violence can be prevented; in the less violent cultures (for example, every other democracy and every other economically developed nation on earth, outside of the United States), it is already being prevented. And my own work over the past twenty-five years, in violence-prevention programs with the most violent homicidal and suicidal men that our own unusually violent American society produces—the inmates of our maximum-security prisons and mental hospitals—has convinced me that it is possible to eliminate most of the violence that now plagues us if we really want to.

I am far from alone in reaching the conclusion that violence prevention is being limited more by lack of will than by lack of know-how. Elliott Currie,[4] in one of the best American studies of criminal violence that has yet been written, also concludes that

> It is not lack of knowledge or technical prowess that keeps us from launching an honest and serious fight against crime; the obstacles are much more . . . ideological and political. What seem on the surface to be technical arguments about what we can and cannot do about crime . . . turn out, on closer inspection, to be moral or political arguments about what we should or should not do . . .
>
> We have the level of criminal violence we do because we have arranged our social and economic life in certain ways rather than others. The brutality and violence of American life are a signal . . . that there are profound social costs to maintaining those arrangements. But by the same token, altering them also has a price; and if we continue to tolerate the conditions that have made us the most violent of industrial societies, it is not because the problem is overwhelmingly mysterious or because we do not know what to do, but because we have decided that the benefits of changing those conditions aren't worth the costs.

Why do we continue to doom ourselves to so much unnecessary and preventable death and suffering? How can we understand why we as a nation behave collectively like the protagonist of a tragedy, bringing violence and destruction on ourselves and those we love, and all in the

name of morality? Since the royal road to the understanding of character, whether individual or national, is through the study of the great
mythic and tragic paradigms that exemplify the archetypal forms it
takes, I return to Melville's masterpiece of the American obsession with
retributive justice, *Moby-Dick*. When I think of the mentality that is
willing to sacrifice even rational self-interest, not to mention concern
for others, for the sake of some abstractly conceived notion of justice
and the punishment of evil, I can only think of Captain Ahab. Like any
tragic hero, Ahab was convinced that he knew the difference between
good and evil, he knew that Moby-Dick was evil, and he knew that if
only he could kill Moby-Dick he would destroy evil and restore justice
to the world. In exactly the same way, we know that "criminals" represent and symbolize evil, that if we can only kill or immobilize them all,
we will have destroyed evil and attained justice. What else are our
endless, futile, and self-defeating crusades, called the "War on Crime"
and the "War on Drugs," but our version of the voyage of the *Pequod*?
What else has "Crime" (or "Drugs") come to symbolize, in the American
mind, that wasn't already contained in Ahab's image of that symbol of
absolute evil, the great white whale, Moby-Dick? And where else are
we sailing our ship of state except toward exactly the same kind of
tragic and self-destructive shipwreck to which Ahab sailed the *Pequod*?

American violence is the result of our collective "moral choice" to
maintain those social policies that in turn maintain our uniquely high
level of violence; and I call that choice a moral choice because it is very
explicitly rationalized, justified, and legitimized on moral grounds, in
moral terms. Let me give you an example of what I mean. America has
for many years had the highest per capita imprisonment rate in the
world, substantially higher than our closest rivals for that "distinction"
during this period—two police states: the former Soviet Union, and the
former South Africa. The conditions in many of our prisons are so
cruel, inhumane, and degrading, with severe overcrowding, frequent
rapes and beatings, prolonged and arbitrary use of solitary confinement,
grossly unsanitary, disease-inducing living conditions, and deprivation

of elementary medical care, that the United States is now among the nations, along with Iran and Iraq, that Human Rights Watch is monitoring for "numerous human rights abuses and frequent violations of the United Nations Standard Minimum Rules for the Treatment of Prisoners."[5] But even running a brutalizing and dehumanizing prison system is enormously expensive when it holds as many human beings as ours does (well over a million people at last count, and increasing every day). All the expenses associated with even the most miserable penal system cost the country tens of billions of dollars every year (and the cost has been rising with each passing year), money which of necessity gets drained away from programs in the community that have been demonstrated to prevent violence. Despite these facts (or rather, in part because of them), the United States also has by far the highest rates of criminal violence of any Western democracy or, for that matter, of any economically developed nation on earth.

Moral approaches to violence do not help us to understand the causes and prevention of violence; and what is worse, some of the moral assumptions about violence actually inhibit us in our attempts to learn about its causes and prevention. The most popular moral ways of thinking about violence lead to the mistaken conclusion that to understand violent behavior is to excuse it; or as the French proverb puts it, *Tout comprendre c'est tout pardonner,* to understand all is to forgive all. This proverb might be called the bogeyman of every effort to understand violence; it hovers in the wings, ready to be brought out whenever an attempt is made to learn what causes violence so that we can prevent it, rather than being limited to punishing it. Punishing requires much less effort than does understanding the many different forms of violence: learning what variety and interaction of biological, psychological, and social forces cause the different forms of violence. It is easier and less threatening to condemn violence (morally and legally) so that we can punish it, rather than seeking its causes and working to prevent it.

What those who quote the French proverb have not grasped is that when one takes a naturalistic, nonmoralistic approach to violence, "forgiveness" is simply beside the point, since the concept of forgiveness is meaningless if one has not condemned in the first place. "Condemning" violence is as irrelevant as it would be to "condemn" cancer or heart disease. And yet no one supposes that because doctors do not "condemn" or "punish" cancer and heart disease (or the people who suffer from those life-threatening illnesses) that they are somehow "soft on cancer" or "permissive" toward heart disease.

Often, I have been asked by friends and colleagues how I happened to have become involved in the study of violence. My interest began early on, growing up in my family, in Nebraska. Professionally, my interest in understanding violent people quickened when I signed up for an elective rotation in "Prison Psychiatry," while in training at the Harvard Medical School. The program was organized and supervised by an inspiring psychoanalyst, Dr. Gerald Adler.

When I entered this training program, it was with the conscious assumption that prison inmates were likely to be untreatable "con artists" with little interest in anything except manipulating us. To my surprise, I discovered that working with violent men was one of the most intellectually challenging and emotionally moving experiences in my years to that point. I quickly learned that most of what I had previously been taught about so-called "sociopaths" or "antisocial personalities" was either wrong, or else so superficial as to be more misleading than helpful. I found that the relationship between the life histories of the violent men who wound up in prison, beginning with their childhoods, and their adult behavior, was considerably more understandable and comprehensible than was the corresponding relationship in many of the more seriously "mentally ill" patients I was treating in the university teaching hospital—perhaps because there is a greater biological component in the etiology of severe mental illnesses, in contrast to the predominantly social and psychological causes of most violence.

When one of the Harvard teaching hospitals was awarded a contract by the state to provide psychiatric services at a newly opened prison mental hospital, in the late 1970s, I became its medical director, leading a team of psychiatrists, psychologists, and social workers. Four years later, I became the clinical director of a program of psychiatric services throughout the state prison system and ran that program for the next ten years, from 1981 to 1991. Perhaps the most encouraging thing I feel I learned from that experience is that it is indeed possible to prevent violence. In the Massachusetts state prison system, the level of lethal violence, both homicidal and suicidal, was reduced nearly to zero, while some other types of violence, both individual and collective, such as riots and hostage taking, which had also been common during the 1970s, had simply become nonexistent by the last half of the 1980s, throughout the entire state prison system.

One of the main purposes of this book is to try to describe what I have learned about the causes and prevention of violent behavior, from twenty-five years of working with violent men, and from a lifetime of pondering questions about violence. It is my hope that we might apply some of those lessons more generally, with the goal of reducing the level of violence to which the community at large, indeed the world as a whole, not just the population of the prisons, is exposed and vulnerable.

PART I

THE

PATHOLOGY

OF VIOLENCE

CHAPTER 1

Visits to Hell:

Entering

the World

of the Prison

VISITS TO THE MAXIMUM-SECURITY PRISON IN MASSACHUSETTS ARE VISITS to hell. Like Dante's inferno, it too has its lowest circle for the most damned, the infamous Cell Block Number Ten, a solitary confinement unit. And as Dante realized, it is helpful to have a guide so that we can bridge the gap in this underworld between the human and the inhuman, the living and the "living dead." We need help to fathom what conceivable or inconceivable state of despair or damage could have led its inhabitants to become so dead to the humanity they no longer share with others.

I have written this book to offer myself as your guide on a journey into the universe of violence. To do justice to so vast a topic requires a discussion large enough to encompass its epic, mythic dimensions. When we talk about violence, we are talking about hell. This is the world of the Inferno, Golgotha, King Lear—of Auschwitz and Armenia, Andersonville and Attica, the "Middle Passage" and Wounded Knee. This is the world of individual atrocities so disturbing to contemplate that I have to ask myself: How can I expect you to accompany me into this terrible place? And yet I know that we have to be willing to look horror in the face if we are ever to understand the causes of the human propensity toward violence well enough to prevent its most destructive manifestations.

Our responses to violence are as complex as the subject itself is. Many respond to violence with a mixture of horror, revulsion, outrage, fascination, arousal, and valorization. Our horror can lead us to distance ourselves from violence. If we have had some personal experience of violence, we may find it too disturbing to speak of or think about. Or our personal experience may draw us deep into research, study, and action against violence. Whatever our response, each of us has a working theory of violence—conscious or unconscious—that steers our attitudes, behavior, and judgments. For example, many may already have concluded that it is only a few crazy, abnormal, and freakish people who are violent. We may find ourselves abhorring violence and at the same time fascinated by it, drawn to sadistic movies and tabloid newspapers. The "pornography of violence"—the sensationalizing of violence—is a means by which we distance ourselves from it, perhaps render it less frightening and more manageable by reducing it to the dimensions of titillation and entertainment. Historically, many people have felt a kind of awe in relation to violence and war, so that they glorify the heroes who excel in killing others. Both men and women commemorate war heroes for their courage to commit violent acts as soldiers at war. A man is often thought to be more "manly" if he has been to war and seen violent action. And yet, I think it would be a serious mistake if we let this concept of heroism keep us from asking hard and necessary questions about the viability of violence as a survival strategy. Knowing what we now know, we have to ask ourselves: Is violence, as a personal, social, and political strategy, compatible with human survival at this stage in our evolutionary development?

Among the readers of a book on violence, there are inevitably those whose lives have been marked forever by a personal exposure to violence—as victims, as survivors of victims, as family members of someone who has committed a violent act (against himself or another), or as those who have felt compelled to commit serious violence themselves, whether legally or illegally, in wartime or in peace. For those of us to whom this applies—and of course all of us are vulnerable to violence—we have an obligation not to trivialize this subject, not to distance ourselves from it, and not to withdraw from it. For while we may wish to avoid violence, it does not always avoid us.

What I am attempting in this book is to lay the foundations for a theory that can identify the root causes of violent behavior, isolate the pathogenic forces that are necessary prerequisites for the development of violence, and describe the ravages of this disease and the lives of those who are claimed by it, be they "victims" or "perpetrators" (or, as is more often the case, both).

The City of The Living Dead

Let me take you now into the universe of violence, as I have seen it in the maximum-security prison. I cannot enter this underworld without being reminded of Dante's rueful comment on his first glimpse of the damned: "I should never have believed death had undone so many."[1]

For twenty-five years now, I have been passing through the metal detectors and steel doors of this and other prisons. I know perfectly well how many men will be inside. And still, I never cease to be amazed and appalled by the sheer number of men who are buried alive here, often because of behavior so murderous that we have not yet figured out what else to do with them. There are thousands upon thousands of these men, even in a small and relatively peaceful state like Massachusetts. In the United States there are more than a million, a total population of condemned men larger than that of many cities, most armies, some states in this country, and some entire nations. Among the dead, I count not only the victims of these men but also the men themselves.

For only the living dead could want to kill the living. No one who loves life, who cherishes and feels his own aliveness, could want to kill another human being. But the living dead need to kill others, because for them the most unendurable anguish is the pain of seeing that others are still alive.

Entering this woeful city feels like entering the underworld, even though it is mostly above ground. The architecture creates the illusion of being buried alive in an underground concrete bunker. A man cannot see out of doors or get a glimpse of sky or sun, for he is surrounded by windowless walls of solid concrete. The only openings through which daylight can enter at all are small apertures near the ceiling, ten to thirty feet above eye level, which function neither as air vents nor as windows. Some of the cell blocks in this prison are in a claustrophobic, windowless basement. Their use as long-term "living" facilities for inmates has finally been banned by the courts as cruel and unusual punishment. And yet, the maximum-security prison for the Federal prison system in Marion, Illinois—the spiritual model or archetype, one might suppose, for the various state prisons—is actually underground. Even today, prisoners in the solitary confinement cell blocks in some of the remaining (and still used) nineteenth-century Massachusetts prisons can see nothing from their cell doors but a solid wall—rather like the jails of Czarist Russia that a nineteenth-century physician, Anton Chekhov, visited and described.[2] The whole system has a military feel to it; it is like a state of civil war that never ends, in which there are no victors, neither side surrenders, and there is not even the possibility of a peace treaty.

Looking at the gate leading into the Massachusetts prison you do not see inscribed over it Dante's motto, "Abandon all hope ye who enter here,"[3] but it does not need to be, for most of those whom I see there had already abandoned all hope. That is why they committed the crimes that sent them there. These most desperate and incorrigibly violent prison inmates, the ones who become concentrated in the maximum security prisons and prison hospitals, exemplify most clearly, because most extremely, the fundamental features of violent behavior. It is from these men that we most need to learn.

To speak of these men as "the living dead" is not a metaphor I have invented, but rather the most direct and literal, least distorted way to summarize what these men have told me when describing their subjective experience of themselves. Many murderers, both sane and insane, have told me that "they" have died, that their personality has died, usually at some identifiable time in the past, so that they feel dead, even though their bodies live on. When they say they feel dead they mean they cannot feel anything—neither emotions nor even physical sensations. I have seen many who admit to killing others without so much as a flicker of remorse or any other emotion. Moreover, they themselves have been battered in fights and have mutilated themselves horribly (enucleated their eyes, castrated or emasculated their genitals, torn out their toenails) without feeling any physical pain at the time. Common sense suggests that these men are "dead" inside. For how else could they possibly murder others and mutilate themselves as they do—unless they had no feelings?

Some have told me they feel like robots or zombies, that they feel their bodies are empty or filled with straw, not flesh and blood, that instead of having veins and nerves they have ropes or cords. One inmate told me he feels like "food that is decomposing."

Another murderer I worked with says he is a "vampire." If I call him the living dead I am only paraphrasing his description of himself, since a vampire is by definition dead, even though he walks and talks. When this man says he is a vampire, he means it literally, as the most precise way to describe himself. This man strangled and stabbed his grandmother to death and then drank her blood. Knowing that about him, we can see that his experience of himself as a dead thing is directly related to the specific kind of violence he committed.

These men do not look like "zombies" or "vampires," nor do they necessarily behave differently from anyone else in the course of an ordinary conversation. In fact, the most extraordinary thing about these

violent men is how ordinary they often appear on the surface.[4] No
matter how many violent people I have worked with, I still find myself
amazed by these ordinary-looking men, who have actually committed
extraordinarily brutal, violent crimes. Of course, everyone who reads
the newspapers knows that many horrific acts turn out to have been
committed by men whose most remarkable feature is how unremark-
able they appear to be: Bland, polite, timid, soft-spoken, they make no
waves, bother no one, attract little attention, and rarely let anyone get
very close to them.

THE CASE OF RALPH W.

Ralph W. is an example of such an ordinary man. He is a middle-aged,
middle-class family man from the midwestern "Bible Belt"; a husband,
the father of sons and daughters; a Sunday-school teacher and director
of his church choir; and a career government bureaucrat (although he
never got much beyond the lower levels of the civil-service hierarchy).
On the surface, Ralph W. appears conventional, passive, unassertive,
and unambitious.

One summer afternoon, Ralph W. raped and murdered a fourteen-
year-old girl who sang in the church choir, then buried her body in his
backyard. Following the murder, before the girl's body was discovered,
Ralph W. joined a large group of his fellow townspeople, pretending to
help them find the missing teenager. No one suspected he was any less
sincere than they were. Obviously, neither they nor anyone else had any
idea who Ralph W. actually was. (He is now suspected of having committed similar crimes on previous occasions, completely undetected.)
Ralph W.'s wife, who worked as the personnel director of an insurance
company, was so dumbfounded when her husband's behavior was exposed that she said she could never practice her profession again. How
could she imagine, she said, that she had even the slightest understanding of anyone, when she had been living, and having daughters, with a
"monster" without even realizing it?

When I ask Ralph W. who he is, he says over and over again, "I am

nothing, a nobody. I always felt I was a nothing, that I was not important—a non-entity." Consistent with his image of himself—or his non-
self—Ralph W. also describes a remarkable absence of feelings. He
reports: "From the time I entered military service I always wondered
what it'd be like to kill someone. I wanted to do it. What I wondered
was, whether I'd have feelings or not." He then said, "I wanted not to
have feelings, because I thought 'that was me'—you know, 'nothing,'
'I'm a nothing.' " He said, "After I had sex with" the girl he later killed,
"I had no feelings. I just felt empty—no love, hate, sadness, remorse. If
anything, perhaps, a little fear. But mostly just the thought, 'Now what
do I do?' " He insisted that when he then went on to kill her, "I felt
nothing," he said. "I was not angry at her. I was just afraid of being
found out." But even his fear was so minimal that between the time he
killed the girl and the time he buried her he did not forget that a
football game he wanted to watch was on television, and he took the
time to watch it.

Did Ralph W. really know what fear is, or had he the capacity for
what most people refer to when they speak of fear? He certainly had no
capacity for one kind of normal fear—the fear of one's own conscience,
the capacity for empathy, remorse, and guilt. Instead, he went on to say
that "what most bothers and puzzles me is that I have no feelings about
what I did—no remorse or repentance. Does that mean I'm heartless?"
When I ask him what he means, he says he is "like a stone. Heartless.
Not alive." And then he adds, "I've never shown feelings because I
haven't had them."

But there is one exception in Ralph W.'s report of himself: the rage
he says he felt toward his mother during his childhood. He was "filled
with rage" at his mother, because she revealed to his friends that he had
a "crush" on a girl who was a classmate in school. He says he was
furious at being exposed by his mother because he felt so inadequate
sexually, so incapable of "satisfying" anyone or of being attractive to any
girl his age. He felt he could only be ridiculed, humiliated, and rejected
now that his feelings of attraction to the girl had been publicly exposed.

He says that he never did find a way to express his rage in words or by any other means, but that following his childhood his rage disappeared.

How can we make sense of what Ralph W. is saying? A standard psychiatric explanation would suggest that Ralph W. repressed his rage toward his mother and acted it out on a surrogate instead, on a less frightening and foreboding female, so that his rage by-passed his conscious awareness altogether. That may be a partial explanation of this man's behavior, but I wonder whether Ralph W. and others like him have even the capacity for genuine anger. This absence of feelings is described consistently by murderers throughout the world and throughout history. Moreover, the more violent the criminal, the more notable the lack of feelings. The most violent men already feel numb and dead by the time they begin killing.

In order to understand the psychology of violence, we need to turn many of our most basic assumptions about human behavior upside down and inside out—assumptions that are perfectly valid when applied to normal, nonviolent people and totally misleading when applied to the violent. For example, for healthy people, life is life and death is death, and the difference between them is generally understood. Death does not exist while life continues, it does not coexist with life; and life does not continue after death. Even for most religious believers, this world is this world; the "afterworld" comes after the death of the body. For the violent, none of these assumptions holds true, none of these mutually exclusive categories apply. The usual dichotomies between life and death, this world and the other world, rationality and irrationality, pleasure and pain, reward and punishment, the body and the soul, self-preservation and self-destruction, have totally broken down.[5] For the violent, "death" neither waits for the death of the body, nor is it incompatible with the continued life of the body. Death refers to the death of the self, which has occurred while the body is still living. So we speak of them as "the living dead," biologically alive yet spiritually and emotionally dead.

THE CASE OF STARKWEATHER

For example, in 1957, a mass murderer, all too aptly named Starkweather, killed and mutilated eleven people in a week-long shooting
spree across my home state of Nebraska. (A movie was later made
about his crimes, entitled *Badlands*.) Charles Starkweather was a nineteen-year-old whose whole identity, in his own eyes and in the eyes of
others, was all too aptly summed up in the conventional title of his
occupation: "garbage man." He saw himself and his life as "garbage."
But there is one notable act that Starkweather accomplished in his brief
and otherwise destructive life, which was to write and dictate his autobiography before being executed. It is a significant document in the
study of violence, for it corroborates the perspective on violence I have
been discussing.

In this grim document, Starkweather comments on his mother's reaction to hearing her son being sentenced to death. He comments:
"When she cried at the court house . . . she was crying for something
already dead. . . . I was already dead, or the same as dead . . . nobody ever gets back hisself again."[6] Starkweather was not referring to
the fact that he was soon to be executed; he meant that he had "died"
long before he ever murdered anyone: "The people I murdered had
murdered me. They murdered me slow like. I was better to them. I
killed them in a hurry."[7] At another point, he wrote, "I don't know
life. . . ."[8]

What is so clear from Starkweather's writings is that not only did he
feel dead emotionally, but that he wanted to be dead physically as well.
His continuing biological life, since he was already spiritually dead, was
for him the equivalent of being buried alive: "Soon, I'll be buried with
the dead days. Better to be left to rot on some high hill behind a rock,
and be remembered, than to be buried alive in some stinking place
[that is, his home and community, his world], and go to bed smelly like
a garbage can every night."[9]

Starkweather's attitude is characteristic of all the most violent men I have known over the years. These men find the death of the self so intolerable that they prefer physical death (their own and other people's) to the continuation of the living torment that the rest of us refer to as "life." It is no exaggeration to say that violent men come to hate life—their own and other peoples'. Starkweather stated explicitly that he did not know what life was good for. According to one of the criminologists who spoke with him at length, by the time Starkweather was seventeen he had become "obsessed with a recurring delusion that Death had him 'marked,'" a thought in which he took a "strange, bewildering delight."[10] In fact, he became so preoccupied with the thought that his real agenda was death, not life, that he began to resist any involvement with life that might tempt him away from death.

Those who kill others do so in part because they cannot stand to think that others are alive while they are not, and they cannot bear their living death, either. Starkweather refused to let his lawyer enter any of the pleas that might have spared him the death penalty. In the end, Starkweather got his wish—at the cost of eleven other lives.

"SON OF SAM"

David Berkowitz, alias "Son of Sam," also spoke and wrote repeatedly of his identification with virtually every variety of living death—zombies, vampires, devils, demons, monsters, and so on. He described himself and the world as both dead or dying, and himself as no longer human. The fact that we speak of the most violent criminals (and war criminals) as "inhuman" may only reflect our intuitive awareness of murderers' own subjective experience of themselves. "Son of Sam" also described himself as having lost his soul, which is yet another way of describing the death of the self.

> I am a monster. I am the "Son of Sam." I have a fear now that I
> . . . will become a demon or, I may be a demon right now. . . .
> I fear that with the loss of my humanness I will become like a

zombie. . . . Some people thought I was void of emotions when they examined me. This is exactly what happens to those possessed. I want my soul back! I want what was taken from me! I have a right to be human. . . . I am willing to die to be at peace. . . . I must be put to death.[11]

Self-Mutilation: Trying to Bring the Dead Back to Life

Once they have seen that killing others does not bring them back to life, many murderers find that the only way to feel alive, since they cannot feel anything emotionally, is to feel physical pain. So they attempt to induce such feelings by cutting or otherwise injuring their bodies.

Over the years, innumerable inmates have told me that the experience of physical pain is preferable to feeling nothing. Self-mutilating people typically do not feel physical pain at the time of injuring themselves, but only later, when their bodies start to heal. Yet, as one man put it, the only time he felt any relief, any sense (fleeting though it was) of being alive, was immediately after he had cut or otherwise injured himself. For another young inmate, only the sight of his own blood, and the awareness that he would feel something eventually, reassured him that he was alive, not a robot. Until then he felt he had no nerves and blood vessels, only wires or cords. (This particular man's mother doused herself with gasoline and set herself on fire in front of his eyes while her son looked on. He then ran away from home, supporting himself as a homosexual prostitute.) His dilemma, faced with his history and with his life, was: Which is worse, to feel or not to feel?

Many of the most violent men in prisons mutilate themselves at least as viciously as they mutilate their victims (that is to say, very viciously). I take such actions to be an answer to the question I just posed, that it is worse to feel "nothing" than it is to feel "something," even if that "something" is pain. The things these men do to themselves are the most common, "everyday" events in the world of the maximum-security prisons. They keep the emergency room surgeons in the prisons busy, repairing the damage these men inflict on themselves.

At the least violent end of the self-mutilative spectrum, these men cut their wrists or forearms or other areas of their bodies. Then they escalate to swallowing razor blades, screws, or other injurious objects; I have seen many X-rays of such men whose abdomens look like hardware stores. So common is this practice that surgeons ordinarily are reluctant to remove these objects surgically unless and until so many have accumulated inside the body that they threaten to cause intestinal obstruction or perforation. When that is not sufficient, many escalate to the point of repeatedly inserting bed springs or screws or ball-point pens into their urethras, causing urethral scarring which can cause urinary obstruction and the need for a permanent indwelling catheter, which in turn tends to cause urinary tract infections, kidney failure, and death. But even before that point has been reached, the self-inflicted damage has sometimes become so severe as to leave the treating urologists with little choice but to recommend the complete amputation of the penis. On the other hand, I have also known prison inmates who have cut off their own penis and testicles, others who have torn out their own toenails, and others who have blinded themselves.

When these various forms of self-mutilation no longer bring feeling, many of these men come to realize that the only way to kill the pain in their souls is to kill the whole body. For these men, their living death is an intolerable, zombielike existence, like the tormented shades of the formerly living who inhabit the underworld in Homer, Virgil, Dante, and the Bible—a situation of such distress that many decide to end their own bodily lives as well as those of others. Like the dead souls in the Book of Job (26:5–7), these men live in a universe of violence and despair:

In the underworld the dead things writhe in fear,
The waters and all that live in them are struck with terror.
Hell is laid bare,
And destruction hath no covering.
God spreads the canopy of the sky over chaos,
And suspends earth in the void.

The death of the self—which is what we are talking about here—brings with it a sense of the intolerability of existence—one's own and everyone else's. Murder is an attempt not just to rescue one's self—for many, it is already too late for that; the self has already died—but to bring one's dead self back to life. When that does not happen, then one's own physical death can seem to promise the only relief possible.

It is for these sorts of reasons that many more murderers kill themselves than are ever killed by the state, even when capital punishment is the usual penalty for murder. The suicide rate among men who have just committed a murder is several hundred times greater than it is among ordinary men of the same age, sex, and race, in this country and elsewhere.

The fact that so many men killed themselves in Massachusetts prisons in the 1970s caused the prison mental health service which I directed for ten years to come into being. In the early 1980s, Judge W. Arthur Garrity of the U.S. District Court—in response to a class action suit brought on behalf of prison inmates—ordered the Department of Correction to allow mental health professionals to establish psychiatric clinics and emergency rooms in the prisons, to guarantee that inmates would not be denied access to psychiatric care simply because they were incarcerated. The misery of this group is so constant, and their attempts to end their misery by means of violent action (toward others and themselves) so repetitive, that our struggle to prevent their suicides at first seemed hopeless.

The state of despair of these violent men does not result simply from their being imprisoned (although that frequently exacerbates it). Many have made suicide attempts before they were jailed, others attempt or complete suicide after their release, and a certain percentage of murderers never enter prison because they kill themselves before they are even arrested or convicted. Also, more inmates are killed by other inmates than were ever killed by the State. In other words, no group is more strongly and widely in favor of capital punishment than are the murderers and other prison inmates. They will even impose it on themselves and each other when the State fails to do so, which is why I feel I am living in "cloud-cuckoo-land" when I hear people suggesting that capital punishment will deter murder and induce more "reverence for life." The men I know already feel so spiritually dead that they long for physical death as well.[12] For many, the only means capable of expressing in a final catharsis the rage that is within them, so as to settle at last their accounts with the world, is the fantasy of dying in a shoot-out with the police in which they would at least take as many people as possible into death with them before they die—an acting out of the Bonnie and Clyde myth, the Götterdämmerung myth. Every year in this country, hundreds of violent criminals go to their deaths in exactly this way.

Perhaps this should not be so surprising if one thinks of all the male warriors throughout history who have lived and died, or made it clear they were willing to die, by the same code—from Hector to Hitler, from Achilles to the Ayatollahs, from Samson and Julius Caesar to the Japanese samurai and kamikaze pilots. For a healthy man, the threat of death would be a powerful deterrent to forbidden behavior (but then, healthy men do not commit murder even in the absence of such a threat), but for the men who do commit murders, death is not a threat. If anything, death is a promise of peace, which makes it understandable that executions and capital punishment encourage more murders than they deter, as judged by the fact that the only Western industrialized nation that still retains the death penalty—the United States—also has a murder rate many times higher than do those nations which have sufficient reverence for life to have abolished punishment by death.

I speak of the violent men I have known as the "living dead." But how can we understand the sense of inner deadness of the kind of man I am describing? These men's souls did not just die. They have dead souls because their souls were murdered. How did it happen? How were they murdered? As we shall come to see in the next chapter, the degree of violence and cruelty to which these men have been subjected in childhood is so extreme and so unusual that it gives a whole new meaning to the term "child abuse."

Dead Souls

IN THE COURSE OF MY WORK WITH THE MOST VIOLENT MEN IN MAXIMUM-security settings, not a day goes by that I do not hear reports—often confirmed by independent sources—of how these men were victimized during childhood. Physical violence, neglect, abandonment, rejection, sexual exploitation and violation occurred on a scale so extreme, so bizarre, and so frequent that one cannot fail to see that the men who occupy the extreme end of the continuum of violent behavior in adulthood occupied an equally extreme end of the continuum of violent child abuse earlier in life.

The violent criminals I have known have been objects of violence from early childhood. They have seen their closest relatives—their fathers and mothers and sisters and brothers—murdered in front of their eyes, often by other family members. As children, these men were shot, axed, scalded, beaten, strangled, tortured, drugged, starved, suffocated, set on fire, thrown out of windows, raped, or prostituted by mothers who were their "pimps"; their bones have been broken; they have been locked in closets or attics for extended periods, and one man I know was deliberately locked by his parents in an empty icebox until he suffered brain damage from oxygen deprivation before he was let out.

The face and body of one Massachusetts prison inmate I know are covered with grotesque scars, despite many plastic surgical procedures, from burns caused by scalding water his mother had thrown on him repeatedly. It was her method of discipline during his childhood. Another man, who brutally raped and murdered a young woman whose apartment he had broken into one day while she was napping, has bullet-hole scars on his arms and legs. He said they were inflicted on him in childhood by his mother, whose idea of "spanking" him was to take out her pistol and shoot him. This same man also described in vivid detail seeing his father murdered in front of his eyes by two other relatives when he was a child. (His descriptions were confirmed by his brother, who was also in prison at the same time for his own violent crime.)

In fact, the first violent criminal I ever saw in therapy, twenty-five years ago, Randolph W., began his description of his life by describing how his father used to beat and terrorize every member of the family. At first, I thought this man was a "con artist," fabricating these stories to win my sympathy, until I discovered that his father was in prison at the same time for having murdered his own daughter—Randolph W.'s sister. Not only were Randolph W.'s stories of family violence not exaggerated, the accuracy of them was corroborated "beyond a reasonable doubt" by an independent source, a court of law.

Another inmate, Harold R., was transferred to Massachusetts from another state after killing several people there in the prison system (and in the community before that). Harold R.'s body is scarred, his limbs misshapen, which he accounts for by describing how his mother repeatedly assaulted him as a child—in his sleep, with an axe; by throwing him out a window; by setting him on fire; and so on. He said reflectively, but more bemusedly than with self-pity, "I guess she wanted to kill me, but I just didn't die."

An inmate whom I never saw, Donald C., but whose "psychological autopsy" I attended after his suicide in prison, described having been subjected in childhood to both heterosexual and homosexual incest and pedophilia by both parents and several other relatives and friends of the family, being passed around nude from adult to adult at parties as a kind of sexual "party favor." Donald C. had described this to a member of the correctional staff in the prison. Following his suicide, Donald C.'s brother, who was also in prison at the same time, corroborated these biographical details.

How can violence to the body kill the soul, even if it does not kill the body? Having heard hundreds of men describe the experience of being beaten nearly to death, I believe the answer to that question is that violence—whatever else it may mean—is the ultimate means of communicating the absence of love by the person inflicting the violence. Even a pet dog knows it is unloved when it is beaten. A child would have to be out of touch with reality (as many do in fact become) not to realize on some level that to be beaten deliberately is to be rejected and unloved. But the self cannot survive without love. The self starved of love dies. That is how violence can cause the death of the self even when it does not kill the body.

The two possible sources of love for the self are love from others, and one's own love for oneself. Children who fail to receive sufficient love from others fail to build those reserves of self-love, and the capacity for self-love, which enable them to survive the inevitable rejections and humiliations which even the most fortunate of people cannot avoid. Without feelings of love, the self feels numb, empty, and dead.

The word I use in this book to refer to the absence or deficiency of self-love is *shame;* its opposite is pride, by which I mean a healthy sense of self-esteem, self-respect, and self-love. When self-love is sufficiently diminished, one feels shame. But it may be somewhat paradoxical to refer to shame as a "feeling," for while shame is initially painful, constant shaming leads to a deadening of feeling, an absence of feeling. An analogous image comes to mind if we think about our experience of cold. If we say we are "cold," we experience cold as a feeling, as something that exists and is painful. But we know from physics that cold is really the absence of heat, or warmth. Shame is also experienced as a feeling, and an intensely painful one; but like cold, it is, in essence, the absence of warmth, emotional warmth, or love for the self. And when it reaches overwhelming intensity, shame is experienced, like cold, as a feeling of numbness and deadness. We know that cold starts out feeling painful, but when it reaches an intolerable extreme, it results in complete numbness and physical death. At first only a limb may die, but when the cold is sufficiently severe, the whole body dies. In the same way, the self dies when exposed to more shame than it can tolerate. This is why Dante was profoundly psychologically correct when he stated that the lowest circle of hell was a region not of flames, but of ice—absolute coldness.

All of us know what it is to experience feelings of shame and humiliation, rejection and ridicule. These are painful feelings, to be sure, but most people are not disastrously overwhelmed by those feelings to the degree that violent people are, which may be one reason why we find it so difficult to understand those who become so deeply shamed as to undergo the death of the self. It may be difficult to understand, let alone imagine, how the feeling of shame could actually lead to a total inability to feel; and to know how intolerable that emptiness and absence actually "feels" when one has experienced a total loss of self-love. To suffer the loss of love from others, by being rejected or abandoned, assaulted or insulted, slighted or demeaned, humiliated or ridiculed, dishonored or disrespected, is to be shamed by them. To be overwhelmed by shame and humiliation is to experience the destruction of self-esteem; and without a certain minimal amount of self-esteem, the self collapses and the soul dies. Violence to the body causes the death of the self because it is so inescapably humiliating. When we cannot fend off, undo, or escape from such overwhelmingly unloving acts, when we cannot protect ourselves from them, whether by violent or nonviolent means, something gets killed within us—our souls are murdered. All this is implicit in the double meaning of the word that most directly and literally refers both to the death of the self, and to what causes the death of the self: namely, *mortification*, which means both humiliation and causing death.

It is also true, of course, that actions that do not directly cause physical injury or death can constitute the kind of psychological torture that can destroy a human personality in ways that are likely to lead to violent behavior in later life—such as locking a child in a closet, verbally threatening him or her with death or mutilation, ridiculing and taunting the child, and so on. Such actions constitute a form of psychological violence which, even in the absence of physical injury, can kill the self. Thus, people do not need to have been physically attacked in order to become violent. Violent child abuse is not a necessary precursor to adult violence for the simple reason that violence is not the only way in which an adult can shame and humiliate a child. Words alone can shame and reject, insult and humiliate, dishonor and disgrace, tear down self-esteem, and murder the soul.

Not all violent adults were subjected to violent child abuse. Nor do all who were subjected to violent child abuse grow up to commit deadly violence. Child abuse is neither a necessary nor a sufficient condition for adult violence, anymore than smoking is a necessary or sufficient cause for the development of lung cancer. There are, however, plenty of statistical studies showing that acts of actual and extreme physical violence, such as beatings and attempted murders, are regular experiences in the childhoods of those who grow up to become violent, just as we know that smoking is a major, and preventable, cause of lung cancer.[1]

The Mythic Roots of Violence

Before there were statistics, there were myths. The story of Oedipus is a myth that has much to teach us about the origins of violence. Freud taught us to recognize the similarity between Oedipus and the rest of us by alerting us to pay attention to, and become consciously aware of, wishes and temptations to engage in both violent and sexual behaviors that are illicit, destructive, and self-destructive. But Oedipus's homicidal and illicit sexual behavior is not so hard to understand if one remembers that Oedipus, like so many of our prison inmates, was a survivor of the most extreme form of violent child abuse—attempted murder. Laius and Jocasta had, after all, deliberately exposed and abandoned their child, whom they left on a hillside to die, after having driven a stake through his foot (hence the name Oedipus, or "swollen foot"). That Oedipus, like many severely abused prison inmates, later grew up to commit murder and incest is perhaps the least surprising outcome of such a childhood.

When emotional pain is overwhelming, it provokes an automatic, unconscious, reflexlike self-anesthetization, a self-deadening. The image of intolerable distress that those who are trapped in this struggle evoke in me is captured by Tennessee Williams's phrase "cat on a hot tin roof," the feeling that no matter where you put your foot down, the result is excruciating and intolerable, so that life becomes an endless and futile attempt to find a spot comfortable enough that one can finally come to rest. This is the image I often have when I sit with violent men, in the prison and the prison hospital. They are often certain that if only they (and we) could bring about some change—any change—in their environment, there would be an improvement in the way they feel. As a consequence, these men will go to any length—they will cut themselves, cut others, pretend to be crazy, pretend to be sane, go berserk, threaten to kill us, threaten to kill themselves, take hostages, start a riot—whatever it takes to force someone to transfer them to another environment. The assumption I hear over and over is, "If only I can get moved somewhere else—to another cell block, to another prison, to the hospital [if they are in prison], back to prison [if they are in the hospital], to the community [if they are in prison], back to prison [if they are in the community]—I will feel better, things will be tolerable." But when they are in the new environment, when they do succeed in being transferred elsewhere, it usually turns out to be just as intolerable as the old one.

This distortion is especially difficult for these men to correct when the only environments currently available to them are brutalizing and dehumanizing. That makes it harder for them to see that the most intractable component of their present distress is not, ultimately, caused by their immediate current environment but by their inner emptiness and deadness and past victimization, so that no amount of moving to different environments alone will relieve their distress. If the current environment were actually more humane, it would at least be a bit easier for many of these men to recognize that the source of their most intolerable distress is not in their present environment, bad as that is, but in themselves: i.e., in their memories of past experiences, and in the means by which they attempt and are still attempting to protect themselves from the pain of those experiences and their memories. This is one reason why a humane environment is an absolute prerequisite for the healing of violent men, and why punitive environments only perpetuate the violence of the criminals who are placed in them.

The soul needs love as vitally and urgently as the lungs need oxygen; without it the soul dies, just as the body does without oxygen. It may not be self-evident to healthy people just how literally true this is, for healthy people have resources of love that are sufficient to tide them over periods of severe and painful rejection or loss. Similarly, one does not realize how dependent the body is on oxygen until one has nearly suffocated, or has had to resuscitate someone who is gasping for breath. But when one has worked with deeply and seriously ill human beings, the evidence of the need for both oxygen and love is overwhelming.

The kind of man I am describing protects himself from the emotional suffocation of living in a loveless atmosphere by withdrawing the love he has begun to feel from everyone and everything, in an attempt to reserve for himself whatever capacity for love he may have. But his supply of self-love is also deficient. And it cannot grow to the dimen-

sions that are necessary for health when it is not fed by love from
others. If it were not deficient, he could afford to love others. But his
withdrawal of love from everyone and everything around him not only
protects him from emotional pain, it also condemns him to the absence
of emotional pleasure or joy; for we cannot enjoy the people who make
up our world, cannot enjoy being with them, except to the degree that
we love them. So the person who cannot love cannot have *any* feelings—pain *or* joy.[2]

But a joyless life is a synonym for hell. A man who does not love and
cannot love, is, in effect, condemned to hell.[3] His entire environment,
from which—without love—he is cut off, is without enjoyment for him,
and thus the world he "lives" in is a source of emptiness and emotional
suffocation for him. Both the world and the self are experienced and
perceived emotionally as being dead, inanimate, without a soul—without feelings.

Again, these are not abstractions. Most of the cuts that inmates
inflict on themselves are not meant as punishment to relieve guilt feelings but rather, as stimuli to create physical sensations, so as to
counteract the feeling of deadness, the absence of feelings, which these
men describe as the most intolerable of their various torments. The
men who experience the deepest distress are those who feel so dead
they are incapable of feeling physical pain even when they mutilate
themselves. I cannot believe that the people I see could have been
capable of the atrocities they have committed on other living beings if
they perceived and experienced their victims as live, sentient human
beings in the same sense that any normal person identifies and em-
pathizes with others as sharing a common human sensibility. But how
can one know that others have feelings, or be moved by the feelings of
others, if one does not experience any feelings oneself?

Since the sense of aliveness and humanness that comes from loving
includes a vulnerability to pain, only those who are capable of risking
pain can experience joy. Emotional health is not the absence of pain. It
is the capacity to bear painful feelings when they occur, without letting

them stop us from loving others and continuing to feel worthy of love ourselves. A person can expose himself to the vulnerability of loving another person only if he has enough self-esteem to protect himself from the devastation he would suffer if that love were not reciprocated. He cannot afford to give to another what no one has previously given him. Nor can he give to another the love which he cannot give himself. If he has taken the chance and lost, the results can be immediately and devastatingly lethal, to others and to himself. Without love (by which I mean here love for oneself), the self collapses, the soul dies, the psyche goes to hell. Men will quickly and ferociously attack others, even kill them, if they think it will prevent their own souls from being murdered. What they immediately discover when they commit a violent act, however, is that this strategy is self-defeating. And that is why so many murderers finally decide to end their own lives as well.

The kind of man I am describing protects himself from the risk of being deprived of love by emptying his soul of love for others to an unimaginable degree. And a soul empty of love fills with hate instead. This is exactly what "Son of Sam" described when he wrote that "the unclean spirits will fill the very same void which they so subtly created with evil light [darkness] and evil knowledge. 'The void has been filled' . . . replaced with a dark, foul substance [hate] that resulted in death and destruction." For the only way a man can stop himself from what he experiences as the danger of loving others is by hating them instead.

When I speak of murderers as feeling engulfed by hate, and the world as entirely hateful, I am quoting what these men have told me. Sidney B. was a middle-aged editor of a small community magazine on the West Coast, who described himself as having barely managed to survive financially, in spite of what he perceived to be his wife's repeated efforts to sabotage his career. In the days leading up to their twentieth wedding anniversary, his wife said, "Twenty years—what a waste!" And he showed me a card she had bought, which she gave him as her anniversary "present," in which she had crossed out the printed phrase "Love is" and replaced it with "Love was." After that particularly unhappy anniversary, he reports that he awakened from a fitful sleep with the sensation that he was "drowning in an ocean of hate," and that before he was even fully awake, feeling as if he were performing his actions while still in a dream or a nightmare, he grabbed the leash of his wife's dog and strangled his wife to death.

Needless to say, his wife's actions left him feeling rejected, unloved, and humiliated. That is, of course, no justification of his homicidal behavior, either morally or legally; it is intended merely as a partial *explanation* of the *cause* of that behavior, one factor among the many that led up to this tragedy. Explanations are not to be confused with exculpations, or justifications; they serve an altogether different set of purposes, namely, causal understanding and primary prevention.

What I think lies behind this intense hate is the unmet wish to be loved, the inability actively to love anyone (self or other), and the consequent abject dependency on others to magically fill with love a bottomless pit, an inferno—the self—that is utterly empty of love. There is a wish on the part of murderous men to be loved by others, a wish which is insatiable, grounded as it is in an inability to love oneself or others. We only need to hear the life stories of these men to see the tragic way in which they have been treated with the most extreme lack of love from their earliest remembered and unremembered beginnings by the very people from whom they most needed and wanted to be loved.

I began this book by trying to show why only a tragic point of view was adequate for thinking about the problem of human violence; that we needed to look within the laboratory of the prison and the prison hospital to learn from the violent actions and psychology of those men in our society who have been quarantined because of their violence; that we need to see that violence is the ultimate humiliation, one that cuts so deep it can kill the soul even when it does not kill the body; that those who kill have been "murdered" themselves, or else fear that they are about to be destroyed, and so they kill for what appears to them as self-defense.

Violence "speaks" of an intolerable condition of human shame and rage, a blinding rage that speaks through the body. In order to "hear" and understand it more clearly, I need to turn our attention now to a more detailed study of the bodily language of violence.

Violent Action as

Symbolic Language:

Myth, Ritual,

and Tragedy

It is neither easy nor agreeable to dredge this abyss of viciousness, and yet I think it must be done, because what could be perpetrated yesterday could be attempted again tomorrow, could overwhelm us and our children. One is tempted to turn away with a grimace and close one's mind: this is a temptation one must resist.[1]

—PRIMO LEVI

IN MY EFFORT TO UNDERSTAND THE PSYCHOLOGY OF VIOLENT MEN, I OFTEN find myself turning to mythic and tragic literature. Only the Greek tragedies and those of Shakespeare, the horrors described in Thucydides and the Bible, map with fidelity the universe of human violence that I have seen in the prisons. It is only through thinking in terms of that literature that I have managed to find a way to mediate between ordinary sanity and humanity on the one hand, and unimaginable horror and monstrosity on the other. Compared to the tragedies I see and hear of daily, the abstractions of the "social sciences" seem like pale imitations of reality, like the shadows in Plato's cave. In the worlds I work in, Oedipus is not a theory, or a "complex." I have *seen* Oedipus—a man who killed his father and then blinded himself, not on the stage and not in a textbook, but in real life. I have seen Medea—a woman who killed her children in response to her husband's abandoning her for another woman. I have seen Othello—a man who murdered his wife and then took his own life. I have seen Samson (the archetypal "son of Sam"), and I have seen him many times—men who have brought the roof down on their own heads as the only means of expressing their boundless rage, when the whole world appeared to them as their enemy and they wanted to kill everyone, even, or perhaps especially, if it meant ending their own lives as well.

These experiences in the prison have led me to think that the classical myths and tragedies may have originated not so much as products of fantasy, the symbolic, "conscious" representation of the unconscious fantasies of healthy people, but as attempts to describe and represent, to cope with and make sense of—indeed to survive, emotionally and mentally—the actual crimes and atrocities that people have inflicted on one another for as far back into history as our collective memories extend.

"In the beginning was the deed," says Goethe, in *Faust*.[2] He may well be right. In the violent men I have studied, the violent act precedes the thought and the word. Much of the therapy we do with violent men consists of trying to facilitate their ability to think about and talk about their thoughts and feelings before, and instead of, committing impulsive, unreasoned, unthinkable acts of violence. The blinding of Samson, Tiresias, and the Cyclops, the blinding of Gloucester in *King Lear*, are not so much mythic "fictions" as depictions of real acts that real people commit in real life.

Violence, Myth, and Tragedy

I say this as preface to my attempt to understand what could possibly have caused one particular act of violence that seemed to me to have pushed violence to the limit beyond which physical reality does not permit humans to go, just as it exemplifies the immemorial human propensity to push violence to the limit of what is physically possible. I am speaking of a twenty-year-old man named Ross L., who was referred for psychiatric evaluation because he had cut his wrist in court, just prior to being sentenced to prison, in what he later admitted had been an attempt to delay the sentencing. His attempt was unsuccessful, and he was sentenced to prison for the rest of his natural life, for the crime of murder.

What had happened was this. On a cold winter night, he had run into a former high-school classmate in a convenience store. As his car was broken, she offered him a ride home, and during the ride he took out a knife and stabbed her to death. He then mutilated her eyes, cut out her tongue, and threw her out of the car. He was neither stealing her money nor her car; nor had he raped her. His crime stood out for me not only for its brutality and its horror, but because it displayed the most extreme loss of the human feelings that make up what we mean when we speak of "humanity" itself. Beyond that, it was utterly and totally senseless. If by some miracle the woman had lived, she still could have identified him, even without eyes or tongue, for she knew him. But in fact he had killed her, beyond any possibility of doubt. So why did he feel the need to stab out her eyes and cut her tongue apart as well? This did not protect him from being discovered; it created even more evidence of his guilt. And of course he did not "have" to kill her in the first place. The only effect of his doing so (from the standpoint of his own "self-interest") is that now he can look forward to spending the rest of his life in prison.

The very extremity of both the violence and the irrationality contained in his crime seemed to me to imply the possibility that it might reveal, more clearly than a more limited or moderate act of violence could, the psychological forces that underlie all violence; so that if we could learn to understand the emotional logic that underlay this man's crime, we might come upon factors common to all murders. What makes it worthwhile to think about this man and his motivation at all is the importance of learning to understand what causes people to behave in ways that are inhuman so that we can gain some better means of preventing such behavior in the future. It is important to learn from the human beings who commit such crimes, and it is more important, the more horrible the crimes.

In this case, the sheer inhumanity of Ross L.'s crime was so extreme that he had become barely, if at all, recognizable or identifiable as a human being. I found it very difficult to see him as a person—his crime kept getting in the way, concealing him, so to speak. It occurred to me that this elemental fact might be the first clue in my effort to understand what could have caused him to do what he did.

Reflecting further on this man, talking with him at more length, and seeing his utter absence of remorse or guilt and his feeling not only of total innocence but of wounded innocence (despite the fact that he did not deny that he had committed the acts of which he was found guilty); his feeling that other people were treating him unfairly and picking on him and always had; his attribution to others of all responsibility for his problems; his feelling that all the justification he needed for his crime was that "I didn't like the way she was looking at me" and "I didn't want her talking about me"; his extreme sensitivity to insult; his boasting and grandiosity; his assumption that he was entitled to have special privileges; his reiterated threats that if he did not get what he wanted he would kill himself or us and that whatever he did would be our fault; his unwillingness to accept responsibility for anything that would make him "look bad"; coupled with a repeated litany of complaints describing his constant, intolerable personal frustration and torment (all of which he attributed to his environment and the people in it, not to any inner conflict or dissatisfaction with himself), I began to realize that his crime makes all too much sense, when one grasps the special logic that lies behind it.

How can we go about learning to see what that logic is? I will start with Freud's insight that thoughts and fantasies are symbolic representations of actions, so they can precede actions and serve as substitutes for them as well. And then I will add that the opposite is also true: *Actions are symbolic representations of thoughts.* That is, actions can precede and serve as substitutes for conscious thoughts. They can take the place of thinking in words, if the behavior is never interpreted or translated into words and ideas. The philosopher and literary critic Kenneth Burke wrote that in order to understand literature, we must learn to interpret *language as symbolic action.*[3] I am suggesting that in order to understand violence we must reverse that procedure and learn to interpret *action as symbolic language*—with a "symbolic logic" of its own.

Individuals or groups engaging in any given behavior may or may not be able to state consciously the meaning of their action. They may not be able to translate a symbolic action, such as a ritual, into that other symbolic medium called language. Nevertheless, all behavior is meaningful. All behavior is the embodiment or enactment of a purpose or wish—that is, a wishful fantasy or myth, a plot or narrative, and sometimes a nightmare or delusion—that can also be expressed, by means of language, as a thought. Actions also serve as a means of expressing the feelings associated with the thought, such as love, hate, sadness, or fear, though again the symbolic medium is physical action rather than words.

Freud pointed out that people with disorders of character, whose psychopathology manifests itself in the form of abnormal, destructive, or life-threatening behavior, act out in their *behavior* the *fantasies* that normal and neurotic people experience only in their *unconscious* minds (such as in nightmares, or in the dreams of incest to which Plato refers). They can also be described as acting out the fantasies that psychotic people experience *consciously* in their *delusions.*[4]

To understand murder and the other forms of violent behavior, then, we must learn to interpret that behavior—translate its purpose and meaning into words and thoughts, just as Freud uncoded the somatic symptoms of his hysterical patients as the symbolic speech by means of which they spoke through their bodies, so that the body itself became the medium of communication. Now we need to do the same with violence, applying the same principles to the understanding of violence that Freud did to the explanation of compulsive behaviors, repetitive accidents, magical rituals, slips of the tongue, delusions, superstitions, myths, dreams, and so on.

Understanding violence requires understanding what thought or fantasy the violent behavior symbolically represents. Doing this is especially difficult in the case of most violent people, because they are so oriented toward expressing their thoughts in the form of actions rather than words. Their verbal inarticulateness prevents them from telling us in words the thought their behavior symbolically expresses.

But this task is important because regardless of whatever subjective, symbolic meaning violent behavior has to the murderer, the objective consequence of it is not symbolic at all; it is all too literal and real. It is also so senseless as to defy our efforts at comprehension through the usual means and the ordinary assumptions of rational thought, common sense, and self-interest. Yet until we can learn to make sense of this senselessness, to comprehend this incomprehensible, how can we ever understand it? And if we cannot understand violence, how can we ever prevent it? Understanding violence ultimately requires learning how to translate violent actions into words.

My hope was that if I could learn to understand this one murder, then the same principles of interpretation could be applied to other acts of violence. My first clue to the thought being expressed in Ross L.'s senseless and apparently unmotivated murder and mutilation was that the more time I spent with him, the clearer it became that his character—his habits and behavior patterns, the moral value system in terms of which he justified his behavior and goals—served as a defense against the threat of being treated with scorn and disrespect, of being perceived as a weakling, not a "real man," someone who could be laughed at or gossiped about. This suggested that he might suffer from feelings of impotence and inadequacy as a man, and that as a result he might feel vulnerable and hypersensitive to any experience that would reflect that image of himself back to him. And as I talked with him further, he confirmed that he had indeed had such experiences, and had indeed found them intolerable.

For example, before puberty he was regularly beaten up and teased by other boys, who taunted him as a "wimp," a "punk," and a "pussy." "Punk" is the derogatory, homophobic prison slang term for the passive homosexual sex object, or "kid," of a more powerful man; and "pussy" is, of course, the equally derogatory slang term for the female genitals. So he was being called an inadequate man, or non-man, in every possible way.

When he was thirteen, however, he began drinking and taking street drugs, which helped him behave violently, which bolstered his self-respect as a man. He also boasted that he could rebuild the engine of any car within three hours. Mechanical expertise with cars was important to him, as it is to many teenage males, as a means of proving his adequacy as a man. But he committed his crime when he was without a car, because he had been unable to pay the mechanic who was rebuilding its engine. The girl he murdered was a high-school senior, a former classmate of his. In his own eyes, by accepting her offer of a ride on a cold night, he had been forced to admit that he lacked both the money and the mechanical skills to have a car of his own, and he had to depend on her for help.

He also boasted of having become "the Don Juan" of his hometown, a "real stud" who had no trouble "getting girls." He claimed that he had not been hurt when ever he had been rejected by a girl, though he insisted that that had very seldom occurred. Despite this braggadocio, he was nevertheless sexually frustrated and unsuccessful enough, and angry enough at women, to tell an acquaintance shortly before the crime that he wanted to get a woman, any woman, into a car, "screw" her and then kill her and throw her out of the car. In the event, raping proved to be beyond his abilities, so he "only" killed and mutilated her. He made the police's task of finding the murderer easier because he could not resist attempting to impress one of his acquaintances with his manhood by bragging about the brutal crime he had just committed.

All of this suggests to me that the logic that underlay this murder and mutilation was the emotional logic of the family of painful feelings called shame and humiliation, which, when they become overwhelming because a person has no basis for self-respect, can be intolerable, and so devastating as to bring about the collapse of self-esteem and thus the death of the self. His behavior, as we explore it further, can be seen as a desperate attempt—what could be more desperate?—to ward off these catastrophic experiences; and I will suggest that we cannot understand his grotesque crime without understanding the logic of shame. But what is that logic?

We all know that shame motivates the wish for concealment, the wish not to be seen; the word itself comes from Old Germanic roots meaning to clothe or cover oneself.[5] Darwin pointed out that "under a keen sense of shame there is a strong desire for concealment. . . . An ashamed person can hardly endure to meet the gaze of those present. . . ."[6]

Erik Erikson takes this insight a step further, in a way that may help us to understand our murderer more deeply. "Shame supposes," Erikson says,[7] "that one is completely exposed and conscious of being looked at. . . . One is visible and not ready to be visible; which is why we dream of shame as a situation in which we are stared at in a condition of incomplete dress, . . . with one's pants down. . . . He who is ashamed would like to force the world not to look at him, not to notice his exposure. He would like to destroy the eyes of the world."

Erikson quotes the folk song about a murderer who is standing under the gallows waiting to be hanged:

"My name it is Sam Hall,
And I hate you one and all,
God damn your eyes!"

All of which is less surprising when we reflect that, as Aristotle[8] realized long ago, ". . . we feel more shame about a thing if it is done openly, before all men's eyes. Hence the proverb, 'shame dwells in the eyes.'" But not only the eyes—for as Aristotle also realized, we feel more shame "before those who are likely to tell everybody about you"; and since "not telling others is as good as not believing you wrong," we can understand why preventing them from telling others about you, such as by preventing them from talking at all, is one of the oldest and most powerful ways of reducing one's risk of being shamed.

The fear and anger and paranoia that shame provokes, and specifically toward eyes, is also captured in folk beliefs (and occasional individual delusions) about the "Evil Eye"; though this anger can also, as in the case of this murderer, be directed toward the gossiping tongue that can repeat to others what the eye has seen. To understand or make sense of this man's mutilation of his victim, which is senseless from any rational standpoint, we need to see it as the concrete, nonverbal expression of the following thought (which has the structure, like all unconscious thought, of magical thinking): "If I destroy eyes, I will destroy shame" (for one can only be shamed in the [evil] eyes of others); in other words, "If I destroy eyes, I cannot be shamed"; and "if I destroy tongues, then I cannot be talked about, ridiculed or laughed at; my shamefulness cannot be revealed to others."

The emotional logic that underlies this particular crime, then, which I called the logic of shame, takes the form of magical thinking that says, "If I kill this person in this way, I will kill shame—I will be able to protect myself from being exposed and vulnerable to and potentially overwhelmed by the feeling of shame" (the "objective correlative" of which consists of being observed and talked about).

My point here is not that violent people focus their hostility exclusively on eyes or tongues, for, of course, they do not.[9] Rather, I am attempting, by analyzing one of the most extreme examples of apparently unmotivated and irrational, senseless violence, to find symptoms that can serve as clues to what is going on, and can help us to begin to make sense of the senseless. The fact that Ross L. focused his attention and hostility on his victim's eyes and tongue is a valuable clue to his corresponding preoccupation with and morbid hypersensitivity to the fear of being overwhelmed by shame and ridicule; and that at least suggests the plausibility of looking further to see if there is evidence that it might be this fear which ultimately motivated not only this particular murder but all aggressive, apparently unprovoked violence. If Ross L. is at all typical of other murderers, then we would have to conclude that the most dangerous men on earth are those who are afraid that they are wimps. Wars have been started for less.

The Symbolism of Collective Violence

To draw out this parallel between murder and war, I had hoped that an analysis of Ross L.'s violence, precisely because it was so extreme and unlimited, might throw light on other acts of extreme violence, wherever they might occur. Upon reflection, his individual atrocity seemed to match, in its cruelty, irrationality, and ultimate self-destructiveness, the equally incomprehensible collective atrocities such as those committed by Nazi Germany; to represent a kind of parallel, on a microcosmic scale, to what the Nazis did on a macrocosmic one.

As a political movement, Nazism focused so predominantly on violence (on the scale of genocide), virtually as an end in itself, that it might almost be considered a "pure culture" of violence. That is why it is so relevant to note the centrality of shame as the main-motive force, or emotive force, behind one of the most lethal forms of collective violence in this century or any other. Hitler came to power on the campaign promise to undo "the shame of Versailles"[10]—and clearly that promise, and the sensitivity to shame from which it derived its power, struck a responsive chord in the German people as a whole.

As Seymour Martin Lipset[11] and others have shown, by the time of the Depression on the crest of which Hitler rode to power in 1933, the group who supported him most strongly at the polls were the lower middle classes. The members of this group felt in danger of losing their capital and suffering a loss of social and economic status, a degradation, by becoming part of the humiliated, inferior, poverty-stricken lower class, or felt they had already suffered that humiliating sea-change into something poor and strange, and were eager for revenge—for a way of re-establishing their status or sense of power—which Hitler and his Nazi party promised them in abundance. Downward social mobility, unemployment, and homelessness are among the most potent stimuli of shame, and are a key to the politics of violence.

But why was the anger that shame stimulates directed so strongly against the Jews? One reason was that Jews came to be the scapegoats for the status-envies generated by the economic inequities that were in turn generated by the social and economic system, since they had come to symbolize and be identified with wealth and the capitalist system (as symbolized most powerfully, perhaps, by the Rothschild banking family). This process was facilitated by the fact that Jews were the only group that had been permitted to lend money at interest, and prohibited from practicing most other professions or owning most other forms of capital, throughout the Christian era and world. At the same time that wealthy Jews were seen as threatening the economic status and security of the middle class from above, other Jews—Marx and his followers—were seen as threatening them from below, with threats to overturn the entire economic system and dispossess the middle class in the name of the proletariat. In response to all this, the lower middle classes focused their resentment over their threatened humiliation on those who, in their minds, had come to symbolize the social forces responsible for their plight—the Jews. Those are among the reasons that anti-Semitism was the central pillar of Nazi ideology, so that destroying the Jews became arguably more important to Hitler than winning the war.

But many of these social forces, and the envy, fear, and hatred of the Jews that were stimulated by those forces, had been around for the past two thousand years or more. It is especially relevant, given the analysis of violence presented just above, to remember that throughout most of European history, as Leonard Moss and Stephen Cappannari have pointed out,

> the Jewish people as a whole were viewed as . . . the source of the evil eye. . . . The Council of Elvira (Spain, fourth century) . . . forbade Jews to stand among ripening crops belonging to Christians lest they cause the crops to rot and wither with their malevolent glances. The Jews of England were forbidden to attend the coronation of Richard the Lion-Hearted (1189) for fear that an evil eye might harm the crown. So feared was the purported power of the Jew that the German word for evil eye remains to this day *Judenblick* (Jew's glance).[12]

But why was that so? Why did Gentiles in general, and Nazis in particular, feel so threatened by the Jews, and specifically by being gazed at by Jewish eyes? To answer those questions, it is relevant to note that anthropologists have found throughout the world that envy is at the root of folk beliefs in the evil eye. And the "word, envy, [itself] is linked to the evil eye. The Latin word for envy, *invidia*, from which our word envy derives, consists of the verb *videre*, 'to see,' and the prefix *in*, meaning 'against.' "[13] And as Hannah Arendt pointed out, it is virtually "a 'truism' that . . . anti-Semitism is . . . a form of envy"—though the fact that it is a truism does not mean that it is not true.[14]

One does not have to speculate about this link between envy and anti-Semitism in the Nazi mind; it can be confirmed and documented empirically by reading Hitler's many envious comments about Jews. For example, in one particularly vivid passage, he contrasts with bitterness and rage his own poverty as a failed artist with the wealth of a "rich Jewish couple" whose luxurious motor car he would see arriving at concerts in Vienna during his youth.[15] In fact, Hitler's writings in general constitute one long chronicle of complaints about the shame and humiliation to which both he, in his youth, and the German-speaking peoples after World War I, had been subjected—all of which he managed to blame mostly on the Jews, for whom it is hard to say which he felt more strongly, envy or hate. It is also relevant to note that envy, like jealousy, is a form of shame, a member of the same family of feelings. For to feel envious of someone is to feel inferior to that person, with respect to whatever it is one envies about the other.

The fact that the Nazis felt both intense shame and envy, and especially envy of the Jews, is consistent with, and would indeed be expected, when it reaches the intensity of paranoia, to result in the superstition (or collective paranoid delusion) that the Jews were the bearers of the evil eye. But that also clarifies something else—namely, the meaning and motivation, or cause, of the Nazis' irrational and otherwise incomprehensible, and even self-defeating, preoccupation with destroying the entire Jewish people. The collective murder of the Jews can be seen as a symbolic representation of the thought: "If we destroy the Jews, we will destroy the evil eye (because they are the bearers of the evil eye)"; or in other words, "If we destroy the Jews, we will destroy shame—we cannot be shamed." Their motivation was, like Ross L.'s, to destroy their vulnerability to being shamed.

At this point we have come full circle, from individual murder (homicide) to collective murder (genocide). The Holocaust, the Nazi genocide of the Jews, follows exactly the same emotional logic, and has the same symbolic structure, as the individual murder and mutilation with which we began this discussion of the symbolism of violence.

The Symbolism of Shame and Violence in Myth and Tragedy

Another clue that the emotional symbolism of Ross L.'s crime reveals a general psychological truth about violence can be found in the frequent references in the Bible and in Shakespeare to the destruction of eyes and tongues, in response to being shamed. For example, what is the emotion (the motive) that leads Delilah to have Samson blinded? Of course, she and the other Philistines are already eager to avenge themselves on Samson for his past violence toward them, but why do they specifically want to blind him, as opposed to any of the many other ways they could have injured or even killed him once they were able to overpower him? Delilah tells us the answer to this question over and over again, uttering exactly the same reproach against Samson on three separate occasions (to make sure we don't miss the point?): "Behold, thou hast mocked me" (in the King James version); or, as it is translated in the New English Bible: "I see you have made a fool of me" (Judges 16:10, 13, 15). To feel mocked, or made a fool of, is to feel shamed. The story teaches us that the most direct, literal, and "figurative" way to put an end to that feeling of shame is to blind the person in whose eyes one feels shamed—which is exactly what she does.

The Bible is full of images of eyes and tongues being plucked out or cut out in response to words or actions that expose someone to disrespect, insolence, haughtiness, boasting, or anything else that causes, or constitutes, shaming them. For example, what did the angels do to the men of Sodom who tried to rape (and thus dishonour) them? "They smote the men that were at the door of the house with blindness" (Genesis 19:11). What happens to "the eye that *mocketh* at his father, and *despiseth* to obey his mother (or "*scorns* a mother's old age")?" "The ravens of the valley shall pick it out, and the young eagles shall eat it"

(Proverbs 30:17). The penalty for *mocking, despising, and scorning* (three synonyms for *"shaming"*) is to have one's eyes picked out and eaten. What happens to those who shame, insult, or disrespect others by being proud and boastful toward them; who make fools of them by telling lies; who "talk with smooth lip and double heart"? The Psalmist tells us that "the Lord shall cut off all smooth [deceptive] lips, and the tongue that speaketh proud things [or "talks so boastfully"]" (Psalm 12). Similarly, the Psalmist prays to God, with reference to his enemies, "Destroy, O Lord, and divide their tongues." Why does the Psalmist want God to destroy their tongues? "Because of the voice of the enemy . . .: for they cast iniquity upon me [or "they revile me," or in other words, "they denounce me with abusive language"]" (Psalm 55). The solution to the problem of being shamed verbally is written on the body: "Destroy . . . and divide their tongues."

Why there should be so much violence directed toward tongues and lips is less surprising when we read also how much destructive power is attributed to those organs. For example, we read in the Psalms that "your slanderous tongue is sharp as a razor" (Psalm 52), and we read of "my persecutors . . . whose tongues are sharp swords" (Psalm 57), and so on.

This is, of course, poetry, not literal description. But what the poet does verbally, using one set of words and ideas as a symbol or metaphor for another, the violent person does literally and physically, using tongues and eyes as his symbol or metaphor for the same emotions and motives that the poet is speaking of—shame, pride, fear, hatred, and so on. It is precisely because the great poets have such an extraordinary ability to express, represent, and evoke these emotions in words and, more specifically, in words that represent actions (such as cutting out eyes or tongues) which serve as "objective correlatives" for these emotions, that we are able, with their help, to translate the actions of violent people into the words and ideas, emotions and motives, of which violent acts are the physical symbols.

Shakespeare, with his usual profound psychological insight, also understood that when people feel shamed by another person, when they feel inferior, envious, jealous, rejected, insulted, ridiculed, or taunted, they feel an impulse to put out that person's eyes and tongue. For example, in *Antony and Cleopatra,* when a messenger exposes the Egyptian queen to feelings of shame and humiliation by informing her that her lover, Antony, has married another woman, Cleopatra attempts to diminish her feelings of shame by threatening to destroy the messenger's eyes: "Hence, horrible villain, or I'll spurn ["kick"] thine eyes/Like balls before me" (II.v.63–64).

But these are only verbal threats. A much more gruesome scene appears in *King Lear,* when Edmund arranges to have his father, Gloucester, actually blinded. Why does Edmund do this? and especially, to his own father? Edmund explains this reason, quite explicitly: His father has shamed him; his father is the source of his feelings of shame. Gloucester has shamed Edmund by fathering him out of wedlock; Edmund is socially and legally a bastard. Edmund realizes that his bastardy constitutes, as he realizes the word itself implies, baseness and debasement; his father has made him base, of inferior or humble (humiliated) social and economic status, in a society that values "legitimacy." Shakespeare depicts Edmund's preoccupation with this theme:

> Why bastard? Wherefore base?
> When my dimensions are as well compact,
> My mind as generous, and my shape as true,
> As honest madam's issue? Why brand they us
> With base? with baseness? bastardy? base, base?
>
> (*King Lear,* I.ii.6–10)

Furthermore, Gloucester has added shame to shame by feeling ashamed of Edmund; that is, ashamed of having fathered a bastard. When Kent sees Edmund with Gloucester and says, "Is not this your son, my lord?" Gloucester replies, "His breeding, sir, hath been at my charge. I have so often *blush'd* [i.e., felt ashamed] *to acknowledge him,* that now I am braz'd to it" (I.i.8–11). Speaking of Edmund's bastardy, he says, "Do you smell a fault?" and adds "yet . . . the whoreson must be acknowledg'd" (I.i.16–24). All this he says in front of Edmund—at the eventual cost of his eyes.

And tongues are just as important. Men who feel sufficiently shamed by another person's words (by their raillery, ridicule, gossip, or slander) will be tempted to cut out that person's tongue, particularly if they do not feel articulate or witty enough to defend themselves adequately with words or nonviolent actions of their own. In *Troilus and Cressida*, for example, Ajax responds to the insults by which Thersites has been shaming him by threatening: "I shall cut out your tongue" (2.1.107). Verbal shame is the stimulus; cutting out the tongue is the expressive response. But it is also true that the man who already feels overwhelmed by shame (and that means, at the extreme, the paranoid person) does not have to be confronted by a Thersites in order to feel insulted and disrespected. The shame-driven person is quite capable of hearing shame—and may be incapable of hearing anything else—in even the most benign of words.

The Behavioral Symbolism of Violence

Even if it is clear that eyes and tongues are symbolic vehicles for, and communicators of, shame, envy, and related feelings, what does this have to do with violent actions? What desires drive us to communicate symbolically through the body? To answer that question, we will look a bit more deeply into bodily actions as a mode of communication and symbolization that can function as an alternative to language.

Darwin[16] was perhaps the first major thinker to demonstrate in detail how the bodily movements and actions of animals (including humans) serve as a kind of proto-language, expressing and communicating emotions, information, and intentions. Darwin limited himself to explicating relatively simple behavior patterns such as facial expressions, and nonvolitional physiological/emotional reactions such as blushing. But a generation later, Sir Julian Huxley[17] borrowed the term *ritual*—which previously referred to the rules of religious behavior—to describe the more complex behavior patterns of animals which had lost their original primarily physiological function (locomotion, copulation, nutrition, etc.) by becoming purely symbolic ceremonies, taking on the new function of communication.

In many species, staring at another animal with a fixed gaze serves the purpose not of looking but of communicating a message of intimidation and threats. In virtually every species studied, including humans, staring eyes communicate the extreme emotions of both love and hate. Staring is perceived throughout the animal kingdom as hostile and intimidating, as a means of establishing dominance. Fights that male animals, including humans, engage in with other members of their own species are almost always status contests, to establish which male is higher or lower in the pecking order, which determines access to sexual and economic privileges, such as desirable mates or better hunting grounds. In other contexts, staring expresses tenderness and love.

However, in both contexts—hostile and affectionate—staring eyes set the stage for intense intimacy. Averting one's eyes is a universal sign of submission, appeasement, or surrender in the context of hostility or rivalry. But it also means the absence of hostile intent, or the absence of any intention to establish greater intimacy than the other is ready for. Paradoxically, it can also signal, in a sexual or potentially sexual context, a lack of interest or the withdrawal of erotic interest; or, on the other hand, a willingness for sexual intimacy. The message may well be, "I am not available for that"; or, it can be a form of sexual teasing, part of a ritual courtship ceremony—"I am running away in order to provoke you to pursue me."

Illustrations of the symbolic, expressive, and communicative function of violent behavior could be multiplied endlessly with examples from throughout the animal kingdom. But my point here is simply to remind the reader that behavior can be just as symbolic as words; that like words, bodily behavior communicates meanings, often of astonishing specificity, about matters of life-and-death importance, which can be understood quite clearly, consistently, and reliably by those to whom the behavioral signs and signals are directed. Long before words and language were invented, symbolic behavior patterns served the same function that words later came to serve—albeit with vastly less flexibility.

Interpreting the Language of Violence

If we return for a moment to the murderous acts of Ross L., we can now see that it would be impossible to understand the mutilation of a young woman's eyes and tongue, except by seeing it as a concrete, nonverbal expression of unconscious magical thinking, in the service of trying to escape overwhelming, annihilating shame. His actions say: "If I destroy eyes I cannot be shamed"; and "if I destroy tongues I cannot be talked about, ridiculed, or laughed at; nor will my shamefulness, my shameful secrets, be revealed to others."

In bodily language, murder is to behavior what paranoia is to thought, and hate is to feelings. Murder is the symbolic representation of a paranoid thought, but by means of actions rather than words, in people who are not necessarily delusional, psychotic, or insane (at least in terms of the conventional psychiatric and legal definitions of those terms). Violence toward others may be thought of as the behavioral equivalent of paranoia, or the behavioral version of it—its hypostasis, the translation into terms of physical reality of the waking dream (or nightmare) which paranoia represents in terms of words and thoughts, fantasies and delusions.

But paranoia itself is the form of psychopathology that results when a person's ability to differentiate between feelings and facts is overwhelmed by feelings of shame, so that even ordinary experiences may be perceived mistakenly as shameful, culminating in the increasing delusion that one is actually being shamed or exposed, spied on and observed, held up to ridicule and scorn, criticism, and scurrilous gossip.

Murder represents (for the murderer) the ultimate act of self-defense, a last resort against being overwhelmed by shame and "losing one's mind," an attempt to ward off psychosis or "going crazy." The subjective sense on the part of the murderer is that he must commit this act or lose everything—his mind, his sanity, himself. It is an attempt to hold off paranoid delusions; the riddling, tormented feeling that one is being spied on, watched, hexed by an evil eye, gossiped about, ridiculed, and accused of possessing character traits that shame-driven men find intolerably shameful, such as weakness, cowardice, impotence, homosexuality, sexual inadequacy, and so on.

Again, the point is not that violent men focus their hostility exclusively on eyes or tongues, for, of course, they do not. Nor are their actions necessarily accompanied consciously by the interpretive language which I have suggested in the course of my discussion. On the contrary, the capacity to "control" one's impulses by expressing them in words rather than actions could prevent murder, in the sense that words are often the only alternatives to violent actions (which is one reason why both psychotherapy and education can help to prevent violence).

By analyzing the detailed phenomenology of any given act of violence, we can discover clues that can help us to understand the emotional forces that motivate such behavior. The fact that Ross L. focused his attention and hostility on his victim's eyes and tongue signified or symbolized his morbid hypersensitivity to the fear of being overwhelmed by shame and ridicule.

One cannot read the newspapers without coming across the same pattern of behavior in one form or another. For example, during a highly publicized murder trial in New York a few years ago, the defendant, Joel

Steinberg, was convicted of the inexplicable and horrendous crime of beating to death his adopted daughter, Lisa, and of beating and intimidating his common law wife, Hedda Nussbaum. As Nussbaum described his behavior in the weeks and months leading up to the murder, it became clear that Steinberg had "developed a fear of being stared at," so that he "repeatedly poked [her] in the eyes for this offense, causing . . . damage to her [eyes]." In the weeks before he killed Lisa, he reportedly complained about her staring at him also. "Joel had been saying I was staring and the children were staring at him, that we were trying to hypnotize him," Ms. Nussbaum testified. Finally, Steinberg explained his fatal blows to Lisa by saying, "The staring business had gotten to be too much," that he had "knocked down Lisa to protect" himself from her stares.

At the end of Steinberg's trial, an incident occurred which would seem to reveal both his deficient capacity for feeling guilty together with an extreme hypersensitivity to ridicule. As Steinberg was delivering a self-exculpatory plea for a light sentence, in the course of which he described himself as the victim, and, instead of expressing guilt for killing his daughter, said he had remorse for himself, for losing his own life, he interrupted himself to accuse the judge of laughing at him. The judge replied that he was not laughing at the defendant, he was merely astonished at what he was saying.[18]

These personality traits are, in my experience, the main motives for violence: the fear of shame and ridicule, and the overbearing need to prevent others from laughing at oneself by making them weep instead.

When the criminologist Jack Katz[19] described murderers' conception of what they were doing as performing an act of "righteous slaughter," he was not exaggerating. Murderers have simply gone back to the behavioral origins of the ritual sacrifice of humans, which is why, in order to understand murderers, we need to understand these same origins.

The purpose of rituals, whether of animals or of humans, is to communicate, by means of behavior rather than words, an "idea," which is why "the two basic characteristics of ritual behavior" (and we are talking about nothing in this murder if we are not talking about ritual) are, as Walter Burkert says,

> repetition and theatrical exaggeration. For the essentially immutable patterns do not transmit differentiated and complex information but, rather, just one piece of information each. This single piece of information is considered so important that it is reinforced by constant repetition [and theatrical exaggeration] so as to avoid misunderstanding. . . .[20]

The "theatrical exaggeration"—the sheer extremity and bizarreness of the murder committed by Ross L. and the behavior associated with it—could hardly be more pronounced. And the murderer was certainly engaged in "repetition" as well: destroying the eyes of his sacrificial victim was not enough; he had to destroy her tongue as well, in order to communicate his point so clearly that no one could miss it. The "single piece of information" he intended to communicate by means of these actions may be expressed in this interpretation: "I am not a wimp, a punk, and a pussy"—though that sentence itself can be paraphrased or translated into any of a variety of synonymous messages: "I am not shameful," "I cannot be shamed by others, I will shame them instead," and so forth.

But, for the fullest exemplification of these points, we may need to turn to a murderer who surpassed even the one we have already discussed—in both psychopathology and violence. If his behavior illustrates even more comprehensively the symbolism of violence, perhaps it is because this man was not only violent but also psychotic.

THE CASE OF DENNIS X.

At the age of nineteen, Dennis X. developed "delusions of grandeur," and came to believe that he was God. Over the next thirteen years, whenever he was not in a mental hospital, he would get high on marijuana, LSD, or alcohol, have sexual escapades (usually with other males) about which he felt great shame and conflict, following which he would go into a "homosexual panic," become psychotic, agitated, and assaultive, get arrested, and become rehospitalized. As a result, because of his fear that he would not be able to resist repeating this cycle, Dennis X. began spending most of his time at home in his pajamas, where his mother (and, when she was home, his sister) took care of him. He would become acutely and grossly psychotic whenever he felt "unsupported," such as when his mother would criticize him, worry about his ability to take care of himself, or pressure him to be more active and independent. At these times he would become delusional, insisting rather desperately that he was God and that if people did not believe in Him or lost faith in Him, he would cause earthquakes and cataclysms, wipe out whole populations, and cause hell for all eternity. Sometimes he would also claim to be a number of different heroes from history, such as Alexander, Caesar, and others, and say that he had been reincarnated many times. However, he did tend to calm down when his caretakers, whether at home or in the hospital, appeared not to notice or criticize or draw his attention to his lack of activity and independence, but simply took care of him in the unqualified and un-demanding way that they usually did.

Be that as it may, at the same time that Dennis X. resisted leaving the house and clung to his life-style of virtually complete passivity and dependency, he described himself as feeling smothered by what he perceived as his mother's and sister's overprotectiveness. At these times he believed he could read sexual thoughts in their minds, and would accuse them of having sexual desires for him, calling his sister "the bitch of Buchenwald" because "she castrates men."

During a recent hospitalization, Dennis X. had met a woman to whom he was attracted and whom he had fantasies of marrying. He called this woman his "divine and holy love," and felt strongly that sex should not be part of their relationship until they were married. On one last occasion, his mother finally succeeded in persuading him to aban-

don his self-imposed hibernation at home and persuaded him to go out
of the house, where he became increasingly convinced that a man in
the neighborhood was the Devil, and that this man/Devil was tor-
menting him by placing into his mind unacceptable sexual thoughts
about his girlfriend. He also believed that the Devil himself wanted to
have sex with his girlfriend.

In this context, Dennis X. had repeated nightmares that the Devil
was cuckolding him by having sex with the woman he was interested in.
These dreams increased his feelings of shame over his masculine sexual
inadequacy to the breaking point, or perhaps it would be more accurate
to say that the dreams themselves were caused by the fact that his
feelings were coming to the breaking point. On the morning of the
murder, Dennis X. awoke with more sexual thoughts about his girlfriend, decided he had "had enough" with this Devil, and set out to find
and destroy him, for which purpose he armed himself with the knife
with which he did exactly that. The police report indicated that the
victim had been killed "in what appeared to be . . . a ritualistic manner."

One always hesitates to report violent behavior that is bizarre and
distressing. Still, we have to confront acts that are being committed
every day around the globe. For if we are to increase our ability to
prevent such atrocities, then we have to examine them and attempt to
learn from them until we get some deeper understanding of what could
possibly bring some men to the point where they could do such things.
The way this man described his plan, after he was arrested for killing
"the Devil," was to say that he had intended to "gouge out his eyes, cut
off his ears, cut out his tongue, cut off his penis and testicles, and then
stuff all these up his anus." He was unable to complete that project
only because the knife broke. Following the murder, Dennis X. experienced no feelings of guilt or remorse, and there was also a diminishing
of his feelings of shame. In fact, it would appear that Dennis X.'s
violent behavior actually increased his self-esteem. It had the effect of
replacing his chronic feelings of inferiority with feelings of pride. This

is, I believe, the most common reason for engaging in violence. As Dennis X. put it, "I wanted to get credit for killing the Devil; I was crazy, bragging about it." If ever there was a case of committing righteous slaughter, doing God's work, or performing a sacred act or ritual, this was it, except that in this case, the murder was not committed for God, but by God.

After his arrest, Dennis X. felt the police were bullying him, as a result of which, as he admitted with great embarrassment, "I wanted my Mom." He also stated that he felt "weak, not like a full man" when his mother arrived at the jailhouse. At that point he "gave up hope" of being either God or a man, for everyone "had found out the truth about me"—that he was not God. His mother's presence made him feel weak, leading him to confess to the police.

That feelings of worthlessness, failure, embarrassment, weakness, and being less than a man were central to Dennis X.'s experience of himself, is, I think, reasonably clear from this account. He appears also to have been deeply ashamed of giving in to his wish to let himself be taken care of by his mother and sister, which he could only see as unacceptably passive and dependent behavior for a grown man. He had tried to fend off that image of himself as little more than a big baby by imagining that they saw him as a sexually desirable man instead, in fact so attractive that they desired him sexually and wanted to keep him for themselves.

Dennis X.'s strategy for diminishing his feelings of shame did not work, since the sexual thoughts he was projecting onto his sister and mother, and eventually, onto the "Devil," were a disguise for his underlying wish not to be a sexually mature man, capable of entering into mature sexual relationships. He wanted to remain at home in his pajamas like a perpetual infant. As a result, Dennis X.'s sexual feelings and thoughts, both "heterosexual" and "homosexual," only increased his feelings of shame, perhaps because he had not devised any way to integrate them into a life plan consistent with being an independent, socially and sexually adequate adult man; rather, they seemed more like failed attempts to disguise his real but unacceptable, shame-provoking wish, which was to be taken care of like a baby.

Dennis X. tried to fend off these feelings of shame by imagining that his own wishes were really those of others. He tried to blame his mother and his sister for rendering him impotent, making him weak, controlling him, desiring him, and so on, in an attempt to avoid owning up to his own feelings of being unmanly and weak, wanting to stay at home with his mother and be a baby, not a man.

When people perceive their wishes as rendering them passive or powerless, dependent, helpless, immature, and inadequate both sexually and socially, those wishes are shameful, and they feel that they themselves are contemptible. When that happens, they are likely to project those wishes onto others, experiencing others as wanting to control them. In Dennis's case, he acted those needs and wishes out by behaving so as to assure that people would take care of him for the rest of his life—first his family, then mental hospitals, and finally, more definitively and permanently, a prison mental hospital.

Attributing to others the fact that he was weak, unmanned, and controlled seems to have been a way to save face; for Dennis X. could only feel shame over his own desire for others to take care of him. Only if those wishes were other peoples'—initially his mother's and sister's, then the Devil's, and finally the legal and psychiatric authorities'—would he not need to feel so ashamed.

Murder itself was part of his defensive system, for by behaving in a way that was active, independent, powerful, and aggressive, Dennis X. felt he could negate or wipe out the opposite image of himself as passive, dependent, impotent, and needing love and care. After all, what could possibly be more aggressive than killing someone? What clearer statement could a man make that he needs no one than saying in the language of violent action, "See, I don't need you—I will even kill you to show how little I need you."

But if his assault on his victim's eyes and tongue were also part of this strategy for avoiding and undoing the shame that he felt over his lack of competency, potency, and maturity, why did Dennis X. also want to engage in the other mutilations he planned? Destroying the victim's ears is most simply understood, I would think, as the counterpart and extension of destroying his tongue; for just as the tongue is the organ by means of which people laugh at and spread gossip about others, so the ears are the organs by means of which they hear slander and ridicule—so that to increase even further one's safety against being shamed and ridiculed, one would want to destroy not only the eyes and tongues of the world but also the ears.

But why would he also want to emasculate his victim? Because shame dwells not only in the eyes but also in the genitals. The relationship between shame and genitals is so close and inextricable that the words for the two are identical in most languages. In Greek, for example, *pudenda* means both shame and genitals; the French word for shame, *pudeur,* and the English word for genitals, pudenda, both derive from the Greek. In German, one expression for the genitals is *Schamteile,* "parts of shame." In early translations of the Bible, according to the *Oxford English Dictionary,* the word shame was used to refer interchangeably to the genitals and to the emotion, shame, that is so closely associated with the genitals. Even in contemporary English, the use of the word "privates" to refer to the genitals communicates this same connotation—that the genitals are sources of shame, and are hence (like anything that is shameful) to be concealed or kept private. And, of course, we are all familiar with the first recorded description of the origin of the feeling of shame—namely, Adam and Eve's discovery that they were naked, i.e., their genitals were exposed. Indeed, the association between shame and genitals is so close that the word shame is often used as if it referred only to sexual modesty (i.e., the desire to cover the genitals), rather than to the whole range of other issues that it arises in response to, such as feelings of weakness, sexual and social inadequacy, worthlessness, rejection, immaturity, incompetence, inferiority, passivity, dependency, impotence, homosexuality, failure, and so on.

Dennis X, as I have indicated, experienced all these shame-provoking feelings, wishes, and images of himself. Thus his idea to emasculate his victim and place the castrated genitals into the man's anus (the site of anal intercourse among gay men, as Dennis was well aware) can be seen as being the condensed and concentrated symbolic expression of a large number of closely related thoughts or messages, such as, for example: "I am not castrated (unmanly, or sexually inadequate as a man), or homosexual, or defective, or weak, or vulnerable to being cuckolded, and therefore shameful—you are!"

But it is not only male genitals that the shame-driven may focus on. After Ross L. had been in prison for a few months, an additional autopsy report on his victim arrived, indicating that he had also stabbed her perineum and labia severely and deeply. He, who had talked of wanting to rape a woman, apparently had an even stronger wish to destroy her genitals. It has often been pointed out that the motive behind the desire to commit rape is hostility, not sex. That truth has seldom been confirmed more unmistakably than in this case. But knowing just how deeply Ross L. feared that he was not only a wimp and a punk but also a pussy himself may help us to understand the depth of his narcissistic rage over the power he felt a woman had to make him feel like less than a man; and the paranoid fear, amounting to panic and desperation, that if he did not destroy her femininity she would destroy his masculinity. A man would have to feel that his own genitals were almost inconceivably inadequate or damaged in order to feel that they would be safe only in a universe in which there were no intact female genitals. But, of course, genitals per se are not the real issue here; they merely symbolize the presence or absence of feelings of sexual adequacy, self-esteem, and pride, and thus, of an intact, coherent sense of self. Given what a core, central constituent of one's sense of self one's sexual identity is, the total absence of those feelings can create a panicky urgency to set things right; and if that task seems nearly hopeless, the individual may feel that he has to take desperate measures in order to survive—such as making sure that someone else does not survive,

and that one destroys whatever parts of another person's body correspond to the parts of one's own that one felt were inadequate.

The rituals surrounding violence, then, like all rituals, are profoundly
symbolic and hence profoundly meaningful (that is, they express many
highly specific and closely related meanings, which can be translated
into words). In fact, they are more symbolic, and hence more meaningful, the more "senseless" they appear to the rational mind, because they
follow the laws of magical rather than rational thinking. Cutting off
someone's ears, for example, does not actually make him deaf, and
prevent him from "hearing" bad things about oneself, it only symbolizes
doing so; just as actually making someone deaf would not prevent him
from learning bad things about oneself. Killing a person is the one
"necessary" and "sufficient" act that will prevent someone forever from
either transmitting or receiving one's shameful secrets. But since killing
alone will do that, why did Ross L. and Dennis X. feel a need to
mutilate their victims as well? I interpret that as a way of communicating *why* they killed their victims, what they felt they were accomplishing through the killing: that is, the mutilation served as a magical means
of accomplishing something that even killing one's victim cannot do,
namely, that of destroying the feeling of shame itself. Why does killing
alone not destroy shame? Because even killing someone cannot truly
eradicate the feelings of shame. One is left still knowing one's own
shameful secrets; there are always others who may discover them, and
so on. So an intensification of the whole project through the introduc-
tion of magic, by means of ritual, is necessary, if it is to be powerful
enough to enable the murderer to stave off the tidal wave of shame that
threatens to engulf him and bring about the death of his own self.

PART II

THE "GERM THEORY" OF

VIOLENCE

How to

Think About

Violence

WE LIVE IN AN AGE IN WHICH THERE IS A DEEP MISTRUST OF THEORIES; THE very idea of theorizing itself is suspect. This powerful and widespread skepticism emanates from both ends of the current intellectual spectrum. From the more traditional, conservative wing of conventional science and scholarship—the positivist-empiricist wing—there is a common assumption that only "facts" are reliable and trustworthy, that any attempt to go beyond raw empirical data to the realm of principles or generalizations is hopelessly idealistic or fatally overambitious. The conservative criminologist, James Q. Wilson,[1] for example, has written that there is no such thing as "underlying causes" of crime; that we should abandon the attempt to discover and ameliorate or eradicate those so-called causes, and simply continue with our customary approach to crime, namely imprisonment and punishment.

Skepticism about theory emanates from the opposite wing as well, the current avant-garde or, as it calls itself, the post-modernist or deconstructionist wing, which rejects and distrusts any and all possible theories (except its own, if I understand it correctly) as inevitably being corrupted and distorted by the power interests which they unavoidably, if unconsciously, both serve and conceal, or mystify (unlike its own theory, which is presumably free from such distortions, for reasons that I am not sure I do understand). One statement of this distrust of any and all possible theories was recently articulated with reference to theories about crime by Carol Smart[2] who stated that

> the [post-modernist] challenge to modernist thought . . . does not entail a denial of poverty, inequality, repression, racism, sexual violence, and so on. Rather it denies that the intellectual can divine the answer to these through the demand for more scientific activity and bigger and better theories . . . in particular, that we can establish a causal explanation which will in turn provide us with objective methods for intervening in the events defined as problematic.

Smart's essay concludes that "the continuing search for the theory, the cause, and the solution" is simply futile, misguided, and counter-productive—a hopeless waste of time and energy. Ironically, it reaches the same point of intellectual exhaustion as does the conservative view, providing a remarkable example of that well-known phenomenon, the meeting of opposites. Both approaches would have us abandon the search for causes and strategies for the prevention of crime and violence.

On the other hand, a group of behavioral scientists appointed by the National Academy of Sciences[3] found that one of the main limitations and obstacles to our ability to understand and prevent violence was the lack of an adequate general theory on the subject:

> The panel found that a substantial knowledge base exists regarding some aspects of violent events and behaviors. . . . However, we were frustrated to realize that it was still not possible to link these fields of knowledge together in a manner that would provide a strong theoretical base on which to build prevention and intervention programs. . . . (p. 21)

[We are still] Lacking a testable general theory of violence. . . .
(p. 39)

While there is a consensus that we lack a theory of violence adequate to enable us to explain, predict, and prevent violent behavior, disagreement concerns whether it will ever be possible to build such a theory. I believe this question can not be answered a priori. It can only be answered by attempting to create such a theory. Even to say that all existing theories are inadequate is not to say that we have no theory. In fact, my main objection to the arguments against theory that I have mentioned is the fact that it is impossible *not* to have a theory on this subject; because we cannot avoid dealing with violence, whatever assumptions we make about it constitute at least an implicit or inchoate theory of violence. So our choice is not between having a theory of violence and not having one; it is between having a conscious theory, which we can then examine, question, criticize, and improve; or an unconscious theory, which will remain forever untested, neither provable nor disprovable, and therefore unimprovable.

If we are going to outline a theory of violence, it might be worthwhile to pause for a moment, to reflect on what characteristics such a theory would need to possess in order to constitute an adequate explanation of violence. What I mean by an explanation is an account of an empirical (observable) phenomenon that is able to show the relation of cause to effect. Some common types of statements about violence, that are often made as if they were explanations of it, can be seen on closer examination to be lacking in explanatory content.

Value Judgments Are Not Explanations

For example, I have often heard people explain a person's violence by saying, "He must just be evil." This usually happens when no one understands why the individual committed the crime, when there appears to be no obvious motive for it, or when the crime, even if there is an apparent motive, is so heinous as to defy "ordinary human understanding." But moral and legal judgments about violent behavior that deem it "bad" or "evil" or "guilty" are *value judgments* about it, not *explanations* of it.

Why do I say that? Let me suggest an analogy. In one of his plays, Molière[4] illustrates the difference between the philosophy (scholasticism) of the Middle Ages and the scientific thinking that was just beginning to be applied in the world of his time. One of his characters, a physician, "explains" why morphine makes people sleepy by attributing that property to its "dormative principle." "Dormative" (or soporific) merely means sleep-inducing; obviously, this is not an explanation, it is a tautology—morphine makes you sleepy because it is sleep-inducing. But we already know that morphine induces sleep; what we don't know is *why* morphine makes people sleepy.

In the same way, to say that the cause of a murder was the fact that the murderer was an evil person, or had an evil mind, or that the cause of the murder was the evil that existed in the mind or character of the murderer, is a tautology. To say that the cause of the evil act (actus reus) is the evil mind of the actor (mens rea) is merely to say the same thing: a tautology adds nothing to what we already know. The question of causation is: *Why* was he "evil"? Why did his personality take on the attributes we are calling evil? Why did he commit the violent act that we are calling evil? These are the kinds of questions a theory of violence should be able to answer; these are the questions I want to answer. But to do so, I think we have to remove (or at least bracket) moral language from our discussion.

I am suggesting that the only way to explain the causes of violence, so that we can learn how to prevent it, is to approach violence as a problem in public health and preventive medicine, and to think of violence as a symptom of life-threatening (and often lethal) pathology, which, like all forms of illness, has an etiology or cause, a pathogen. To think of violence as evil—if we confuse that value judgment about violence with an explanation of it—can only confuse us into thinking that we have an explanation when we do not.

The analogy of smoking and lung cancer can help us here. We know that some people get lung cancer even though they have never smoked, and that some people smoke and never get lung cancer; and yet no one (except perhaps the tobacco industry) really doubts that smoking is a "cause," in a scientifically valid and practically important sense, of lung cancer: neither necessary nor sufficient, but a cause. Nor does anyone "explain" the nonsmoker's lung cancer with the statement that he must therefore be "sinful." No theory can explain everything about the phenomenon it is explaining (and fortunately, as this example shows, it does not have to be able to, in order to generate life-saving methods of prevention—such as the recommendation to quit smoking). In the absence of complete explanation, moral condemnation need not follow.

We face another obstacle in trying to clear our thinking about violence of moral judgment. Suggesting that we avoid the categories of "evil," "guilt," or "crime" is all too often misinterpreted as being "soft on crime," as if in attempting to understand violence, we were forgiving violent behavior. My attempt to understand violent behavior should not be mistakenly interpreted as an effort to excuse or forgive people who commit heinous acts of violence.

The naturalistic, nonmoralistic approach to violence neither supports nor opposes the "forgiveness" of violent behavior—since one has not condemned in the first place. Condemning violence or forgiving it are irrelevant, once you see violence as a problem in public health and preventive medicine. No one supposes that because doctors do not waste their time and energy on "condemnations" or "punishments" of cancer and heart disease that they are somehow "soft on cancer" or "permissive" toward heart disease. They need all their time and energy to prevent and cure those diseases, which one does first and foremost by learning whatever one can about what causes them and how one might prevent them. It can be productive of knowledge to conceptualize violence as a health problem; but as long as we think of it as a moral problem, we will never be able to learn what causes it or what prevents it.

For three millennia our main social hypothesis—that the moral and legal way of thinking about and responding to violence (by calling it evil, forbidding it—"just say no"—and punishing it) will prevent violence (or at least bring it under control)—has been singularly unsuccessful in reducing the level of violence. Three thousand years should be an adequate length of time to test any hypothesis. That is why I am suggesting that it is time now to retire the moral way of thinking about violence for one capable of utilizing all the methods and concepts of the human sciences; time, in fact, to build a truly humane science, for the first time, for the study of violence.

The Rational Self-Interest Theory of Violence

As a nation, our institutions have been acting on an underlying theory of violence, which I call the "rational self-interest" theory. This set of assumptions pervades our criminal justice system. Rational self-interest theory assumes that those who engage in violence do so for reasons of rational self-interest and common sense: Like anyone else in possession of rationality and common sense, those who commit violent acts do not want to go to prison, do not want to be subjected to physical violence themselves, and do not want to die. They will do anything to avoid any of these fates, and all we need do to prevent violence is to threaten to punish those who would commit such acts with greater violence of our own, such as imprisonment and capital punishment.

There are only four things wrong with this theory: It is totally incorrect, hopelessly naive, dangerously misleading, and based on complete and utter ignorance of what violent people are actually like. In addition, the rational self-interest theory of violence has had two disastrous and very expensive consequences. First, it has led us to shift our attention and resources from prevention to punishment. I am not saying that we do not need to use force to restrain the violent when our efforts to prevent violence by other means have failed. But this theory has distracted us from attempting to learn what actually causes violence; and what conditions would be necessary in order to reduce the need for violence; and from applying that knowledge to eliminating or ameliorating those conditions which lead to violence.

It is obvious that the policies we have adopted on the basis of this theory have led to an enormous and still escalating increase in violence. For example, the murder rate in the United States has repeatedly risen, to the point where it is now almost ten times as high as it was at the turn of the century and is still climbing. Like a macabre Dow-Jones average, it fluctuates from year to year, but the long-term trend is up. The murder rate in the United States is from five to twenty times higher than it is in any other industrialized democracy, even though we imprison proportionately five to twenty times more people than any other country on earth except Russia; and despite (or because of) the fact that we are the only Western democracy that still practices capital punishment (another respect in which we are like Russia).

To imagine that violence is "rational" and dictated by "self-interest" can only blind us to the reality of those forms of violence that have been most horrendously destructive of human life around the world in this century—the violence of Hitler, Stalin, Pol Pot, Idi Amin, Khomeini, Saddam Hussein; of the kamikaze pilots, the Baader-Meinhof gang, the Red Brigades; of Beirut, Belfast, Bogotá, and Bosnia; and of the endless legion of mass murderers and assassins, both "public" and "private," who are as ready to be killed as to kill—whose rage is so passionate and so blinding that it has caused the subjective distinction between killing and being killed to be all but obliterated and mean-

ingless. As Dostoevsky[5] put it with uncanny prophetic power even before the terrible century through which we have just lived proved him
right:

> . . . one may say anything about the history of the world—any-
> thing that might enter the most disordered imagination. The only
> thing one can't say is that it's rational. The very word sticks in
> one's throat. . . . very often, and even most often, choice is ut-
> terly and stubbornly opposed to reason. . . .

Toward a Theory of Violence

In the course of this book, I hope to show how much of what appears
anomalous, inexplicable, and incomprehensible about violence
(whether individual or collective) is not anomalous at all, but all too
ominously exactly what we might expect—given a certain set of conditions.

Let me begin with the common empirical observation that people
feel incomparably more alarmed by a threat to the psyche or the soul or
the self than they are by a threat to the body. The death of the self is of
far greater concern than the death of the body. People will willingly
sacrifice their bodies if they perceive it as the only way to avoid "losing
their souls," "losing their minds," or "losing face."

In addition, a person only develops a stable, integrated, and differen-
tiated sense of selfhood or identity through the process of interacting
with other humans in the community, or culture. The psyche is as
dependent on being nurtured by those modes of relationships and community, of child-rearing and education, which we call culture, as the
body is on being nourished by food. The relationship between culture
and character is an unavoidable sociopsychological reality.

One consequence of that fact is that a perceived threat to the integrity and survival of a person's culture is perceived as a threat to the

integrity and survival of the individual's personality or character, and to the viability of one's ethical value system which is a central and essential component of both personality and culture, and is what most intimately links the self and its culture, the culture and its selves. Those are among the reasons why the death of one's culture is tantamount to the death of one's self.

The worlds I know where people have experienced the actual or threatened death of self and community are the maximum-security prisons and mental hospitals for the criminally insane—"extreme environments," where soul and mind and conscience, racial pride and self-respect, are incomparably more damaged, vulnerable, and threatened than anywhere else. Here it becomes especially clear that the priority humans place on honor and self-respect (including the honor of one's group and one's culture) over that of physical comfort and even survival is not only humanity's most unique and essential attribute, but also our most dangerous.

It is not a coincidence that our human propensity to create morality and civilization, and to commit homicide and suicide, are the two characteristics that most specifically differentiate us from all other species. These two sides of human nature are inextricably related. They are caused by the same complex of interacting emotional forces, which operate both individually and collectively in human psychology and culture—shame, pride, guilt, and innocence. When individuals and groups feel their "honor" is at stake, and an intolerable degree of humiliation or "loss of face" would result from a failure to fight for that honor, they may act violently. The loss of self-esteem is experienced subjectively as the death of the self. People will sacrifice anything to prevent the death and disintegration of their individual or group identity.

If our primary goal is to prevent violence, we have no rational alternative but to view violence as a problem in public health and preventive medicine. We can define disease, broadly enough to include violence, as any force or process at work within an organism or species that tends to cause the death of the organism or, especially, the extinction of the species. Health refers to those forces or processes within organisms and species that tend to sustain, protect, and preserve life, individual and collective. I use the term violence to refer to the infliction of physical injury on a human being by a human being, whether oneself or another, especially when the injury is lethal, but also when it is life-threatening, mutilating, or disabling; and whether it is caused by deliberate, conscious intention or by careless disregard and unconcern for the safety of oneself or others. From the perspective of public health and preventive medicine, violence is death or disability that is inflicted by means of physical injury, or trauma, caused by human behavior and choice, and thus by the human mind or psyche. Thus, a violent, as opposed to a natural, death is one caused by an act of man (or woman), not an act of God, and by culture, rather than by nature.

Violence, then, can be seen as a symptom of individual or group psychopathology, whether it is an individual case (murder, suicide) or an epidemic (war, genocide). This is true even if we make the distinction, as J. P. Scott[6] and other students of animal behavior have done, between aggressive or offensive violence—initiated by the aggressor—and the defensive type—warding off an attack. Defensive violence can be seen as the effect of the aggressor's violence. Defense—even defensive violence—can be a necessary (though it is not always a sufficient) component of health. It can be adaptive—acting in the service of survival. The defense mechanisms of the body, the immune system, or the defense mechanisms of the individual mind, or of the group, the body politic, act in the same way.

But if some violence is defensive, and defensive violence can be healthy, then how can violence be both healthy and pathological at the same time? Not all mechanisms of defense do function adaptively, therapeutically, so as to heal illness and save life. In many physical illnesses, the natural defense can easily become maladaptive and self-defeating, as with pneumonia patients who drown in their own secretions, even though those secretions are an intrinsic part of their mechanisms of defense. The same is true of much "defensive" violence, which can easily become suicidal, rather than self-protective. However, even when it is adaptive and self-preserving, defensive violence can still be considered as a symptom of pathology; in this situation it is the aggressor's pathology, not the defender's. Human nature being what it is, one's own violence is almost always perceived as defensive, while other peoples' is likely to be seen as aggressive. This is the reason why the utility of the distinction between the two types of violence among humans has always been limited.

Modern technology has tragically made this problem of deciding whose violence is defensive and whose is aggressive a moot point. For now that weapons have become so destructive that there is no effective defense against them, and now that defensive violence utilizing nuclear weapons could destroy the defender as well as the aggressor, it is clear that defensive violence can no longer be healthy or adaptive enough to solve the problem. The only solution now is to apply the established principles of public health and preventive medicine to this type of pathology by learning how to achieve primary prevention of violence— that is, to prevent those social and psychological conditions that cause aggressive violence in the first place—so that defensive violence (secondary prevention) is not necessary.

I am not using the terms "illness" and "disease" as metaphors when I apply them to the subject of violence: I mean them literally. Violence, and also the social and psychological forces that cause violence, create biological pain, injury, mutilation, disability, and death just as literally as does any bacillus or malignancy. If violence is to be conceptualized as a bio-medical problem, a problem in public health and preventive psychiatry, what structure does this imply for a theory of violence cast in these terms? What kinds of facts must such a theory of violence be capable of explaining? I believe the best answer to these questions was suggested some years ago by the American psychiatrist George Engel, when he argued that all medical problems, all diseases (and he was not even speaking specifically of violence) can only be understood and conceptualized adequately if they are seen as "bio-psycho-social" problems, as phenomena that are simultaneously caused by, and have effects on, biological, psychological, and social systems. Certainly this is true of violence, a term that refers to an enormously complex, multidetermined range of phenomena. Some of the data concerning violence can only be explained in biological terms, some in psychological ones, and some in social, cultural, historical, and socioeconomic terms, such as class-stratification, and discrimination on the basis of age, sex, or race. No theory of violence could be considered adequate except to the extent that it is capable of integrating all three levels of abstraction.

In order to clarify the nature of the theory I am presenting here, it will also be helpful, I think, to point out that a comprehensive theory of violence cannot be solely a theory in criminology, nor solely in clinical or forensic psychiatry. It cannot be a theory in criminology because most crimes are not violent, and most violence is not criminal. Most of the crimes that are committed are property crimes. And most of the violent (that is, man-made, nonnatural) injuries and deaths that occur, both in the United States and throughout the world, are not caused by activities that the legal system defines as criminal. For example, in the United States and every other developed country, many more deaths are caused by suicides than by homicides. An even larger number of violent deaths are caused by carelessness. Although these deaths are usually, and often misleadingly, called "accidental" or "unintentional," most of them are actually the predictable (and preventable) effects of deliberate human choices and intentions, such as hazardous working conditions, substandard housing, violent sports, risk-taking avocations, and so on. These kill twice as many people as die from homicide and suicide combined. The collective violence called warfare is, with rare exceptions, entirely legal, not only according to the legal system of the nation on whose side any given soldier is fighting, but also according to that of the enemy nation. If one adds to all those the deaths caused by structural violence (that is, the excess death rates among the poor caused by the socioeconomic structure, i.e., class and caste stratification), which produces far more deaths than all of the previously mentioned categories combined, one begins to see why any theory of violence, if it is to deal at all with the medical reality involved, cannot limit itself to the subject matter of criminology.

But a theory of violence cannot be solely a theory of clinical psychiatry either, because most violence is not committed by the mentally ill (as either the psychiatrists or the courts of law have defined mental illness), and most mentally ill people are not violent. The vast majority of murders are committed by people with severe disorders of personality or character, not people who are "insane" in the sense of being out of touch with reality, or experiencing hallucinations or delusions; thus, it is no surprise that no more than about one percent of murderers in the United States are found "not guilty by reason of insanity." And only a fraction of the mentally ill commit either homicide or suicide (although the proportion who die by suicide is higher than in the general population).

Finally, the theory I am presenting here is not solely a theory in forensic psychiatry, that subspecialty that serves to assist the courts in deciding whether a given individual was "criminally responsible" for his violent act, or should be found "not guilty by reason of insanity"— whether he committed his violence while he was "sane" or "insane" at the time of the act. It is not just that the vast majority are "sane," as I just mentioned, but also because I am attempting to discover causes of violence that cut across "diagnostic" boundaries, and that are responsible for the resort to violence in both the "sane" and the "insane." In addition, I regard such terminology as so arbitrary as to be of limited usefulness and relevance anyway, when applied to violent behavior. For example, I tend to sympathize with the commonsense view that I think many people have when they respond to a particularly bizarre or brutal murder, or series of murders, with the expression, "Someone would have to be crazy to do such a thing." That most such murderers are not "crazy," as either law or psychiatry define "crazy," reveals the limitations in the standard legal and psychiatric vocabularies, and in the conventional approaches of both fields to both violence and "craziness"; or, at least, their limited usefulness for my purposes in this book. I think that the individuals (and groups) who committed much of the violence I discuss here (or much of the violence that one reads about in the newspapers every day) would have to be "sick" or "crazy," in some meaningful sense of those terms, to have done what they have done. To confine our discourse to the question of whether the behavior of such persons meets certain legal or psychiatric definitions of what constitutes madness versus badness, or psychosis versus perversion versus borderline personality may be a way of avoiding the more radical implications of understanding both their sickness and their violence.

I am convinced that violent behavior, even at its most apparently senseless, incomprehensible, and psychotic, is an understandable response to an identifiable, specifiable set of conditions; and that even when it seems motivated by "rational" self-interest, it is the end product of a series of irrational, self-destructive, and unconscious motives that can be studied, identified, and understood.

Shame:

The Emotions and

Morality of

Violence

I think the tragic feeling is evoked in us when we are in the presence of a character who is ready to lay down his life, if need be, to secure one thing—his sense of personal dignity.

—ARTHUR MILLER, *TRAGEDY AND THE COMMON MAN*

WE KNOW FROM PAST EXPERIENCE HOW EFFECTIVE THE PUBLIC HEALTH approach has been in our struggles against epidemics. In the nineteenth century, for example, strategies such as cleaning up the sewer system and the water supply were far more effective in the battle against diseases than all the doctors, medicines, and hospitals in the world. In addition, discovering the specific pathogen in the water supply that was killing people guided our preventive efforts both by clarifying what specifically needed to be removed from the contaminated water, and by enabling us to know when it had been removed. Identifying the causes of the various forms of disease is the first step in prevention.

Using what I have come to think of as a "germ theory" of violence, I will identify the pathogen that causes the most lethal form of pathology of our time, except that the pathogens under the microscope are not microorganisms but emotions. After I have examined them in this chapter, I will spend the remainder of this book illustrating the explanatory and predictive power of this theory by examining where the pathogens are to be found in our society at large. In keeping with the public health approach, I will devote the next two chapters to examining the "sewer system," identifying all the places where the pathogens exist—not the physical sewer system, but the social one, the "sewer system" of our society, the prison system (and the prison mental hospital), which are the receptacles and conduits into which we as a society dump the human beings whom we treat like garbage and waste products.

I will then examine the water supply as a whole, as it exists outside (but feeds into) the sewer system—namely, our social and economic system. I will identify where the pathogen that causes violence is concentrated, whom it infects, and how it is grown and distributed. I will try to show how our social and economic structure is permeated with this pathogen, and spreads it in identifiable ways—just as concretely as any contaminated water supply does. And I will also show whose interests it serves to keep the water supply contaminated.

I will then raise the question: Granted that the pathogen that causes violence exerts its destructive effects at the level of individual psychology (just as any microbe exerts its effects at the level of the organism—the individual body); and granted that the spread of this pathogen might best be stopped by cleaning up the water supply and the sewer system (that is, by reforming our social and economic system and our criminal justice and penal system); isn't it still possible that the pathogen really and ultimately is biological? Is violence caused, for instance, by ineradicable biological instincts, or by heredity, or brain damage (such as some forms of epilepsy), or drug abuse, or the biological differences between the different races, or sexes, or age groups? In this chapter I will argue that the public health approach is the appropriate model to show that violence is a contagious disease, not an hereditary one. The pathogen is psychological, not biological, and it is spread primarily by means of social, economic, and cultural vectors, not biological ones. Biological factors are far less important as causes of violence (in the instances in which they have some effect) than are social and psychological ones. For example, I will show that the hormonal patterns characteristic of the male sex exert a much less powerful effect on the patterns of violent behavior than do certain cultural factors, which I will then go on to specify in Chapter 10, examining how the gender asymmetry which characterizes patriarchal cultures stimulates violence toward both men and women, much more powerfully than do the biological differences between them.

In the Epilogue, I will link all the preceding chapters together, showing how this theory of violence, and the understanding of violence that it makes possible, can illuminate aspects of the history and dynamics of civilization, patriarchy, and morality that cannot be as easily discerned from other perspectives.

How might we discover what that pathogen is? My own approach to the study of violence has been to sit down and talk with violent people, and ask them why they have been violent. What I have discovered is that many of them tell me. Not all of them do. Some—like Ross L., whose mutilation of his victim I discussed in Chapter Three—do not tell me in words; and many may not understand why they committed the violence that sent them to prison. With them I have had to decode the symbolic language of their violent acts, like a cryptologist, or an anthropologist who tries to decipher the meaning of a bizarre and gruesome ritual. Still, surprisingly many men do tell me, simply and directly.

For example, the prison inmates I work with have told me repeatedly, when I asked them why they had assaulted someone, that it was because "he disrespected me," or "he disrespected my visit" (meaning "visitor"). The word "disrespect" is so central in the vocabulary, moral value system, and psychodynamics of these chronically violent men that they have abbreviated it into the slang term, "he dis'ed me."

Chester T., a very angry and violent inmate in his thirties, in prison for armed robbery, was referred to me because he had been yelling at, insulting, threatening, and assaulting another inmate. He had been doing this kind of thing for the past several weeks, and, off and on, for years. But he was usually so inarticulate and disorganized that neither I nor anyone else had been able to figure out what he wanted or what was fueling these repetitive acts of violence; nor had I had much success in persuading him to stop his endlessly self-defeating power struggles with everyone around him, which inevitably resulted in his being punished more and more severely. This very pattern is extremely common among men in prison. In prisons, the more violent people are, the more harshly the prison authorities punish them; and, the more harshly they are punished, the more violent they become, so that both the inmates and the prison authorities are engaged in a constantly repeated, counterproductive power struggle—the ultimate "vicious" cycle.

In an attempt to break through that vicious cycle with this man, I finally asked him "What do you want so badly that you would sacrifice everything else in order to get it?" And he, who was usually so inarticulate, disorganized, and agitated that it was difficult to get a clear answer to any question, stood up to his full height and replied with calm assurance, with perfect coherence and even a kind of eloquence: "Pride. Dignity. Self-esteem." And then he went on to say, again more clearly than before: "And I'll kill every mother-fucker in that cell block if I have to in order to get it! My life ain't worth nothin' if I take somebody disrespectin' me and callin' me punk asshole faggot and goin' 'Ha! Ha!' at me. Life ain't worth livin' if there ain't nothin' worth dyin' for. If you ain't got pride, you got nothin'. That's all you got! I've already got my pride." He explained that the other prisoner was "tryin' to take that away from me. I'm not a total idiot. I'm not a coward. There ain't nothin' I can do except snuff him. I'll throw gasoline on him and light him." He went on to say that the other man had challenged him to a fight, and he was afraid not to accept the challenge because he thought "I'll look like a coward and a punk if I don't fight him."

One hears this from violent men in one variation or another again and again. Billy A., a man in his mid-forties, came in to see me because he also had been involved in a running battle with most of the prisoners and correction officers on his cell block. He began his explanation as to why he was doing this by saying that he didn't care if he lived or died, because the screws and the other prisoners had treated him so badly— "worse than animals in zoos are treated"—that they had taken all his property away from him and he had nothing left to lose; but what he couldn't afford to lose was his self-respect, because that was all he had left, and "If you don't have your self-respect, you don't have nothing." One way they took his self-respect was that another man threw water on him, and the officer who saw this happen did nothing to intervene. So the only way Billy A. felt he could regain his self-respect was to throw water on the officer and the other prisoner—as a result of which they sentenced him to solitary confinement. Still, he remained implacable in his expression of defiance: "Death is a positive in this situation, not a negative, because I'm so tired of all this bullshit that death seems thrilling by comparison. I'm not depressed. I don't have any feelings or wants, but I've got to have my self-respect, and I've declared war on the whole world till I get it!"

This man had a very severe paranoid personality, and was extremely dangerous because of it, in prison and before he was sent to prison. Billy A. had attempted—with no provocation or warning—to murder a woman by whom he felt persecuted. Although he, like most of the violent mentally ill, was sentenced to prison rather than a mental hospital, he was clearly in a state of paranoid delusion. A letter he wrote to a judge illustrates how the prison system made this man even more paranoid and more dangerous by systematically humiliating him. He apparently wrote this letter more for the purpose of unburdening himself and clarifying his thoughts than with any intention of mailing it, although he did finally show it to a prison psychiatrist so that she could help get the situation described in it resolved.

He expresses in the letter his desperation, his feeling that the way he was being treated was bringing him closer and closer to his limit, and his sense that he was running out of time. He describes feeling spiritually and mentally defeated, and writes that he had no fear of anyone or anything, including death. Rather, he felt that his life in solitary confinement, subjected to the mental and physical torment of the guards and other inmates, was not worth living.

Billy A. goes on in the letter to describe a specific incident that took place over three days, days that he describes as having been "the most mentally debilitating" of his whole life, worse even than death. To begin with, eight other inmates had insulted him by calling him "all sorts of unmentionable names." When he told an officer that he wished to bring charges against those prisoners for harassing him, he was ordered to go to the visitors' room and strip. He was left there for half an hour, then was marched back to his cell "buck naked." The prisoners who had exposed him to this "humiliation" began "laughing and making catcalls" at him. He discovered that his cell had also been stripped of all his personal possessions, including his toilet articles (toothbrush, soap, washcloth). What especially distressed him about this was its effect on his self-esteem—that he had been unable to take a shower for more than a week, and "the way I keep my self-respect is by keeping my body clean." Finally, in desperation he began banging on his desk because "I really needed cosmetics." In retaliation, officers again ordered him to stand naked in the visitors' room for fifteen minutes while they laughed at him and made "snide remarks." He said "the laughter really troubled me because I did not see a damn thing funny." He thought they were "getting some untold pleasure" out of treating him this way. Eventually they gave him a pair of overalls, but no shoes.

He then described how they strapped him to a bench, tightened (too tightly) the handcuffs and leg irons that all inmates are required to wear whenever they leave a solitary confinement cell, opened all the windows, and opened his overalls so that his bare skin was exposed to the cold air. He said "that brought tears to my eyes. Not because he unzipped my jumpsuit but because he looked at the other hoodlums and winked his eye and smiled." They left him shivering there (this was in January) for three hours. Then an officer grinned and said, "I do not want to get mean"—following which he stepped on and off his bare toes with his boots, as the other officers laughed at him as if he were "a freak." He went on to say that perhaps he was as dumb as everyone treated him as being, or as insane as everyone seemed to think he was—he no longer knew or cared. That was when he resolved to "declare war on the whole world" until he was able to restore his self-respect. While his self-esteem was already so damaged that he was already antisocial, it is also true that prison was only rendering someone who was already wounded, and therefore dangerous, even more so.

Some people think armed robbers commit their crimes in order to get money. And of course, sometimes, that is the way they rationalize their behavior. But when you sit down and talk with people who repeatedly commit such crimes, what you hear is, "I never got so much respect before in my life as I did when I first pointed a gun at somebody," or, "You wouldn't believe how much respect you get when you have a gun pointed at some dude's face." For men who have lived for a lifetime on a diet of contempt and disdain, the temptation to gain instant respect in this way can be worth far more than the cost of going to prison, or even of dying.

Should we really be so surprised at all this? Doesn't the Bible, in describing the first recorded murder in history, tell us that Cain killed Abel because he was treated with disrespect? "The Lord had respect unto Abel and to his offering: But unto Cain . . . he had not respect" (Gen. 4:4–5). In other words, God "dis'ed" Cain! Or rather, Cain was "dis'ed" because of Abel. The inextricable connection between disrespect and shame is emphasized by the anthropologist Julian Pitt-Rivers, who concluded that in all known cultures "the withdrawal of respect dishonors, . . . and this inspires the sentiment of shame."[1]

In maximum security prisons, this is the story of men's lives.

I have yet to see a serious act of violence that was not provoked by the experience of feeling shamed and humiliated, disrespected and ridiculed, and that did not represent the attempt to prevent or undo this "loss of face"—no matter how severe the punishment, even if it includes death. For we misunderstand these men, at our peril, if we do not realize they mean it literally when they say they would rather kill or mutilate others, be killed or mutilated themselves, than live without pride, dignity, and self-respect. They literally prefer death to dishonor. That hunger strikes in prison go on when inmates feel their pride has been irredeemably wounded, and they see refusing to eat as their only way of asserting their dignity and autonomy and protesting the injustices of which they perceive themselves to be the victims, suggests to me that Frantz Fanon[2] was expressing a psychological truth for many when he said "hunger with dignity is preferable to bread eaten in slavery."

Perhaps the lesson of all this for society is that when men feel sufficiently impotent and humiliated, the usual assumptions one makes about human behavior and motivation, such as the wish to eat when starving, the wish to live or stay out of prison at all costs, no longer hold. Einstein taught us that Newton's laws do not hold when objects approach the speed of light; what I have learned about humans is that the "instinct of (physiological) self-preservation" does not hold when one approaches the point of being so overwhelmed by shame that one can only preserve one's self (as a psychological entity) by sacrificing one's body (or those of others).

The emotion of shame is the primary or ultimate cause of all violence, whether toward others or toward the self. Shame is a necessary but not a sufficient cause of violence, just as the tubercle bacillus is necessary

but not sufficient for the development of tuberculosis. Several preconditions have to be met before shame can lead to the full pathogenesis of
violent behavior. The pathogenic, or violence-inducing, effects of
shame can be stimulated, inhibited, or redirected, both by the presence
or absence of other feelings, such as guilt or innocence, and by the
specific social and psychological circumstances in which shame is experienced.

The different forms of violence, whether toward individuals or entire
populations, are motivated (caused) by the feeling of shame. The purpose of violence is to diminish the intensity of shame and replace it as
far as possible with its opposite, pride, thus preventing the individual
from being overwhelmed by the feeling of shame. Violence toward others, such as homicide, is an attempt to replace shame with pride. It is
important to add that men who feel ashamed are not likely to become
seriously violent toward others and inflict lethal or life-threatening, mutilating or disabling injuries on others unless several preconditions are
met.

The first precondition is probably the most carefully guarded secret
held by violent men, which it took me years of working with them to
recognize, precisely because they guard it so fiercely. This is a secret
that many of them would rather die than reveal; I put it that extremely
because many of them, in fact, do die in order not to reveal it. They try
so hard to conceal this secret precisely because it is so deeply shameful
to them, and of course shame further motivates the need to conceal.
The secret is that they feel ashamed—deeply ashamed, chronically
ashamed, acutely ashamed, over matters that are so trivial that their
very triviality makes it even more shameful to feel ashamed about them,
so that they are ashamed even to reveal what shames them. And why
are they so ashamed of feeling ashamed? Because nothing is more
shameful than to feel ashamed. Often violent men will hide this secret behind a defensive mask of bravado, arrogance, "machismo," self-
satisfaction, insouciance, or studied indifference. Many violent men
would rather die than let you know what is distressing them, or even

that anything is distressing them. Behind the mask of "cool" or self-assurance that many violent men clamp onto their faces—with a desperation born of the certain knowledge that they would "lose face" if they ever let it slip—is a person who feels vulnerable not just to "loss of face" but to the total loss of honor, prestige, respect, and status—the disintegration of identity, especially their adult, masculine, heterosexual identity; their selfhood, personhood, rationality, and sanity.

The assertion that men do not kill for no reason is often truer the more "unprovoked" the killing appears to be. A man only kills another when he is, as he sees it, fighting to save himself, his own self—when he feels he is in danger of experiencing what I referred to earlier as "the death of the self," unless he engages in violence. Murderers see themselves as literally having no other choice; to them, "it's him or me" (or "her or me"). This is what I mean when I say that the degree of shame that a man needs to be experiencing in order to become homicidal is so intense and so painful that it threatens to overwhelm him and bring about the death of the self, cause him to lose his mind, his soul, or his sacred honor (all of which are merely different ways of expressing the same thought).

This should not be confused with the triviality of the incident that provokes or precipitates a man's shame, which is a completely different matter. In fact, it is well known to anyone who reads the newspapers that people often seem to become seriously violent, even homicidal, over what are patently "trivial" events. Paradoxically it is the very triviality of those precipitants that makes them overwhelmingly shameful.

The second precondition for violence is met when these men perceive themselves as having no nonviolent means of warding off or diminishing their feelings of shame or low self-esteem—such as socially rewarded economic or cultural achievement, or high social status, position, and prestige. Violence is a "last resort," a strategy they will use only when no other alternatives appear possible. But that should hardly be surprising; after all, the costs and risks of engaging in violent behavior are extremely high.

The third precondition for engaging in violent behavior is that the person lacks the emotional capacities or the feelings that normally inhibit the violent impulses that are stimulated by shame. The most important are love and guilt toward others, and fear for the self. What is most startling about the most violent people is how incapable they are, at least at the time they commit their violence, of feeling love, guilt, or fear. The psychology of shame explains this. The person who is overwhelmed by feelings of shame is by definition experiencing a psychically life-threatening lack of love, and someone in that condition has no love left over for anyone else.

With respect to guilt, being assaulted, or punished, or humiliated (the conditions that increase the feeling of shame) decreases the degree of guilt. That is why penance, or self-punishment, alleviates the feeling of sinfulness. Guilt, as Freud saw, motivates the need for punishment, since punishment relieves guilt feelings. That is also why the more harshly we punish criminals, or children, the more violent they become; the punishment increases their feelings of shame and simultaneously decreases their capacities for feelings of love for others, and of guilt toward others.

Freud commented that no one feels as guilty as the saints, to which I would add that no one feels as innocent as the criminals; their lack of guilt feelings, even over the most atrocious of crimes, is one of their most prominent characteristics. But, of course, that would have to be true, for if they had the capacity to feel guilty over hurting other people, they would not have the emotional capacity to hurt them.

With respect to fear, as we have seen, when the psyche is in danger, and overwhelmed by feelings of shame, one will readily sacrifice one's body in order to rescue one's psyche, one's self-respect. That is why so-called psychopaths, or sociopaths, or antisocial personalities have always been described as notably lacking in the capacity to experience fear.

A central precondition for committing violence, then, is the presence of overwhelming shame in the absence of feelings of either love or guilt;

the shame stimulates rage, and violent impulses, toward the person in whose eyes one feels shamed, and the feelings that would normally inhibit the expression of those feelings and the acting out of those impulses, such as love and/or guilt, are absent.

These preconditions explain what would otherwise seem to be two anomalies. The first is that we all experience feelings of shame in one of its many forms (feelings of inferiority, rejection, embarrassment, etc.), and yet not everyone becomes violent. Most people do not commit any acts of significant violence in their entire lives, despite the fact that shame is experienced throughout the life cycle. The theory I am presenting here suggests that most people have nonviolent means available to them to protect or restore their wounded self-esteem. Or else the circumstances in which they find themselves are such that violent behavior would not succeed in accomplishing what they needed; and, finally, because most people possess capacities for guilt and empathy with others that will not permit them to engage in lethal violence except under extremely unlikely circumstances.

The second anomaly is that even the most violent people on earth, the most intractably, frequently, and recurrently assaultive or homicidal criminals or maniacs, are not violent most of the time. Their violence occurs in brief, acute crises, so that even though we have no trouble in identifying them as very dangerous people, most of the time even they hurt no one. It only happens when an incident occurs that intensifies their feelings of being humiliated, disrespected, or dishonored to the point that it threatens the coherence of the self, or when they find themselves in a specific situation from which they feel they cannot withdraw nonviolently except by "losing face" to a catastrophic degree.

I did not enter the world of the prisons knowing this. I had been taught none of it. I reached these conclusions, against much resistance, after the violent men with whom I worked, year after year, had presented me with so much cumulative evidence that these were the only terms in which I could understand them or make any sense of their otherwise unexplained, paradoxical, and anomalous behavior. Ironically, that process began with the very first man I saw in psychotherapy in the prisons, even though it took me at least a year to see what I was seeing.

THE CASE OF RANDOLPH W.

Randolph W. was a big, muscular, "macho" white man from a working-class background, in his mid-thirties, who had the deformed nose that many chronically violent men have after years having their nose repeatedly struck and broken in fights. Randolph said his father was the first one to break his nose. Randolph W. was in prison, and had been several times before, for a variety of violent assaults, "muggings," and armed robberies. The first clue that his violent way of life had something to do with the feeling of shame, and his unwillingness to acknowledge either that feeling or its causes, came when he was asked to read and sign some papers. Then he could no longer conceal the fact that he could neither read nor write. He had never told me this. Once he could no longer conceal it, he then told me the lengths he had gone to conceal this shameful fact from everyone else in the prison. At that point, in my naiveté, I thought: This is progress. This is an important step. Now we have a concrete problem, a source of low self-esteem that Randolph has never acknowledged before; he can solve this; even the prison can help him. For the prison ran a small school, with teachers who could teach him to read and write. I did not imagine the obstacles to that seemingly simple and obvious solution. Randolph was so ashamed of his ignorance that he would not go near the school, because in order to learn how to read and write he would have to tell others that he was illiterate, and he was so ashamed that he would rather remain illiterate than reveal it.

Then Randolph W. had to deal with a complaint from his cell mate, who objected to the smell that came from his bed. He still wet the bed—not every night, but often enough to be a problem. He was so ashamed of this fact that he went to elaborate lengths to conceal it from everyone.

The third clue came toward the end of the first year of therapy, when he requested plastic surgery for his deformed nose. In discussing that request with me, he confided how inadequate it made him feel sexually, since he felt it caused women not to find him attractive. Randolph W. felt ugly, and he believed that if only he had a "perfect" nose, his chances with women would be better, and his self-confidence would improve. He went on to have the operation, and then had to deal with the predictable disappointment of finding that his new nose did not have the magical effects he had hoped for; his nose was indeed less deformed, but neither his overall appearance nor his social success with women was suddenly rendered "perfect."

But perhaps the most surprising clue as to how shame-driven he was—and how related that shame was to Randolph W.'s violence— came at the very end of his year of therapy. For him, as for many men socialized into the sex roles of our culture, dependency is very shameful and incompatible with the image of the sexually adequate male. At that point he seemed to trust me well enough to reveal his biggest secret of all. When he was "free," out in the community (during his brief inter- vals between prison sentences), he would find that he got so tired of being cold and hungry, sleeping in parked cars and in hallways, or on the street, having no job or money, that he would start missing prison, where he knew he could receive at least three meals a day and a bed to sleep in, along with people who "cared" about him enough to make sure that he was there each night. He then went on to tell me that whenever he reached that point, he would then commit some "dumb" crime, a mugging or an armed robbery, knowing full well that he would be sent back to prison (though only if he committed the crime with enough violence to give the judge no choice but to return him to prison). Inter- estingly, the only alternative to prison that held any hope for Randolph W. was his pattern of beginning a relationship with a woman and then moving in with her. These were usually slightly older women who took care of him and provided him with a place to live. Inevitably, the rela- tionships would fall apart when the women got tired of his "sponging" off them, or if they began to insist that he get a job and start helping to

support the household—a demand in the face of which he felt crush-
ingly inadequate and incapable. And, before long, he would be back on
the street, until he committed another violent crime that would take
him back to the prison.

How can we make sense of Mr. W.'s story? Obviously, behind Randolph W.'s "macho" disguise there was a man who felt inadequate and
not very manly; in fact, he seems to have felt more like a big baby in
virtually every way—sexually, educationally, and vocationally. Lacking
competence, skill, knowledge, and training in every sphere, he felt—
and actually was—incapable of taking care of himself. While limited by
his illiteracy, he still could have joined the millions of other illiterate
Americans who work at low-income, low-prestige jobs as manual laborers of one sort or another, but that was far from manageable for him.
His reluctance was not so much that he saw such jobs as more demeaning and humiliating than he was willing or able to tolerate; his chief
resistance came from his desire to be completely taken care of by
others; he felt incapable of taking care of himself, and he certainly
could not have cared for anyone else, certainly not a wife or a child.

In sum, Randolph W. was deeply ashamed of himself. At the same
time, he was so ashamed of feeling shame that for a long time he
engaged in every maneuver he could think of to avoid revealing to
anyone that he had any needy feelings (or that he felt anything but
supreme self-confidence). Of course, concealing the fact that he felt
ashamed necessitated his concealing also the sources of his shame, the
very things he needed help with, but until the therapy he was too
ashamed to ask for help, and any offer of help was experienced as
shameful and therefore was likely to elicit an aggressive, even violent
rebuff.

Randolph's wish to be loved and taken care of by others—which is a
universal human wish, or need—had never been sufficiently met by
anyone, beginning with his violent, depriving, and deprived family.
Since he had come to associate the desire for love and care with the

likelihood of rejection and rebuff, he not surprisingly experienced the wish as likely to expose him to feelings of shame. He assumed that for a grown man to have such wishes was unmanly, or infantile, a sign of weakness, and therefore shameful. The "macho" self-image that he tried to maintain, and with which he attempted to conceal his feelings of being needy, was the only image of himself in which he could take pride. But on some level, he knew that it was a disguise he put on in the attempt to conceal what he perceived as the shameful truth about himself.

Randolph's life pattern has much to teach us about violence. The psychological meaning of his entire life pattern, including both the repeated acts of violence and the repeated imprisonments which were their predictable, indeed inevitable, consequence, can be summed up in terms of the theory of shame and violence being presented here, and illustrate Freud's concept of the "return of the repressed."

This man's behavior makes no sense if he wanted to stay out of prison, but his violent behavior makes complete sense if we understand it as his way of getting himself sent to prison, where his wish to be taken care of (if not loved) could finally be gratified by the prison, at the same time that his manhood was confirmed by his violent act.

But why did he need to be violent? Not simply as a sure way to be sent to prison; for there are also nonviolent crimes for which judges will send people to prison. If all he wanted was to be sent to prison, he could commit a property crime or a drug offense. But by committing violent crimes he could hide his desire to be loved and cared for by others, of which he felt so deeply ashamed, and also disguise the fact that he was unable to take care of himself, about which he felt inferior and inadequate. And violent behavior can be the most powerful disguise for shame-provoking truth.

Why is this so? Because violent behavior is the exact opposite of the wishes of which he felt ashamed, namely, to be loved and cared for by others, which he thought of as being "passive" and "dependent." Violent behavior is not passive, it is active; it is not dependent on others' responses, it is a way of saying, "See, I don't need you at all; and just to prove that, I will kill you (or at least alienate you, potentially permanently, by my violence)." And one way to conceal the vulnerability of the wish to be loved by others is to reveal only the seemingly opposite wish, the wish to be invulnerable to others, by expressing only (active) hate and rage toward them.

The violence specifically provides (and a nonviolent crime could not) a face-saving way of obtaining care. It is face-saving because he does not have to acknowledge to himself or others that he wants care, food, shelter, and everything they stand for. He can believe, and everyone else can believe, that he is in prison for precisely the opposite reason: because he is so active, aggressive, and independent, so big and tough and strong and dangerous that society was actually afraid of him, that he really wants to leave prison, and it is fortunate that they put those walls there and patrol them with armed guards, or otherwise you can be sure that he would escape as soon as he could. And, of course, the whole of society and the criminal justice system, from newspapers and politicians, to courts and prisons, unconsciously colludes with him in concealing the real reason that he is in prison—namely, that no one would take care of him anywhere else, and he himself is so ashamed of that, and of admitting his need for care and his inability to care for himself. So violent behavior accomplishes the return of the repressed wishes to be loved and taken care of by others, but in a way that is face-saving, so that a man who feels ashamed can tolerate letting those wishes be gratified; and it is face-saving because violent behavior is the mirror-image, the exact reversal, of those wishes.

Most of all, anyone who knows how brutal, degrading, and dehumanizing prisons are can only regard it as the severest possible indictment of our society that people would in fact find that they receive more "care" there than "on the street." That latter phrase is prison argot for "in the community"—and it is actually a more accurate term, for many of those who wind up in prison, like Mr. W., were in fact literally living "on the street," not in anything that could be called a "community." We say "Community, community," but there is no community, for many people, in modern America.

Randolph W. is no unique, isolated, or unusual criminal, and he is far from being the most extreme example of how violence offers men a face-saving means for getting institutional care in a society that views men who need care as shameful and unmanly. The violence-engendering ethos of "rugged individualism," and the social Darwinism that continues to dominate so much public discourse, make it almost impossible for us to take care of people without humiliating them first. Our vastly higher rates of violent crime are one of the prices we pay for these attitudes and values.

THE CASE OF KELVIN C.

Another inmate in the maximum-security prison, Kelvin C., had been in prison for sixteen years for killing one policeman and crippling another. He had been convicted of second-degree murder, not first, since the court decided his murders were impulsive, not premeditated. Thus, there was a danger that he might be paroled soon; he had been eligible for parole for three years, and there might be a limit to how many times the Parole Board would refuse to allow him to be released. I say "danger" based as much on the prisoner's view of his prospects as on my own view.

I was influenced by the fact that this large, muscular man was probably the most unremittingly violent individual in the entire prison system. He had spent nearly his entire sentence in solitary confinement, because as soon as he was let out, he assaulted another person. For example, on one of the rare occasions he was in the general prison population, he happened to be walking in the hallway on his way to lunch at the same time as one of the psychologists on the staff. He ran toward her, pushed her onto the floor, and began trying to tear her skirt off as if to rape her. Prison officers had to restrain him and return him to "isolation."

That was typical. He committed his assaults so openly and provoca-

tively, either on officers or in full view of them, that it seemed reasonable to assume that he wanted to be in solitary confinement. There he
could spend the entire day in bed doing nothing. But he could only
arrange such passivity by means of violent activity, which would lead
others to "force" (or allow) him to spend the next six or twelve months
alone in his cell in the solitary confinement unit, the prison within a
prison he seemed to prefer.

This way of life was terrible for this man's mental health, since it
held out little hope of his developing any ability to live with other
people. The longer he spent in solitary, the more his thought processes
became confused, incoherent, and illogical, and while he never seemed
to experience delusions or hallucinations, he seemed to me to be going
"stir crazy" (albeit on a quasi-voluntary basis), as do many men who
spend extended durations in conditions of such sensory deprivation and
social isolation. In an attempt to interrupt that cycle, I would repeatedly
petition the court to order him to be transferred to the prison mental
hospital, and they would comply, but his hospitalizations never lasted
very long, for as soon as he became more coherent he would assault
hospital staff (including a very capable, dedicated, popular, and pregnant social worker), so they would return him to the prison.

When I asked Kelvin C. how he felt about leaving prison and returning to the community, this large, violent, dangerous murderer and
rapist replied, in a voice that could for all the world have belonged to a
small child, "I feel I'd be all alone in the big wide world. It would be
like being in a little boat in the middle of the ocean all alone—alone in
the great big empty wilderness. I'd have to start making new
friends. . . ."

The openness, the nakedness, the vulnerability of his response was
very moving. This man had opened his soul to me, with an eloquence, a
poetry, and an emotional expressiveness that belied the image I had
begun to develop, of someone who wanted to be alone; who wanted
nothing in his relationships with other people except to be violent
toward them; and who had neither the wish nor the ability to reveal his

private thoughts and feelings. This core image of himself as a lonely and lost, helpless child was so at variance with his public persona, both in the prison and in the community, that I could only wonder if he had created the latter in order to conceal the former. Beneath his mask of violence was concealed and protected a self (and a self-image) that was so vulnerable and easily hurt, or even destroyed, by other peoples' laughter, disdain, neglect, indifference, or rejection.

I would be misunderstanding Kelvin C.'s motive for wanting to be in solitary confinement if I thought it was based on a desire to be alone, or on the absence of a desire for friends and relationships. But he was expressing his lack of confidence in his ability to do what he wanted to do; clearly he doubted that other people would want to be his friends, doubted that he was lovable enough to be able to make friends. By this time that doubt had become a self-fulfilling prophecy—he had become a "monster" in the eyes of other people so that of course they did not want to be his friends. In fact, they just wanted to lock him up in solitary confinement and stay as far away from him as possible. But if we look closely, we can see how this whole process of turning into such a "monster" began: with his fear that he would only be rejected by others and that he had no means compatible with his self-respect by which to induce other people to take care of him.

One of the terrible ironies in his statement that he would be "all alone" when he left prison was that in reality he could not conceivably have been more alone than he already was. He had made no friends there, either; the concomitant of his being so constantly violent was that he was regarded as one of the "crazies," even by that population of the most violent men in our society. But I want to focus more on the view of himself that his reply to me reveals. What could possibly be more naked or exposed than to be alone in the world, protected only by a small boat in the middle of the ocean, with a sense of needing to start over by making new friends? What he represented to me was the purest case of the use of violence as a face-saving means of forcing others to take care of himself, while at the same time concealing himself, not only behind the mask of violent behavior and the public persona that created but even more literally and concretely behind a solid steel door, so that no one could see or speak about the self-image that he went to so much trouble to conceal because to him it was so shameful and unmanly.

One difference between him and the more run-of-the-mill violent criminals was that he carried both his violent activity and his solitary inactivity (lying on his bed in a small cell twenty-three hours a day for years at a time) further than anyone else. Most of the other violent men seemed to find sufficient respite from their hunger, homelessness, and humiliation in the jungles of our cities by provoking judges to evacuate them to the jungles of our prisons, where they would at least be provided food and shelter. It is true that no zoo would be permitted to keep animals in the kind of "shelter" that is provided for humans in prisons, and that the price the poor and homeless have to pay even for those ersatz versions of food and shelter is continued humiliation; nevertheless—and surprisingly, given the conditions in which most prisoners "live"—most of them do not continue to be so violent as to provoke prison officials to restrict them even further, to total isolation.

After I resigned from the Prison Mental Health Service, I heard that Kelvin C. was eventually released from prison by the Parole Board. The next piece of news about him, I was saddened to hear: he had been murdered. Apparently his behavior had seemed too provocative, frightening, or "crazy" to someone in the community. So Kelvin had been right all along: he really did not know how to take care of himself; it really was dangerous for him to be released. And his ultimate fate made it more understandable to me why he had regularly become most disturbed, agitated, and incoherent at precisely the times when he was scheduled to meet with the Parole Board—i.e., when he was in most danger (literally) of being released from prison.

This pattern is so common among the most violent men in our pris-

ons and prison mental hospitals that it provides a further illustration of
the overriding need these men have to be taken care of. Inmates experience the period just prior to their impending release from prison as the
time of highest stress. This is the time when they are most likely to
make a homicide or suicide attempt, or to experience acute psychotic
symptoms, or to violate a major regulation of the prison. This was such
a recurring experience that I began to realize that I had to pay special
attention to inmates during this period, in order to anticipate their
"acting out" in some violent way, or to head off a recurring, or even
initial, episode of mental illness.

But then I recalled that I had seen the same phenomenon during my
training in the teaching hospitals of the Harvard Medical School, and in
my private psychiatric practice with hospitalized (but mostly nonviolent) patients. Early in my training I was treating a patient, Ann S., who
had been committed to the hospital against her will because of paranoia, but whose symptoms had remitted to the point where I agreed
with her that it was time to begin making plans for her discharge from
the hospital. At that point, Ms. S., who had been protesting loudly
since she was first admitted that she neither needed nor wanted to be
in the hospital, experienced the most massive return of all her psychotic
symptoms, becoming floridly delusional, assaultive, and hearing voices.
Clearly the thought of discharge was such a stress and a threat to her
that it precipitated the full recurrence of the very symptoms that had
necessitated her being hospitalized in the first place.

I have seen that same pattern repeated, with slight variations, in a
number of other mental hospital patients, particularly those who suffer
from paranoia. What was surprising to me, however, was that exactly
the same pattern turned out to be characteristic of violent prison inmates, whether or not their symptoms took the form of violent behavior, signs of overt paranoia, or both. The intensity these feelings can
reach is illustrated by another inmate in the maximum-security prison,
Charles B., a man in his early twenties, who was about to be released a
few years ago, when he showed us a copy of a letter he had just sent to

the Commissioner of Correction. In it he stated that he had been in institutions all his life (foster homes, juvenile detention centers, etc.), that he did not know how to take care of himself "on the street," and that if the Commissioner allowed him to be forced out of the prison, "I will kill you and all your family—slowly!" Another inmate in the same prison, George T., an habitual armed robber who periodically became assaultive, obstreperous, and somewhat paranoid whenever he dropped out of psychiatric treatment, was soon to be transferred to a "pre-release center"—an unlocked residential facility used to ease the transition back into the community, in which inmates leave during the day to work at a job, returning to sleep at the residence, in the evening. He found the thought of release so frightening that he said to me, as the plans were being finalized, "I want to get back into prison. I'll do anything to. Prison's been my life. I'll walk away from the pre-release center. I'll dig up a dead body if I have to, to get them to send me back."

Two similar incidents happened in interviews that took place in the same prison shortly before the inmates involved were about to be released. In both, I began the interviews, as I routinely did with anyone I was seeing for the first time, with a statement that I would hold everything they told me in confidence, unless they told me they had plans to harm themselves or anyone else, or to commit any criminal offenses. In that case, I would feel compelled to do what I could to prevent any harm from being done to anyone, and that for that purpose I would feel free to divulge what they had told me to a third party, if necessary. Even though (or rather, because) they had clearly heard that "warning" (or reassurance), both immediately told me of plans they had to assault other people.

The first, man, Douglas R., a Vietnam veteran, stated loudly and aggressively that the first thing he was going to do when he got home was to take his gun and "shoot my fucking wife's kneecaps off." When I asked him for clarification, he repeated the statement, presumably to make sure that I hadn't missed his point, and indicated that he knew she was having an affair, and that his jealousy was so intense that when he was sitting in his cell in the prison he could virtually hear her making love with the other man.

The second inmate, Jose L., stated that he had been so convinced that the Commissioner of Correction had discriminated against him, personally persecuting him, that he was going to kill him. He then described how close he had come to doing that the last time he had been out of prison. He had followed the Commissioner from his home to his office and had him in the sights of his high-powered rifle and was about to pull the trigger, when someone came up to the car he was sitting in, so he got frightened and drove away. But he vowed that he would definitely make another attempt, as soon as he was out of prison again.

It seemed to me that their telling me of their plans to be violent toward other people was all the evidence needed to conclude that they did not want to go home, at least not at that time, since I had already told them I would have to intervene to prevent harm from being done to anyone. Thus I did not know how to understand their threats of violence except as requests to be further "taken care of" (if one accepts that being taken care of sometimes includes providing the limits and controls that a person needs and wants when he has trouble controlling himself). As for their claims that they wanted to go home, I see it as a way of "saving face," a way of denying the amount of care they need and yearn for.

I learned all this working in the prisons. Like most people, I had simply taken it for granted that no one wanted to be sent to prison, that people would do anything they could to stay out of them, or to leave them as quickly as possible if they could not avoid being sent to one, which is why the prisons had guards, high walls, and locked metal doors—because none of the prisoners wanted to be there and would escape if we relaxed our guard for a moment. And, of course, it is true that some—though a surprisingly small number—do escape, or make escape attempts. Some of these, however, are face-saving ways of concealing the wish to be in prison. One patient at the prison mental hospital who had recently been discharged into the community actually tried to break *into* the hospital, in order to get back in. And one cannot read the newspapers without reading of similar examples. Recently, one homeless man, in New York, has been nicknamed the "Serial Diner," because he provoked the police into sending him to jail periodically by ordering dinner in the most expensive restaurants, and then being unable to pay for it. He was a man who consciously wanted to be in jail, when he got tired of sleeping in bus stations or on sidewalks. The main difference between him and violent criminals was that he was not ashamed of his wish to be taken care of, so he had no need to conceal it behind the disguise of violence.

Many of the violent criminals who fill our maximum-security prisons would like us to believe that they want to escape; and they need to believe that themselves. They desperately want to feel that they are big, tough, independent, self-assertive, self-reliant men, so as not to feel needy, helpless, frightened, inadequate, unskilled, incompetent, and often illiterate. It is essential that we understand this psychology. For we will never understand violence and violent criminals until we see through what is, in truth, a defensive disguise; and until we understand violence, we cannot prevent it.

Career criminals take it for granted that they will be sent to prison sooner or later; they continue breaking whatever laws they do, and finally they get caught. But more than that, as Charles Silberman pointed out, "Criminals . . . often seem to arrange their own capture."[3] He points out that criminals often take no precautions to keep from being caught; they brag about their crimes to their friends; and many clearly want the police to know what they have done. Silberman describes how "one youngster I met in California had held up a gas station in his own neighborhood without wearing a mask or disguising himself in any way; a few hours later, he stopped by in his car to get a tankful of gas, at which time he was arrested."[4]

Violence is a surer way of getting imprisoned than nonviolence is, which is consistent with the hypothesis that the violence of violent criminals represents an effort to force others to provide care and at the same time covers the wish for such care. Silberman points out that criminals themselves know this. One inmate told Silberman:

> "In the end, everyone gets caught." "I don't care how good you are; you'll end up in the slammer sooner or later," he insists. "The law of averages is against you." Indeed it is. Although a robber has less than a 20 percent chance of being arrested on any one offense, . . . he has a 90 percent chance of being arrested at least once if he commits ten robberies, and the odds go up to 99 percent by the 21st offense.[5]

THE CASE OF WALTER T.

Now I would like to examine a third surprising and paradoxical phenomenon about "violent criminals"—although I hesitate to use that word about the man I am about to describe, for he was about as far removed from the usual stereotype of "violent criminals" as one could imagine. The word "wimp" would better describe the way he presented himself. Nevertheless, he was serving a life sentence in prison for murdering his wife. Walter T. had been the janitor at a nursery school for twenty-five years, during the last ten years or so of which his wife had been having an affair with another man. He was aware of her affair and resented it but took no steps to assert his own feelings or wishes in the situation, nor did he discuss the whole situation with her fully, nor indicate that there were limits to what he would tolerate. On the contrary, he meekly accepted what she was doing, and made no objections until she did one thing that he would not, or could not, tolerate: she threatened to leave him for the other man. At that point he killed her.

How can we make sense of his behavior? Clearly, it was not her cuckolding that he found intolerable, nor was it jealousy. It was her threat to abandon him that made both her life and his no longer worth continuing. But what does it mean to abandon someone? According to my dictionary, it means to "withdraw support or help from" the person being abandoned. Now, of course, everyone needs support and help in life; there is a sense in which one could well say that we all need all the help we can get—that that is true of all human beings.

Nevertheless, not all human beings commit murder, even when their wives threaten to leave them; in fact, the vast majority do not, or else the death rate from homicide would begin to take on the dimensions of the Civil War. So I do not know what else to conclude, except that the degree of support and help that this man felt he needed, and the intensity of shame he felt over it, was of a whole different order of magnitude from the degree that most people feel they need.

To put it bluntly: Walter T.'s image of himself was of a dependent, helpless infant, not of a mature, independent man capable of taking care of himself with or without his wife. And his image of her was of a mother whom he needed to nurse him so that he would not die. When she threatened to leave him, he experienced it as the equivalent of a death threat, in the same sense that an infant abandoned by his mother would die. At that point, he decided that since he could not live without her (because of his dependency on her), and he could not live with her (because of her independence of him, and her decision to leave him), he might as well alleviate the painful wish to be loved and taken care of by her by reversing it into an active hate for her, and kill her, the net effect of which is that now he has somebody else to take care of him for the rest of his life—the prison system.

In my experience, this man is typical of murderers in general, and of men who engage in spousal homicides. One of the special characteristics that predispose these men to commit murder, or other serious physical violence, is an unusually strong wish to be loved and taken care of, and unusually strong feelings of being inadequate and unlovable. And when these wishes and feelings are intensified, then the feelings of shame that they provoke are also further intensified; as are the feelings of rage and hate, and the impulses of violence that shame stimulates. Thus, Walter T.'s murder was a way of saying (through actions, not words), "Since I don't want to grovel to be loved by you, I hate you, actively and independently."

Of course he wanted to be loved by his wife; if he had not wanted her love, he would not have had any reason to kill her. But it was too painful and seemingly hopeless for him to let himself go on wanting her when she did not want him. Instead, the murder becomes a kind of undoing ritual that stops the loss of face and the seemingly hopeless wanting. Like all rituals, murder confers a new identity on the participants. For Walter T., to murder his wife was to change an identity that could only expose him to shame—namely, that of a wimp, a grown man who was "really" a helpless little boy—into an identity in which he could take pride.

When the kind of pain I am calling shame is overwhelming to people, all too many resort to the kind of defense against it that Walter T. did, namely, murderous violence. But is there any other evidence that men who commit murder, and especially those who kill their wives, are unusually dependent, and vulnerable to feelings of being abandoned? I think there is, and it comes in the form of an equally surprising and paradoxical finding.

Over the past decade or so, many of those who have been concerned about the extent of the violence to which women have been subjected have introduced a variety of innovations to help battered women choose alternatives to staying in the abusive relationship, and also to put pressure on the men doing the battering to cease and desist. These innovations have taken a variety of forms: changing the laws so as to facilitate the divorce process; changing legal and social mores concerning women's rights; providing adequate employment and income, so as to make it easier for battered wives to leave abusive husbands. And some 1,200 special shelters for battered women, serving more than 300,000 women and children a year, enable them to leave their violent husbands and to take their children with them. So hundreds of thousands of women, who previously would have had to remain in abusive, violent, and dangerous relationships, can now leave their husbands, or at least make a credible threat to leave.

What changes have occurred since these innovations? Before these changes were introduced, the number of husbands killing wives was about equal to the number of wives killing husbands.[6]

Suddenly, a few years ago, twice as many wives were being killed as husbands. It would be difficult to make sense of this paradoxical find-ing—that the proportion of women being killed, in spousal homicides, has actually doubled precisely at the point when, for the first time, women have a variety of ways to leave abusive, violent relationships— except by concluding that a wife's ability to leave her husband was being experienced by him as an intolerably threatening abandonment leading to murder. But what is so threatening to these husbands? Could it be their secret, hidden dependency on their wives? Like Walter T., these husbands act the way one would expect if their self-image were that of infants who would die if their mothers left them.

Here is further reason to believe that many men are so deeply ashamed of their wishes to be loved and taken care of, which they equate with being infantile, passive, and dependent (as though there is anyone, no matter how mature, who does not need to be loved and taken care of), that their feelings of shame motivate them to repress and ward off these feelings, often by going to the opposite extreme. Those who batter and/or kill their wives are precisely the men who experience a life-death dependency on their wives and an overwhelm-ing shame because of it.

These are the ones, of course, who would be most threatened by their wives' new-found independence, for one way such men have of concealing their dependency on their wives—from themselves and from others—is by doing everything they can to make their wives dependent on them, so that their wives cannot possibly leave them or abandon them. When their wives do leave them, it "smokes out" their secret dependency; it forces them to recognize it; it intensifies the feelings of shame it causes; it increases the intensity of violence that such shame stimulates.

I realize that the standard explanation of battering and homicidal husbands (as well as of men who commit rape) is that they want to "control" the women they abuse. Of course they do, and that is one perfectly valid way of describing an aspect of their motivation. Nothing in my analysis of their behavior contradicts that. But when asking the additional question, Why do they want to control their wives? I can only conclude that their desire for omnipotence is in direct proportion to their feeling of impotence.

Why Do Trivial Incidents Lead to Major Violence?

One reason why we have not up to now understood the causes of violence or taken them seriously is because the reasons given for acts of violence often seem so trivial, by any "objective," rational, comparative criterion, that it is very easy to overlook them. We find it hard to comprehend how a trivial incident could lead to or precipitate serious violence, because such explanations violate our sense of reality and rationality, and they violate our sense of morality and legality (our ethical sense).

Most people are not moved to wipe out their families by the kinds of incidents that provoke those who do, just as a little extra salt in the diet does not precipitate most people into pulmonary edema, or a little extra sugar, into diabetic acidosis; but for those who are predisposed to abnormal, life-threatening pathology, murder can be precipitated by events and circumstances that in another person might simply be incorporated into the ongoing metabolism of everyday life. So-called "incomprehensible" crimes are only incomprehensible because of a failure to comprehend something about them that I will now try to explain.

The central role of shame in the causation of violence has been overlooked for two inextricably related reasons. First, because the magnitude of the resulting violence is so far out of proportion to the triviality of the precipitating cause that it becomes almost impossible for any normal, rational person who operates by the criteria of common sense to recognize that the cause could in fact precipitate it. And second, because an essential but seldom noticed characteristic of the psychology of shame is this: If we want to understand the nature of the incident that typically provokes the most intense shame, and hence the most extreme violence, we need to recognize that it is precisely the triviality of the incident that makes the incident so shameful. And it is the intensity of the shame, as I said, that makes the incident so powerfully productive of violence.

It is the very triviality of the incidents that precipitate violence, the kinds of things that provoke homicide and sometimes suicide, whether in family quarrels or those that occur among friends and lovers on the street or in barrooms, that has often been commented on, with surprise and perplexity—being given a "dirty look," having one's new shoes stepped on, being called a demeaning name, having a spouse or lover flirt with someone else, being shoved by someone at a bar, having someone take food off one's plate, or refuse to move a car that is blocking one's driveway; or, to refer to the cases I mention in this book: to have one's car broken down and have too little money and mechanical expertise to get it operating again; to not like the way a friend or spouse or daughter is looking at one, or the way they are talking about one; to have one's father refuse to postpone going to a movie, when one has just arrived at his house; to have to repeat a high-school geometry course; to have one's sister help herself to things from one's own room; and so on.

These kinds of things are often noticed and commented on in newspaper accounts of so-called "senseless" or "incomprehensible" murders.

But it is the very triviality of the incident that provokes the violence. The more trivial the cause of the shame, the more intense the feeling of shame.

Everybody has experienced "trivial" insults that rankle. A child is teased for a difficult word mispronounced, a professional woman is asked to get the coffee. If these small incidents rankle people with power, prestige, and status, imagine their effect on people who don't have these advantages.[7] It is difficult for many of us to abandon our moral and legal way of thinking about violence, to abandon our habit of assuming that the most important question worth asking about violence is whether or not it was justified—in other words, whether the "cause" was of sufficient magnitude to excuse, or at least mitigate, the person's moral/legal guilt.

It is precisely because the incidents that cause shame are typically so "slight" or "trivial," and hence leave one feeling so ashamed to be ashamed about them, that they leave people feeling so "slight" and "trivial" and "unimportant" themselves; as the shame-sensitive person knows better than anyone else, only an unimportant and slight person would be vulnerable to, and upset over, an unimportant slight. And in fact most people are not overwhelmed by their shame over such incidents, to the point of becoming violent; that is precisely why it is so astonishing and shocking when some do—because in fact everyone experiences slights of greater or lesser degrees of seriousness, inevitably, as an ongoing part of life; everyone knows this, and yet only a small minority ever assault or kill others or themselves because of it.

There are other reasons why an apparently or objectively trivial incident may have the power to trigger or precipitate an act of violence that is out of all proportion, in its effects, to that apparent cause. And yet, while I would agree that these other explanations are valid, I would also argue that they do not invalidate, they are not mutually exclusive with, the analysis I have just offered.

For example, the precipitating incident—the trivial event that provokes an act of violence—may be the equivalent of the proverbial "last straw" that breaks the camel's back. In this interpretation, the final precipitant is only in the most trivial sense the "cause" of the violence; the far greater cause was the stress already placed on the camel's back prior to the last little bit. Or one could think of the trivial incident that precipitates violence as nothing more than the tiny spark that ignites the gasoline can, the match that is thrown onto the powder keg. And I would agree that analogies of this sort also have their place in the full description of the events that lead up to an act of violence. As Shervert Frazier[8] put it, murder is not an event but a process; the "event" we call murder is only one point in that process. Most people do not respond to trivial humiliations or embarrassments with explosive rages. So of course the person who does respond in that way must have been "primed" in some sense, or why else would he have been so "hypersensitive" to experiences that the average person would not respond to with violence?

But the point I am making is that events that are utterly trivial from any moral or legal point of view may be of the very greatest importance and significance from a medical and psychological perspective—literally, of life-and-death importance—for that is precisely their significance. They determine the difference between life and death for millions of human beings. The power of shame is inversely proportional to the magnitude of the precipitating cause; the more trivial the cause of feeling shame, the more shameful it becomes to acknowledge that that is what one feels so ashamed (and hence so enraged) about.

The germ theory of disease can help us here. We know now that the smaller the pathogen attacking us, the more dangerous and deadly it is, and the harder it is to ward off. But when Pasteur first proposed that microorganisms too small to be seen by the naked eye could be killing humans, who are incomparably larger and stronger, the idea seemed to violate every canon of common sense. And yet, what we have discovered over and over again in the course of our evolution is that it was relatively easy to defend ourselves against the large animals of prey, the lions and tigers; and that the larger parasites like tapeworms did not kill nearly as many of us as did those too tiny even to be seen without a microscope. But vastly more dangerous were the even tinier micro-organisms, the bacteria that caused such plagues as the Black Death, and the even deadlier White Death, tuberculosis. And yet we found effective ways to protect ourselves even against these microscopic organisms, compared with those that are smaller yet, the viruses: as the worldwide AIDS epidemic is showing us. Still the even deadlier challenge and much harder to defeat are the tiniest changes of all, those that occur in ultramicroscopic double helices of intra-cellular nucleic acids, producing cancer, aging, degenerative diseases of all sorts. But even those are enormous in size compared to the deadliest challenge of all, the one that endangers not only human but even all organic life: namely, the tiniest atoms in the universe, helium and hydrogen, and their even tinier subatomic particles, their nuclei: the ultimate mechanisms of nuclear weapons, hydrogen bombs.

Truly, the more tiny and trivial the cause, the more powerful, deadly, and violent the result. The Great Chain of Being may go from atoms to God, from the smallest to the greatest, but the Great Chain of Non-Being clearly goes in exactly the opposite direction.

PART III

THE EPIDEMIOLOGY

OF VIOLENCE

CHAPTER 6

The Symbolism

of Punishment

I REALIZE THAT THE MURDERS I HAVE DESCRIBED SEEM SO IRRATIONAL, SO
bizarre, and so idiosyncratic that the reader may well have some doubts
as to how representative they are of violent people in general. Also,
because most murderers are incapable of stating the meaning of their
actions in words (which is why they are limited to expressing themselves by means of actions), the interpretation of the meaning of their
acts often rests on my own inferences.

So I think it would be useful to examine the symbolism of violence
in a different context, where the symbolic meaning of violence is fully
conscious and articulated by those who "commit" it. I have in mind the
violence of punishment—or, as Karl Menninger called it, the crime of
punishment[1]—that form of violence sanctioned by courts of law and
other legal authorities throughout the centuries. Certainly, from the
standpoint of life and death, capital punishment is just as deadly a form
of violence as murder—a man is just as dead if he is killed by the state
as he is if killed by a murderer. Therefore, if we wish to learn more
about the causes of violence in order to do a better job of preventing it,
we need to study the violence of legal punishment. By punishment I

mean the infliction of physical or mental pain or injury on anyone beyond that which is an unavoidable consequence of keeping him from inflicting violence or pain on himself or others.

From my preventive medicine perspective, I see that punishment in this sense—punishment beyond what is necessary for *restraint* (the punishment of retribution, or vengeance)—is an ill-conceived, misdirected, societal crime for which we pay dearly in lives, suffering, and social costs. I will argue that some of the violent measures of legal punishment are a deadly counterpart to the violence that we call crime.

I can understand if you, the reader, are skeptical of my view that punishment is the mirror of crime, emotionally, motivationally, and symbolically. What reason do we have to think that an examination of anything as presumably rational, necessary, and sane as legal punishment might have the same causes, follow the same symbolic logic and thus be as irrational and insane as the terrible and sickening murders and mutilations described above? As a partial answer to that question, let me cite a passage from Freud, which I believe speaks to this issue in a way that is relevant to what I am trying to do here. As he put it (with my own interpolations added in brackets),

> . . . mental processes . . . are actually more familiar to us and more accessible to consciousness as they are seen in the group than they can be in the individual man. In [the individual], when tension arises, it is only . . . aggressiveness . . . which . . . makes itself noisily heard; [the] actual demands [that is, the purposes and goals and meanings of this aggression and their symbolic messages] often remain unconscious in the background.

> If we bring [these demands] to conscious knowledge, we find that they coincide with the precepts of the prevailing cultural superego [which we see in the moral value system of the culture, as

officially embodied in the codes and practices of the criminal
justice system].

At this point the two processes, . . . the . . . development of
the group and that . . . of the individual, are . . . always interlocked.

For that reason some of the manifestations and properties of [the
aggressive drive, as manifested in the cultural] super-ego [includ-
ing the legal and penal systems] can be more easily detected in its
behaviour in the cultural community than in the separate individual.[2]

Punishment, then, is that collective violence which any society defines as legal, just as crime is the individual violence that we define as
illegal. The actual injuries inflicted on criminals by the legal system are
specifically intended to be as identical as possible to the violence committed by the criminal.

But more relevant and important for my purpose is that the psychological parameters of crime and punishment are also interlocked. The
first thing that strikes us when we begin to study the history of legal
punishments is how exactly and literally the symbolism of punishment
corresponds to the symbolism and motivation of crime—even crimes as
terrible as those committed by the murderers I have just described.

For example, from the time law was first invented, the essence of law
and the pursuit of justice has consisted of the attempt to "make the
punishment fit the crime"—often in the form of the most concrete and
literal form of correspondence, as in the biblical phrase "an eye for an
eye." Sometimes the form this takes is to punish the criminal by destroying the organ or body part with which he committed the crime; at
other times the goal is to mutilate the criminal in the same body part
that he had injured in his victim. But in either case, the symbolic
principle is the same (and follows the same laws of "symbolic logic" as

does the kind of violence that is called "criminal")—namely, to undo the shame that had been inflicted on the victim of violence (the person who is now the perpetrator of violence), by the perpetrator of violence (the person who is now the victim of violence).

For example, Saudi Arabian law courts punish thieves by chopping off their hands—for hands are what theft is committed with. On a less extreme scale, but with equally concrete logic, some parents in our own society tell children that if they say dirty words they will wash their mouths out with soap (the mouth being the part of the body that committed the offense, dirty being the metaphorical expression for socially unacceptable, and soap being what we use to remove actual, non-metaphorical dirt).

A similar conflation of categories was made by the murderers I discussed in the last chapter, who treated a metaphor (being shamed "in other people's eyes," in which "eyes" is a metaphor for other people's disdain) as if the offense (shaming) and the disdain were a concrete reality, and one could only destroy it by destroying the other person's actual, concrete, non-metaphorical eyes. But that same mental process, which seems like such an obvious confusion between the metaphoric and the literal, can be seen to run through the whole history of the legal system, where the symbolism of punishment is just as subservient to the laws of magical thinking as is the symbolism of crime.

Thus, the crime of shaming a man, by slandering, insulting, or ridiculing him (and thus "destroying his honor"), has been punished since the dawn of civilization by cutting out the organ by means of which the offender insulted or ridiculed his victim, namely, his tongue. In Spain, for example, in laws operative from the thirteenth century until the Enlightenment, the punishment inflicted on a man who destroyed the reputation and honor of another man by slander, and thus shamed him, was to have his tongue cut out—"according to the custom, at once cruel and symbolic, of punishing a man or woman in the organ with which the crime . . . was committed."[3]

During the Florentine Renaissance,

Official public punishment was often meted out less for its own obvious cruelty than for the symbolic image it engendered. . . . Careful hierarchies of punishment thus evolved which fit . . . the nature of the crime. Not only should they express revenge for the result of the crime (an eye for an eye), but they were expected also to mirror the actual criminal act. For example, a blasphemer [that is, one who insults God] might have his tongue cut out. . . . Dante applied this doctrine in a famous passage in the *Inferno*. . . . In 1441 the painter Pisanello was sentenced . . . to have his tongue cut out for having insulted the government of Venice. . . .[4]

Richard van Dulmen documents the same types of punishments for the same types of offenses in European courts of law from the sixteenth century until well into the nineteenth, which extended so far as to mutilate a prisoner's body even after he had been executed—by tearing out and burning his tongue, for example, if his crime was committed with that organ (as in the case of slander, insults, or blasphemy). He points out that the logic behind these gruesome punishments was that the crime (the evil, the sin) was pictured as a concrete reality that had an objective existence even apart from the person committing it; and that it was the crime or evil itself that had to be marked and destroyed. And that could be done only by destroying the organ of the body that committed the crime. He emphasizes the importance of "execution rituals, without which the death penalty in early modern society would not have been what it was, namely, a form of ritual killing. . . . The issue was purification, indeed the self-purification of society," as if society itself had been polluted by the "crime" that was committed in its midst. "God's disfavour and punishment of town and country was feared if the population did not cleanse itself from the crime. Socio-magical and religious notions amalgamated. . . ."[5]

Throughout the centuries, the penalty for rape has been to destroy the organ that "commited" that crime. In the American South, for example, "it goes almost without saying that the penalty for a slave who dared lust after white women's flesh was castration." Until the Civil War, this was the official law of the slave code, not simply the standard atrocity committed by lynch mobs, as it later became. But even as late as the 1940s, it was still an official, legally sanctioned punishment for rape in several Southern states. As Wyatt-Brown put it, "the moral focus was honor, and the reprisal for its violation was the opposite: the stigma of shame. As a result, there could not be much distinction between the legal and community forms of retribution. Common law and lynch law were ethically compatible"—and as we have seen, both followed the same laws of symbolism as did the original crime for which they were the punishment. For the means by which the stigma of shame was transferred from the rape victim and her family (all of whom had been shamed, or dishonored, by the rape) to the perpetrator was by castrating the rapist. This act had the effect of symbolically restoring the honor of the violated, through the psychological logic of what Freud called primary process or "magical" thinking.

Crime and punishment are reciprocal systems for the symbolic exchange of honor and shame. The currency of these emotional, symbolic, and violent exchanges is the currency of honor and shame. In this case, the currency is not gold but parts of the body, of which eyes and genitals are the most highly valued (although tongues and ears and other body parts may also be used as well). These organs, eyes and genitals, symbolize the emotions in question, honor and shame. For example, intact genitals (not raped, not castrated) symbolize honor and confer pride on the possessor; raped or castrated genitals symbolize shame and confer disgrace.

Since corporal punishments for violent crime have largely been replaced by other sanctions, chiefly imprisonment—aimed at punishing the person as a psychological and social being rather than solely a physical being—the reader might wonder about the relevance of the symbolism of punishment in the modern world. Despite the ways in which punishment has superficially changed, however, we have kept the old symbolism still intact and still operative.

Over the centuries, the subject and object of punishment has shifted from the body to the soul, from dead bodies to dead souls, from the maiming of bodies to the maiming of human souls. How has this shift been brought about?

As punishment was gradually transposed from the physical to the mental plane, it has become even more symbolic, or symbolic at a more "rarefied" level—but the same messages are communicated in no less actual and powerful a way. As Michel Foucault put it:

> If the penalty in its most severe forms no longer addresses itself to the body, on what does it lay hold? The answer of the theoreticians—those who, about 1760, opened up a new period that is not yet at an end—is simple, almost obvious. It seems to be contained in the question itself: since it is no longer the body, it must be the soul. . . . Mably formulated the principle once and for all [in 1789, the year of the French Revolution]: "Punishment . . . should strike the soul rather than the body."[6]

Consider the most powerful model or paradigm of the modern prison, for there we can see how noncorporal punishment continues the same symbolic meanings that corporal means used to. The most notable innovation of the American system "was a rule of absolute, total silence" imposed on the inmates. In one of the two main versions of this system, called the "Pennsylvania" system, after two Philadelphia prisons that pioneered the concept—Walnut Street (1790) and Cherry Hill (1829)—"prisoners were utterly alone, night and day" and "wore hoods whenever they left their cells." At Walnut Street, "The convicts were to be locked in cells that would prevent all external communication with each other."[7]

The other principal version of the "American" system, named after the prison in Auburn, New York, differed from the Pennsylvania system only in that prisoners worked together rather than in isolation during the day. As in Pennsylvania, they slept in solitary cells at night. In both systems, however, the silence apparently was thunderous. Alexis de Tocqueville, who visited and wrote a report on the American penitentiary system together with Gustave de Beaumont, found the silence in these great houses of captivity especially awesome at night. It was, he said, nearly the silence "of death. We have often trod during night those monotonous and dim galleries, where a lamp is always burning: we felt as if we traversed catacombs; there were a thousand living beings, and yet it was a desert solitude."[8]

As Lawrence Friedman has written:

> All the new penitentiaries, whatever their differences, were committed to silence, [and] to a certain amount of isolation. . . . At the Eastern Penitentiary in Philadelphia, the new convict was undressed, his hair cut. . . . Then he put on the prison uniform and a "cap or hood" to blindfold him; in this condition he was led to his cell. No one in the prison could speak. At Sing Sing in New York, officers wore moccasins, so that they could "approach the cells without the convicts being aware of their presence." The rule of silence was so well enforced that "for several years there has not been any case reported of a prisoner talking after he was locked up."[9]

Charles Dickens, who visited the great Philadelphia prison in the early 1840s, was horrified by what he saw: " 'Those who devised this system . . . and those benevolent gentlemen who carry it into execution, do not know what . . . they are doing.' Prison life was nothing but torture and agony. 'I hold this slow and daily tampering with the mysteries of the brain, to be immeasurably worse than any torture of the body.' The wounds it inflicted 'are not upon the surface, and it extorts few cries that human ears can hear'; but there was a 'depth of terrible endurance . . . which none but the sufferers themselves can fathom, and which no man has a right to inflict upon his fellow-creature.' The prisoners, who entered in black hoods, emblems of the 'curtain dropped' between them 'and the living world,' were like men 'buried alive; to be dug out in the slow round of years; and in the meantime dead to everything but torturing anxieties and horrible despair.' "[10]

What effects did this system have on those who were subjected to it? Where the full experiment was tried, with the system of total round-the-clock isolation added to the enforced blindfolding, soundlessness, and muteness (in New York, from 1821 to 1823),

> the results were horrific: one prisoner tried to kill himself by throwing himself "from the fourth gallery, upon the pavement"; another "beat and mangled his head against the walls of his cell, until he destroyed one of his eyes." From then on, hard labor [rather than total and permanent solitary confinement] was the absolute rule.[11]

But once that slight modification was introduced, the system not only continued, it even spread, in this form or worse, throughout most of the young country. And while it is true that the criminals who were subjected to it were no longer punished by being blinded, having their tongues cut out, or their ears cut off, still it is not hard to see that physical mutilations of that sort had simply been replaced by their functional equivalents. To the extent that it was possible to render men effectively blind, deaf, and dumb by means that did not involve their jailers' touching their eyes, ears, or tongues directly or physically, this system "succeeded," although it did not preclude driving the inmates themselves mad enough to lead them to destroy their own eyes, as the example above illustrates.

This is the system that replaced corporal mutilation and the death penalty. I can imagine the reader now saying, But surely, American prisons no longer impose such dehumanizing conditions on anyone?

Presently, there is no rule of total silence for all prisoners anymore, nor are prisoners blindfolded whenever they leave their cells. But the notion that such conditions are not effectively duplicated on a certain fraction of the prison population even today, and with results even more horrific than those mentioned above, would be far too optimistic a conclusion. The following story illustrates my point.

THE CASE OF LLOYD A.

Several years ago, in the late 1970s, Lloyd A., a man who had just been released from prison, after only a few days brutally and without provocation murdered one college student and nearly killed another who had picked Lloyd up when he was hitchhiking. At the conclusion of the murder trial that followed, as he sentenced Lloyd A. to "a natural life" sentence, without any possibility of parole, the judge commented that his only regret was that capital punishment had been stricken from the list of punishments he had the power to mete out, because he thought this crime was so heinous that nothing less than the death penalty was commensurate with it.

Upon reading that comment in the newspaper account of the sentencing, one of my colleagues, a psychologist, commented that he sympathized with the judge's sentiments. But another psychologist, also a colleague, who had known the murderer during the man's previous prison term—which had been for a minor, nonviolent crime—mentioned that he knew something about the conditions under which Lloyd A. had first been incarcerated.

While he had been in prison, during his first sentence, prison officers found Lloyd A. to be a difficult, rebellious, often obnoxious and provocative young man. As a consequence, Lloyd A. had spent virtually his entire previous sentence in solitary confinement. When sufficiently annoyed, the correction officers would punish Lloyd A. by closing a solid steel door which covered the only exit from his tiny concrete cell, and by turning off the only light in his cell, which had the effect of creating the feeling of being buried alive, unable to see or to speak to anyone—the functional equivalent of destroying his eyes and tongue.

When Lloyd A. was particularly offensive to the officers, they would also remove his mattress and back up his toilet (which at that time was a hole in the floor), so that he would have to sleep on the concrete floor in his own excrement, accompanied by the vermin that are naturally attracted to such an environment. Furthermore, since Lloyd A. had broken so many rules, the parole board would not grant him a parole. So, for his minor and nonviolent crime, Lloyd D. ended up serving a longer sentence than he otherwise would have, spending the last two years of his term in the conditions I have just described. Moreover, instead of being released back into the community on parole status in a series of gradual transitions, with increasing levels of freedom, responsibility, and privileges, such as finding a job and beginning work while still living in a supervised and supportive residential facility, Lloyd A. was given no transitional period in which to readjust and adapt to the "outside." He was not eligible for any rehabilitative treatment whatsoever. Instead, one day, his full sentence was "rapped up" (prison slang for "completed"). On the day when the prison could no longer legally keep him, his solid door was opened, and Lloyd A. was led blinking into the daylight, through all the other solid doors that block access to the outside world, until he found himself out on the street.

I am not going to speculate about what his state of mind was at that point; we know what he did within a few days of his release. For to say merely that Lloyd A. was angry, embittered, unprepared to be in the community, and utterly without any of the supports that might have helped him to be less of a menace to the public, may sound like an attempt to "excuse" his horrendous crime, which is far from my intention.

Still, to focus on the character of Lloyd A. or even on his crime, would miss the point of what I think we can learn from his story: namely, that punishing someone in the way that he was punished does not protect the public; it only sends a human time bomb into the community where he is primed to explode the moment he resumes his first contact with other human beings. The conditions of his first prison term did not cause the flaws in his character that got him into trouble, or he would not have been sent to prison in the first place. But he left prison incomparably more violent and dangerous than when he entered. To the extent that his punishment had any effect on him, it was to turn an offensive and antisocial man who had not been seriously violent into an unprovoked murderer, and a would-be multiple murderer at that.

I mention this because it is current wisdom among some politicians today to claim that only punishing criminals more harshly and "coddling" them less will "teach" them to give up their evil ways and behave better. As the British Prime Minister, John Major, put it recently, "It is time to understand less and condemn more." But people who say this have no idea what they are saying, any more than the prison administrators Charles Dickens visited (or those responsible for the punishment of the man I have just described) knew what they were doing.

I have no doubt that we must restrain violent people from injuring anyone, as long as they will not or cannot restrain themselves. That does require restricting their freedom for as long as they are dangerous. But punishment per se—the gratuitous infliction of pain or deprivation above and beyond whatever is unavoidably inherent in the act of re-straining the violent—does not prevent or inhibit further violence, it only stimulates it.

Among the few who do understand that making punishment any harsher than one can avoid doing is not only futile, but even dangerous and counterproductive, are the wiser and more experienced correction officers. One of them said, in explaining why no one should treat inmates the way Lloyd A. was treated, "You can lock a dog in a closet for a month, but I don't want to be the person who's standing there when you let him out."

It would be pointless to blame the correction officers for the conditions maintained in prison. Nothing is easier than to criticize those individuals to whom we, as a society, have given the most dangerous and onerous task of guarding our safety, while we in turn give them virtually no support, training, or supervision, and refuse to listen to what they have to teach us about the men with whom they work every day. Clearly, such a method of handling "crime" is not only dangerous to both officers and inmates, it also endangers the public safety far more than a humane, enlightened system would. In the meantime, prison officers are subjected to constant threats, harassment, attacks, and even occasional murder at the hands of inmates who have themselves been so brutalized and dehumanized that they feel they have nothing to lose.

Ritual Rites of Domination and Submission: Shame and Humiliation

Earlier I mentioned that the sexual organs and the acts associated with them are powerful symbols of shame. It is for this reason that castration (or emasculation) and rape are two of the most powerful ways of inflicting ultimate shame and humiliation on another person. Rites of domination and emasculation are not restricted to the human species. As ethologists have long noted, male baboons signal their submission to a more dominant male by assuming the attitude of a female in heat, who is willing to be mounted. The submissive male animal, the one who has been, in effect, defeated, and is communicating his surrender to the stronger one, turns around, exposing his hind parts to the superior male. This is called "presenting." Mounting and presentation are used as signals among baboons, regardless of sex. For instance, a young male may present to an older and stronger female, and she may mount him. Among the females, presentation and mounting are used in the same way.

Many animal species continually use sexual behavior patterns outside the specifically sexual sphere. Serving as they do to indicate differences in power. . . . a similar pattern exists in humans and . . . its meaning corresponds to that of the mounting-presentation signals in monkeys.[12]

There are, however, two extremely important and closely related differences between animals and humans in this respect. The first is the fact that, as Mark Twain observed, "man is the only animal that blushes."[13] Humankind is the only animal that feels shame—those painful, unacceptable, and sometimes intolerable feelings of inferiority that many men experience when "backed into" a subordinate position. The second difference is that whereas these rituals of dominance and submission, using sexual organs and acts as their symbolic currency, create peace, order, and social stability among animals, they are far more likely to lead to warfare among human beings. Men often fight to the death in order to avoid the fate of the underdog. Or else they experience the death of the self when they submit to another man rather than continuing to fight. Since one's sexual identity is such a central constituent of a person's sense of self, if it is destroyed, so is the self. Animals, by contrast, typically submit shamelessly and peacefully once they realize they are outmatched, and the stronger one ceases to fight as well.

Men will often kill or assault each other in the struggle to avoid being in the submissive position, and experience an almost bottomless sense of degradation—when they do submit—to the point where, effectively, their self has died.

But there is another arena in which this symbolism operates, namely, the "successful degradation ceremony," as the sociologists Garfinkel[14] and Goffman[15] have called it. In the prisons, as I have observed them, this concept describes a particular kind of ritual called the "booking," or admission process, of a new inmate into prison. As Garfinkel defines it, a "status degradation ceremony" consists of "any communicative work between persons, whereby the public identity of an actor is transformed into something looked on as lower in the local scheme of social types." Garfinkel argues that "the structural conditions of status degradation" correspond to "the structural conditions of shame," so that a degradation ceremony provides "in the very features of its organization the conditions sufficient for inducing shame." He adds that "degradation ceremonies fall within the scope of the sociology of moral indignation," which he includes with other "social affects" such as "shame and guilt."

The behavioral paradigm of shame is found in the withdrawal and covering of the portion of the body that socially defines one's public appearance—prominently, at least in our society, the genitals and the face: "I felt I had been caught with my pants down"; "I wanted to fall through the floor." Shame motivates people to conceal or hide themselves from public view, to save the self from further insult. So the forced exposure of the self, or of those parts of the body that make one particularly vulnerable to shame, exposes the person, who is treated in this way, to the experience of shame.

But what is the purpose of exposing someone to the maximum possible amount of shame? Garfinkel suggests that "moral indignation serves to effect the ritual destruction of the person denounced . . . the destruction of the person being denounced is intended literally." What Garfinkel is describing is what I have referred to elsewhere as the "death of the self"—the destruction of the person, or of that person's total identity. And how is this relevant to the symbolism of punishment? As Garfinkel points out, "In our society, . . . the court and its officers have something like a fair monopoly over such ceremonies, and there they have become an occupational routine."

The Ritual Degradation of "Booking"

This "occupational routine" occurs regularly among prison officers in the admission process for new inmates.[16] The central feature of this "total degradation ceremony" consists of stripping the inmate so that he is naked, in front of a group of officers, who then force him to bend over in the attitude of submission (described above as "presentation" when animals do it); and, in addition, to spread the cheeks of his buttocks so that his anal orifice is completely exposed to the group. At that point one of the officers (or a prison doctor, if one is willing) sticks a gloved finger into the man's anus—ostensibly to determine if the man is smuggling drugs into prison by secreting them there. I say "ostensibly" because I know, from having talked with the superintendents of more than one prison and prison mental hospital in the past, that the whole admission ritual, including this part of the ceremony, is consciously and deliberately intended to terrify and humiliate the new inmate or patient, by demonstrating to him the complete and total power the prison or hospital has over him, and to intimidate him into submitting absolutely to the institution and its officers. I should also emphasize, however, that that attitude is by no means universal among either superintendents or officers, and many of them appropriately regard this ceremony as degrading and counterproductive, so that they refuse to allow such behavior in their institutions.

The symbolism is obvious: it is a digital anal rape. But even before the finger is introduced into the anus, it is a public humiliation. It is a total degradation ceremony, a massive assault on and annihilation of manhood. It is also a version of the "presenting" ritual by which both animals and humans symbolize relations of dominance and submission. With at least some inmates it achieves—in conjunction with other components of the admission process and the total incarceration experience—the intended aim of total degradation ceremonies: ritual destruction of the personality or manhood of the inmate, the death of his self, so that he becomes a "non-person," or a "dead soul."

In addition, it is worth remembering what Freud discovered about paranoia, namely, that paranoia is precipitated by fears of homosexuality, so that whatever arouses, stimulates, or intensifies those fears will only increase a person's level of paranoia. Being forced to strip naked in front of a group of other men, having one's anus manually entered by one of them, would increase paranoia. Once one sees the intensity of the paranoia in prisons, and how paranoia in turn stimulates the most extreme levels of violence among these violent men, one understands why this admission ritual is absurdly and tragically counterproductive. To put it another way, if the purpose of imprisonment were to socialize men to become as violent as possible—both while they are there, and after they return to the community—we could hardly find a more effective way to accomplish it.

Again, I am not saying that any one specific practice, like the one I have just mentioned, is "the" cause of the violence these men commit, either in prison or on the outside. For most, they would not be in prison in the first place if they had not already committed some degree or other of antisocial behavior. But I am saying that certain practices stimulate these men's already existing potential for violence and their predisposition to engage in it, and only increase the likelihood that they will escalate their violence in the future to whatever is the maximum level for which they have the potential.

From the time I first walked through the elaborate security apparatus into the prison and began to engage in the diagnosis and treatment of violent men who lived (and sometimes died) there, I noticed that the degree of paranoia in the atmosphere was so thick you could cut it with a knife. It is true that a large amount of paranoia is unavoidable, given the nature of the people who are sent to prison. It stands to reason that to be among men who are, by definition, untrustworthy, one would have to be out of touch with reality oneself to trust them. In the world of the prisons, I have long maintained one needs to be "paranoid" in order to be in touch with reality—"paranoid" in the sense of being acutely mistrustful, of always maintaining a high degree of skepticism and doubt and an awareness that the men you are dealing with are often very dangerous. And, of course, the inmates feel the same way

about each other, only more so. They themselves are far more constantly endangered and far less protected than anyone in a position of
authority.

The principal problem with paranoia is that it tends to become a
self-fulfilling prophecy. The more paranoid a person is, the more he
feels he is surrounded by enemies and needs to be violent toward them
in order to protect himself. The more he behaves this way, the more he
creates enemies, even among people who were initially neutral or
friendly. Doing anything that gratuitously increases the level of paranoia
among violent men is the equivalent of throwing a lighted match into a
gasoline can.

The form in which paranoia manifests itself in prison is not primarily
through delusions. Most inmates are not overtly psychotic, but suffer
instead from a profound and pervasive inability to trust anyone—even
those few people in the prison world who are trustworthy. But a particularly dangerous and acute form of prison paranoia, which is often
responsible for otherwise inexplicable and unprovoked violence on the
part of inmates, is something called "homosexual panic." I suppose one
might say that "homosexual panic" is to "homophobia" as weather is to
climate—it is the emotional/behavioral thunder and lightning storm
that is happening right now, as opposed to the more lasting, stable and
chronic attitude that "homophobia" refers to. "Homosexual panic" is an
acute psychiatric (and security) emergency that happens when an inmate experiences a degree of homosexual stimulation that is intolerable
to his self-esteem and his sense of his own masculinity, a crisis which
can cause a man to prove that far from loving men, he hates them all
and will prove it by being as violent as possible toward them.

If the purpose of our prison system were to create as much homosexual panic as possible among the men who are sent to jail, and, thereby
to increase the level of violence and the predisposition to violence
among these men, we could hardly have designed a more effective plan.
For we have built into the prison system just about every element that
could add to the homosexual panic that inmates experience there. First,

we make it an all-male environment. That alone will do it for some
men, as any psychiatrist with experience of army barracks is aware.
Second, we deprive the inmates of the one thing that might reassure
those who are heterosexual—namely, "conjugal visits" with women.
Third, we fail to protect imprisoned men from actual and frequent
rapes, or (what amounts to the same thing, only worse) of being forced
into submitting to an ongoing sexual relationship with another inmate
who is dominant over them and turns them into his "woman." Fourth,
just to make sure that they get the point, and realize that this is the
essence and purpose of the whole prison system, these men are introduced to the prison with the kind of "total degradation ceremony," or
symbolic anal rape and humiliation, that I described earlier. This is our
culture's initiation ceremony into the civilization of the damned, the
society of dead souls, men who are stripped of their manhood. In sum,
the only thing that is surprising about the world of the prison system,
and its effect on the men sent there, is that these men are not more
violent than they are.

Punishment has yet another symbolism as well. I mentioned earlier
that the prisons I have seen can be compared only to hell. I indicated
that I thought one reason this was so was because many of the violent
criminals I have seen in such places resemble the damned, in terms of
their own emotional condition, as it exists independently of the prison:
many of them were "damned" before they ever got to prison. But I
believe there is much more to it than that, and that prisons resemble
hell as much as they do not just because of the character of the people
who tend to occupy them, but also because throughout history (and
with few exceptions) the societies that construct prisons have specifically wanted to make the prisons resemble hell, as much as possible,
from their architecture to the relationships between the various groups
of people involved in them—especially the inmates, the correctional
staff, and the judges who sentence people to them.

For example, Samuel Edgerton[17] has pointed out the reciprocal or
interchangeable nature of hell and prisons, each of which came to

symbolize the other, in the Italian Renaissance. Artists who painted hell modeled it after contemporary prisons. And the criminal courts modeled their arrangements after paintings of the Last Judgment, at which the Supreme Judge sentenced the guilty to hell.

In these paintings, not only the architecture of hell, but also the various punishments and tortures that went on within it, were portrayed by the artists, in keeping with the penal practices of the time. For example,

> In each of hell's caverns, demons perform specialized horrors upon the damned who are usually without clothes. . . . Trecento artists took pains to show these sinners as naked and not nude—the distinction being that the former is a condition of embarrassment while the latter . . . became a condition of pictorial beauty. Artists of the Middle Ages . . . would frequently have seen living wrongdoers stripped naked in public, as a form of punishment prescribed by the local law courts. Some acts of obscene humiliation often accompanied these sentences in real life, which Giotto and Fra Angelico also reflected. In Giotto's fresco . . . two sinners in hell are shown hanging upside down, a man by a rope attached to his penis and a woman by a hook in her vagina.[18]

These artists were merely portraying the actual punishments inflicted on real people by the criminal courts of that time. Edgerton mentions also that "Dante's own vision of the netherworld . . . indicates a popular belief that a distinct parallel existed between temporal and eternal vindictive justice. Certainly painters of the period borrowed from local images of public chastisement for their own representations of the inferno in the Last Judgment."[19]

Conversely, just as depictions of hell were modeled upon the penal system, so the symbolism of the penal system and the criminal courts that condemned people to punishment was modeled upon the Last Judgment, which condemned people to hell. "A . . . now lost painting

by Taddeo Gaddi once decorated the wall behind the judges of the
Mercanzia court, showing The Judges Tribunal Watching Truth Tear
out the Tongue of Falsehood"[20]—a punishment that, as mentioned
above, was inflicted by the law courts to punish crimes committed with
the tongue, such as perjury, slander, insults, blasphemy, and heresy.
Obviously, these images of hell and damnation were not merely symbolic or allegorical; they were literal depictions of the day-to-day practices of the contemporary penal system itself, in all its vivid reality.

The Wisdom of Judges and God and The Devil's Work of Prison Guards

I would like to mention one other implication of this symbolism, because it may still have a powerful influence on the penal system. If
criminal trials are modeled after the Last Judgment, and prisons after
hell, then judges are modeled after God. Prison officers, however, are
modeled after devils, and may well be expected to act accordingly. For
example, Edgerton points out that

> in spite of his status as an officer of the law, the public execu-
> tioner in late medieval and Renaissance times did not enjoy nor-
> mal social acceptance. In spite of his relatively high salary, he
> often lived the life of an outcast. According to law, he was auto-
> matically infamous. . . . Symbolically, he was regarded as the
> vicar of the devil, counterpart to the judge, who was the vicar of
> Christ. . . . He was also expected to play this vicarious devil's
> role to the letter.[21]

One concrete example of this came to my attention when I was
asked by the Commissioner of Correction in the late 1970s to interview
a prison officer who had apparently became so violent toward one inmate, while working with other officers to quell an incipient riot among

a group of prisoners, that even his fellow officers were worried and concerned that the officer was behaving in a way that was unnecessary, out of control, irrational, and potentially dangerous to everyone concerned.

When I spoke with the officer, he admitted that he was worried about these same issues, felt he was losing his self-control, and was afraid that he would behave toward an inmate in ways that he would later regret as much as anyone else would. After mentioning some personal problems that were adding to his general level of stress, he went on to comment that "no one should have as much power over other human beings as we do over the inmates."

My point is neither to excuse this officer's episode of unnecessary violence, nor to collude with any attempt on his part to avoid taking responsibility for his own behavior—after all, other officers in that same situation had not behaved violently. But officers themselves often do not want to be as punitive toward the "criminals" they have to spend all day working with as they believe they are expected to be—not only by their fellow officers, but by society at large, by virtue of the accepted "stereotype" of the prison officer that is current in our culture now, and has been handed down to us ever since their ancestors were seen as "the vicars of the Devil." My repeated experience in working with these men is that their attitudes toward what works and does not work, in the prevention of violence, and what is appropriate and acceptable or not, in response to violence, is almost always more enlightened and humane than that of many politicians who do not have the same degree of first-hand knowledge, not to mention the rest of us who, as voters, elect those politicians into positions of great power.

Unfortunately, the power of that ancient symbolism of devils punishing sinners in hell may be much greater and longer lasting in our collective cultural unconscious than most of us would ever realize—to the point where we actually build prisons underground (or make them appear that way). That same collective unconscious may well lead us to regard the infliction of gratuitous torments on prisoners as a legitimate and expected part of a prison officer's "job description," supposing them to be performing the same functions that devils do in hell, dividing prisons into different circles of increasing punishment (with solitary confinement as the lowest circle of hell), keeping the resemblance between prisons and hell, and between prisoners and the damned, as close as possible.

How to Increase

the Rate of

Violence—and Why

WITHIN THE PENAL SYSTEM—IN ADDITION TO LEGALLY EXECUTED AND morally defended punishments—there is a dark underside to punishment in the prisons. It occurs regularly, knowingly, and more or less universally. It is a predictable consequence of our policies and punishments. The most egregious example of what I am referring to here is the violence that prisoners routinely inflict on one another.

Now I realize that to hold the prison system itself responsible for "in-house" violence—from the threats, extortion, and robberies to which prisoners are regularly subjected by other prisoners, to the actual mutilations, rapes, and murders that occur in prison—might sound at first like claiming that the "cops" are completely responsible for the violence that the "robbers" commit. This is not my intention. Of course, many prisoners were sent to prison in the first place because they had already made a habit of violence. Still, prison conditions often tolerate and even exacerbate the inmates' pre-existing potential for violence. In fact, the very conditions that occur regularly in most prisons may force prisoners to engage in acts of serious violence in order to avoid being mutilated, raped, or murdered themselves.

All the evidence of which I am aware, both from my own observations, from what I have learned from judges, correctional administrators, prison mental health professionals, and prisoners themselves, and from what has been written, indicates that the responsibility for violence in prisons emanates neither unilaterally from prisoners nor from the prison system alone. It is the predictable and even inevitable outcome of patterns of interaction between prisoners and the penal system. Any characterization of legal punishment as a form of violence, with a symbolism of its own (one it shares more or less interchangeably with "criminal" violence) if it is to be complete must include the violence of prisoners toward each other in the inventory of prison punishment. While that conclusion may seem radical to some, it is supported by a great deal of empirical evidence, some of which I will now review.

Heterosexual deprivation itself leads directly to increased levels of violence, both within the prison and, later, in the community, after the prisoners are released from prison (as ninety percent are). Heterosexual deprivation in itself constitutes a symbolic castration or emasculation of those men who are heterosexual[1]—a shaming of them as men. When coupled with whatever pre-existing homophobia or homosexual panic these men may be vulnerable to, this readily leads to paranoid thoughts and fears, and ultimately, to violent behavior.[2]

But the business of shaming prisoners by symbolically castrating or emasculating them does not end there. Homosexual rape is another even more horrendous and destructive form of punishment endemic to the prisons. For example, in one prison holding close to 700 inmates, one of the prison administrators, who was in a position to know, informed me that out of that total number, probably no more than half a dozen men failed to engage in some form or other of regular sexual encounter with other men. How did he know that? Because in that prison an "observation gallery" overlooks every cell in the three tiers of its maximum-security wing so that the correction officers can observe what goes on within each and every cell.

Since this prison, like almost every other prison in this country, does not permit "conjugal visits," you might assume that such a figure reflects the sexual frustration that must naturally and inevitably accompany a state of enforced heterosexual deprivation. When I first began visiting such institutions, I naively questioned why inmates should not be allowed to participate in sexual relations with each other, as long as they did so voluntarily, since no other sexual relationships were permitted for them. A more experienced colleague answered my question with another: "How could any relationship be 'voluntary' in this kind of environment?" He did not mean that there are no men in prison who voluntarily seek out sexual relationships with other men; a minority of criminals are gay or bisexual, just as a minority of all people are. But all choices and relationships are so constrained and limited in the unfree world of the prison that what is normally meant by such terms as "free" or "voluntary" does not apply. The vast majority of sexual relationships in prison occur in a context of coercion, whether by means of overwhelming physical force and violence, or by means of the credible threat of violence. In other words, most such relationships are, in effect, rape. The fact that many of those relationships are relatively stable "marriages" between dominant and submissive partners merely means that they constitute a form of chronic, ongoing, and repeated rape.

But rape is universally acknowledged to be a crime, and it is seldom if ever openly acknowledged as among the forms of legal punishment legitimately prescribed by governmental authorities. So what would lead me to speak of it as "punishment"—as an intrinsic and universal part of the punishments that our government metes out to those whom it labels as "criminal"? I do this for several reasons. First, the relevant legal authorities, from the judges and prosecutors who send people to prison, to the prison officials who administer them, are all aware of the existence, the reality, and the near-universality of rape in the prisons. Indeed, this is one reason why so many conscientious judges are extremely reluctant to send anyone to prison except when they feel compelled to, either by the violence of the crime or, as is increasingly true, by laws mandating prison sentences even for nonviolent crimes, such as drug offenses. Second, the conditions that stimulate such rapes (the enforced deprivation of other sources of self-esteem, respect, power, and sexual gratification) are consciously and deliberately imposed upon the prison population by the legal authorities. Third, all these authorities tacitly and knowingly tolerate this form of sexual violence, passively delegating to the dominant and most violent inmates the power and authority to deliver this form of punishment to the more submissive and nonviolent ones, so that the rapists in this situation are acting as the vicarious enforcers of a form of punishment that the legal system does not itself enforce formally or directly.

THE CASE OF JEFFREY L.

I first gained some acquaintance with the reality of rape in prison, and of the means through which some inmates are forced into the role of sex slave, when I was asked to see one young man, Jeffrey L., because his behavior had become so bizarre that the prison authorities thought he needed to be evaluated for psychiatric illness. The incident that led to this referral had occurred in the prison Visiting Room, a setting in which inmates sit on one side of a long table and their visitors on the other. Jeffrey L.'s mother had just concluded a visit with him, when instead of merely saying good-bye he leaped over the table in an attempt to follow her out of the Visiting Room and out of the prison, crying hysterically, clinging to her, begging her to take him home with her. Since he would not tell either his mother or the correction officers why he had behaved this way, they asked me to see him.

When I interviewed Jeffrey, I noted that he was a slightly built nineteen-year old white man (or boy) who appeared even younger than his stated age, who was visibly trembling and appeared nearly frightened to death. What he described to me was a pattern of repeated gang rapes to which he had been subjected since first arriving in prison. He was sent to prison for a relatively minor, nonviolent offense. After he was convicted in court, he had first been sent to the medium-security prison to which all of the younger prisoners convicted of nonviolent crimes are initially sent for a brief "diagnostic" evaluation, on the basis of which they are assigned or "classified" to whatever long-term prison setting the authorities deem suitable for that particular individual; soon after arriving there, he was raped by a gang of other inmates. Because he felt overwhelmingly ashamed of what had happened to him, and also because he knew enough about the mores of the prison subculture to know that seeking help from the correctional authorities would be seen as informing or "ratting" on his fellow prisoners, and that the penalty for that in the world of the prison is capital punishment (imposed by the inmates themselves, of course, not by the guards), he refused to reveal to anyone what had happened. As ordinarily happens with nonviolent first offenders, he was soon transferred to a minimum-security prison, where he was again gang-raped. In terror of a repetition of that experience, and in order to provoke the prison officials to transfer him elsewhere, he refused a direct order to return to the cell block to which he had been assigned (and in which he had been raped), and thus was transferred to a third (medium-security) prison, where he was promptly subjected to a gang rape for the third time. It was following that experience that he behaved as I described above in the Visiting Room.

After I referred Jeffrey for surgical repair of the anal tears that the rapes had caused, I informed the Commissioner of Correction of what had happened. He was appropriately, and quite sincerely, horrified, and immediately took steps to make sure that this young man was better protected in the future. It was clear, of course, that the administrators had not engaged in any kind of conspiracy to permit inmates to be subjected to this kind of "punishment." But we need to understand the full meaning of Jeffrey L.'s experience in the larger context. First, it is an integral part of the functioning of the prison system, and hence of the punishment to which prison inmates are regularly subjected; it is no anomalous chance event. Consider these additional facts. Jeffrey L. had only been treated this harshly by the other in-

mates because he refused to submit passively and peacefully. He resisted becoming a sex object. So, many if not most of the inmates who
do submit peacefully to being the passive sex objects of stronger, more
dominant and violent prisoners are not doing so "voluntarily," but simply in order to avoid being subjected to physically injurious violence of
the sort that Jeffrey had suffered.

A second consideration is the degree to which the sexual abuse and
exploitation, or rape (though it is not always recognized and identified
as rape) of inmates is "permitted," by the line-officers on each cellblock. The practice of tolerating and permitting such relationships is
one means by which the officers maintain control of the prison population as a whole. The strategy here can be analyzed into two components: "You scratch my back and I'll scratch yours," and "Divide and
conquer." With respect to the first, the officers are entering into an
implicit, tacit agreement with the rapists, in which the officers will
permit the rapists whatever gratifications they get from raping the
weaker prisoners, and the rapists agree in turn to cooperate with these
officers by submitting to the prison system as a whole (that is, by
renouncing the option of assaulting officers individually, or of collabo-
rating with each other collectively to organize a riot). With respect to
the second, that system of mutually agreed upon trade-offs simultaneously prevents the inmates as a whole from uniting with each other, for
it divides the inmates into two groups—the rapists and the raped—thus
minimizing the chance of their being able to organize an effective pro-
test, rebellion, or riot. It becomes a strategy that officers may use to
"divide and conquer" the inmates.

Conditions in most prisons are such that the officers as a group have
an objective interest in pursuing these two strategies (though the degree to which they acutally do pursue them may vary, from one officer
or prison to another). First of all, there are never as many officers as
there are prisoners, and the officers are perpetually in danger of being
overwhelmed by superior numbers, if the inmates unite. And, then the
prison officers "buy" themselves an hour or two of peace each day—

there is in effect a rest period each afternoon (rest for the officers, that is)—when the inmates are allowed to go into their cells; the whole prison quiets down. The officers know perfectly well what is happening, that roughly half the inmate population submits to being raped.

To what extent are prison officers consciously aware that this is happening, and to what extent do some of them deliberately tolerate these patterns of behavior? All prison officers must be aware of the patterns of prison rape because prisons are small, enclosed communities, and officers form a tightly cohesive clique (of necessity and for their own protection, since those who are not part of that clique do not long survive) so that anything that one officer knows, all know. On the other hand, they are not all equally supportive of the maintenance of this social system; indeed, many are appalled by it. Unfortunately, however, those who disapprove of it cannot stop it, since it is just as dangerous ("suicidal" is perhaps not too strong a word) for an officer to violate the unwritten code of the officers' subculture as it is for an inmate to violate the corresponding (and virtually identical) code of the inmates' subculture—the first principle of which for both is, "Thou shalt not snitch."

I am far from alone in reaching these conclusions. In 1937, Haywood Patterson, chief defendant in the famous Scottsboro rape case, wrote about these behaviors as he observed them at Alabama's Atmore State Prison. In his autobiography, *Scottsboro Boy*,[3] he said that homosexual rape was not only tolerated but actually encouraged by prison authorities, primarily because "it helped them control the men. Especially the tough ones they called devils. They believed that if a devil had a galboy [a sex slave] he would be quiet. He would be a good worker and he wouldn't kill guards and prisoners and try to escape. He would be like a settled married man." He stated that the most valued galboy was a young teenager. "A fifteen-year-old stood no chance at Atmore," he wrote. "I've seen young boys stand up and fight for hours for their rights. Some wouldn't give up"—though eventually they would be overpowered, or lose consciousness. He reported that both prisoners and security guards would watch the assaults with impassive interest. "They knew a young woman was being born. Some just looked forward to using her a little later themselves." Once they were symbolically—socially and psychologically—emasculated in this way, the newly created "galboys" were combination prostitutes and slaves, who could and would be bought and sold by their various pimps, masters, or owners. With reference to the extent of this form of sexual enslavement, Patterson remarked that "I once heard Deputy Warden Lige Lambert tell some state patrolmen that fifty percent of the Negro prisoners in Atmore were galboys—and seventy percent of the white."

Wilbert Rideau, who is himself an inmate at the Angola State Penitentiary in Louisiana, reports that officers there were equally aware of what was going on. These staff members "used to perform prison marriages in which the convict and his galboy-wife would leap over the broomstick together in a mock ceremony."[4]

In his report on sexual violence among the youngsters in Connecticut's juvenile institutions, Anthony Scacco[5] charged that the "administration knows who the victims and aggressors are, and in many instances, the guards are directly responsible for fostering sexual aggression within the institution." Davis's[6] study of the Philadelphia jail system revealed that many security guards discouraged complaints of sexual assault, indicating that they didn't want to be bothered; and, Dinitz, Miller, and Bartollas,[7] in another study of prison rape, charged that "some guards will barter their weaker and younger charges to favored inmates in return for inmate cooperation in keeping the prison under control."

Of course, the active and passive collusion of prison officers and other officials in the vicarious utilization of rape and rapists as a collateral, unofficial supplement to the publicly acknowledged repertoire of punishments that the prison system metes out to inmates does not have to be as overt as these examples suggest, or as overt as the Nazis' delegation of authority to the kapos in the concentration camps, in order to be just as effective in accomplishing the same result. As C. Paul Phelps, the Louisiana Secretary of Correction (and former warden of Angola), shrewdly observed, "Anytime . . . a high level of homosexual rapes and enslavement is taking place, there has to be a tacit trade-off between the inmate power structure and the administration."[8] Most of the trade-off, he says, generally takes place on the lower level of the administration:

When it gets down to the lower level, it's usually an agreement between the inmates and security officers, and the agreement doesn't have to be verbal. Much of the communication between inmates and between staff and inmates is on the nonverbal level. They have their own peculiar method of communicating what they want to say without really saying it, and each understands exactly what the other is saying. It's probably the most sophisticated nonverbal system of communication ever invented in the world."[9]

Thus, prison officers may "play dumb" when one inmate requests to be put in a cell with another whom he can sexually dominate and exploit; they would purchase peace in the cellblock rather than protect the more submissive inmate from rape. But this purchases a relative degree of peace only for the officers, not for the inmates. There is almost universal agreement that one of the major causes of the violence of inmates toward each other—some would say the major cause—is sexual relationships among inmates.[10] Men will fight—often to the death—both in order to commit rape and to avoid being raped; in order to win one "galboy" from another inmate; because of sexual jealousy; in order to prove that they are "real" men and not homosexuals (as those terms are defined in that macho, homophobic subculture); and because the whole system is so degrading, shameful, and humiliating, so damaging to their self-esteem and so destructive of their sense of masculine sexual adequacy and identity; and finally, because some literally go insane, developing paranoid delusions and hallucinations in response to the continual onslaught to their sense of who they are (i.e., whether they are men), and what, if anything, they are worth. That these patterns of violence follow them onto the street, when they are eventually released from prison, goes without saying.

Nevertheless, prison officers have a vested interest in maintaining the system of prison rape because it deflects the violence of the inmates away from the officers and onto each other. As Wilbert Rideau observed at Angola:

> The . . . natural inclination of the institutional security force is to be tolerant of any type of situation that divides the prisoners into predators and prey, with one group of prisoners oppressing another because such a situation prevents the development of any unity among prisoners that could tear down the institution. A "homosexual" jungle-like state of affairs is perfect for that purpose. It's another, perhaps the most effective, means of control."[11]

Of course, it is also true that rape is not the only means by which this goal can be accomplished; it can also be accomplished by dividing the prisoners along racial lines. Dr. Frank L. Rundle, who has served as the chief psychiatrist of the 2,200-man California Training Facility at Soledad, and also as director of psychiatry of the Prison Health Services for all of the correctional institutions, both adult and juvenile, of New York City, observed that the readiness of prison officials to utilize any means to divide inmates from each other went so far as to lead the California prison system to encourage the division of inmates into gangs whose members were selected by race. "The whole system is set up in such a way as to, if not overtly, at least covertly encourage racial war."[12]

Now, however, I want to return to the symbolism of punishment, as revealed by the phenomenon of rape in prison. The term "rape" is customarily applied to the sexual coercion of a female. The Federal Bureau of Investigation defines the crime of rape as: "the carnal knowledge of a female forcibly and against her will"[13]—a formulation that, in effect, defines the phenomenon of male rape out of existence. Those attitudes toward men and women, from which the definition of rape derives, may teach us something about the symbolism of rape. For this definition implies that to be raped is to be treated as a female. Thus, it is no wonder that rape victims in prison are called "galboys," "whores," and "wives," and that men who have been raped almost universally report that they feel emasculated, castrated, and deprived of their masculinity.

The phenomenon of male rape may be far more common than is revealed by any of the conventional statistics on rape. For reasons I have already indicated, rapes in prison are almost never reported, either to the prison authorities or to the district attorneys in the outside world, and are prosecuted only in the rarest and most extreme cases. For example, in an exhaustive investigation of "Sexual Assault in the Philadelphia Prison System and Sheriff's Vans" by the police department and the district attorney's office, in which more than 3,000 prisoners and 500 staff members were interviewed, the Chief Assistant District Attorney, Allan Davis, after hearing repeated accounts of "brutal gang rapes and victimization of young, inexperienced inmates," concluded that sexual violence was "epidemic." Still, he found that only about three percent of the estimated 1,000 sexual assaults, per year, that he uncovered in the Philadelphia jails alone, were ever reported to his office.[14]

And yet, as I have indicated, the rape of males is one of the most widespread—indeed, virtually universal—features of the penal system as I have observed it, and as many others have confirmed. The findings are legion. I will cite some examples: when the Texas Department of Correction became the subject of an investigation, hearings, and a trial, the federal judge in the case, William W. Justice, determined as a "finding of fact" that the brutalization of inmates by other inmates, including forced coercive sexual assault (rape, by any other name), was a "routine" feature of that penal system.[15]

Another court-ordered investigation of conditions of one Florida prison in 1980 found that

> assaults, rapes, robberies, shootings, and stabbings were commonplace even in high-confinement, lock-down areas. So prevalent was the issue of sexual assault that one correction officer quoted in a report to a state legislator said that a young inmate's chances of avoiding rape were "almost zero. . . . He'll get raped within the first twenty-four to forty-eight hours. That's almost standard."[16]

Similarly, in a Pulitzer Prize–winning investigation, Loretta Tofani[17] noted that despite an official figure of less than ten rapes per year among male inmates, on-the-record interviews with ten guards, sixty inmates, and one jail medical worker indicated that there were "approximately a dozen incidents a week" (or more than 600 per year) in the Prince George County Detention Center alone.

In 1968, mass rapes were admitted to be "routine occurrences at Cook County Jail," in Chicago, by officials of the jail themselves. Dr. Anthony M. Scacco, Jr., a criminologist formerly with the Connecticut Department of Correction, reported that rape and other sexual violence was rampant in juvenile and young-adult institutions in that state. Dr. Frank L. Rundle, of the California Training Facility at Soledad, concluded that rape and other sexual violence is universal in the nation's prisons: "I think that that same picture is true of any prison. It's not just Angola or San Quentin or Soledad. It is a feature of prison life everywhere." The director of security at the Angola State Penitentiary, in Louisiana, estimated that "about seven out of ten inmates here [are] now participating or have participated in homosexual activities at one time or another during their confinement." And, as already stated, most of that behavior cannot be considered "voluntary" in any meaningful or legitimate sense, given the atmosphere of threat, danger, and coercion in which it occurs. As C. Paul Phelps, the Louisiana Secretary of Correction, observed, "While the initial rape-emasculation might have been effected by physical force, the ensuing sexual acts are generally done with the galboy's 'consent' and 'cooperation.' "[18]

There are close to two million men in the various penal facilities of this country on any given day, roughly half of whom have already been tried, convicted, and sentenced, while the other half are awaiting trial. And since the turnover of those awaiting trial and those sentenced to short-term incarceration is especially high, the total number of men in custody for at least part of the year, in any one year, comes to more than ten million, with a near equal number released back into our communities.[19]

If any substantial portion of these men are forced to submit to rape, then the number of men who are raped on any given day in America's jails and prisons is astronomical. One investigator estimated some ten years ago, when the total population of the incarcerated was less than half of today's level, that the number was as high as "eighteen adult males raped every minute" of every day.[20] A moment's calculation reveals that that may not be a farfetched figure, particularly with today's even higher rates of incarceration: 18 per minute means roughly 1,000 per hour, 24,000 per day, 168,000 per week, or just under 9,000,000 rapes per year. Even assuming for a moment that the true percentage of those who are raped is below 50 percent; even if some more conservative figure, such as 25 percent, or even 10 percent, is more accurate, the fact remains that most of those who are raped are raped not just once every six weeks, but rather, several times a week (both by their "old man," the rapist to whom they are forced to submit as if they were his "wife," and by those other inmates to whom their "old man" forces them to submit, in exchange for the money or other rewards from those to whom he makes his "whore" available). There is the additional fact that many of those who are raped at the beginning of their sentences, or while they are in short-term incarceration, are gang-raped, so that each incident of rape may incorporate ten or twelve or fourteen individual acts of rape,[21] which would suggest that the figure of 9,000,000 male rapes a year may be, if not conservative, at least not wildly exaggerated. But let us suppose, for the sake of being as conservative as possible, that even that estimate is exaggerated by a factor of ten. That would still leave a total figure of 900,000 (or nearly one million) male rapes a year—as an integral part of the punishment to which prisoners are subjected in the prisons and jails of this country each year.

Is even a figure of ten percent too high? Donald Cotton and Nicholas Groth[22] observed that any "available statistics must be regarded as very conservative at best, since discovery and documentation of this behavior are compromised by the nature of prison conditions, inmate codes and subculture, and staff attitudes." Given that important caveat, with its implication that every estimate is likely to be a significant underestimate, we might note that Daniel Lockwood[23] concluded that 28 percent of the prisoners in one New York state prison had been targets of sexual aggression at least once, and that 20 percent had been targeted more than once. Peter L. Nacci and Thomas Kane[24] estimated that nine percent of state prison inmates nationwide had been "targets" of sexual assault, and Clemens Bartollos and Christopher Sieveides[25] came up with that same percentage among the children who were inmates of juvenile correctional facilities in the southeastern United States. Even Wilbert Rideau has pointed out that "most of the sexual violence occurring not only in Louisiana but across the nation takes place in the . . . county jails, which act as a sieve filtering the strong from the weak and producing the sexual slaves long before they reach the penitentiaries."[26] Thus, the number of incidents of acts of coercive sex, or forcible rape, may be only a fraction of the actual number of sex acts that are participated in because of a realistic awareness that the only alternative is to be seriously injured, mutilated, gang-raped, or killed. One can only comment that rape by any other name is still as coerced and degrading.

Beyond the question of the frequency or quantity of male rape in prisons, the full extent of which is impossible to measure accurately for all the reasons mentioned, we need to consider its nature—the degree of violence and injury it inflicts, and the symbolic message that it communicates. The mere knowledge that one could become a victim of such atrocities can be enough to have a powerful and destructive impact on the entire population living in an environment in which such acts occur, and in which all are potentially vulnerable. And, lest the reader wonder if my examples of sexual exploitation in prison are drawn only from an atypical prison system, let me quote from another observer's account, that of Dr. Anthony Scacco, Jr.:

Many cases could be cited of actual rape of an individual in jail, but one in particular is chosen to let the reader hear the events from an ordinary citizen. He is married with a family, no previous criminal record, and a former Georgia legislator and businessman who found himself the victim of a jail situation. William Laite was indicted and convicted in Texas of perjury relating to a contract he had with the Federal Administration Housing Authority. He was sentenced to the Terrant County Jail in Fort Worth, Texas. The moment he entered the tank, or day room, he was approached by five men. The first comment from one of them was, "I wonder if he has any guts. We'll find out tonight, won't we? Reckon what her name is; she looks ready for about six or eight inches. You figure she will make us fight for it, or is she going to give up to us nice and sweet like a good little girl? Naw, we'll have to work her over first, but hell, that's half the fun, isn't it?" "I couldn't move," said Laite. "I was terrified. This couldn't be real. This couldn't be happening to me." Laite was saved from sexual assault when a seventeen-year-old youth was admitted to the day room as he was about to become the victim of the five men in the tank. The men saw the boy and turned on him, knocked him out, and then, "they were on him at once like jackals, ripping the coveralls off his limp body. Then as I watched in frozen fascination and horror, they sexually assaulted him, savagely and brutally like starving animals after a raw piece of meat. Then I knew what they meant about giving me six or eight inches."

Laite was shocked by the unconcern shown by the guards. He stated that the "guards were protected from the violent prisoners, but I, an inmate myself, was not. The guards never made an attempt to discipline the prisoners. In fact, I suspected that they might pass the time of day watching the fights and sexual activities from some secluded location."[27]

James Dunn,[28] an inmate at Angola, in Louisiana, has described how he first became a sex slave there. At the age of nineteen, he received a three-year sentence for burglary (a nonviolent crime, it should be emphasized, since it involved only the stealing of property, not physical injury to human bodies).

> During my first week here, I saw fourteen guys rape one youngster 'cause he refused to submit. They snatched him up, took him into the TV room, and, man, they did everything to him—I mean, everything, and they wouldn't even use no grease. When they finished with him, he had to be taken to the hospital where they had to sew him back up; then they had to take him to the nuthouse at Jackson 'cause he cracked up.

Three weeks later, Dunn himself

> received a call to go to the library, where an inmate shoved me into a dark room where his partner was waiting. They beat me up and raped me. That was to claim me. . . . When they finished, they told me that I was for them, then went out and told everyone else that they had claimed me.

Dunn recalls his reaction as being "one of fear, of wanting to survive. Once it happened, that was it—unless you killed one of them, and I was short [i.e., had a short sentence] and wanted to go home. So I decided I'd try to make the best of it." Because of his memory of the scene of gang rape that he had witnessed, he did not fight back against his own double rape: "Man, I didn't want none of that kind of action, and my only protection was in sticking with my old man, the guy who raped me." As a result, Dunn had to act as his rapist's "wife" or "slave" doing "whatever the hell he wanted me to do"—wash his old man's clothing, make the beds, prepare meals, and generally do all of the menial things that needed doing.

Wilbert Rideau has commented that "few female rape victims in society must repay their rapist for the violence he inflicted upon them by devoting their existence to servicing his every need for years after—but rape victims in the world of prison must."[29] While that may be true for some female victims of rape, one can readily think of at least two situations in which that is not the case—and here I am thinking of battered wives trapped in a vicious cycle of domestic assault, and of girls who are the victims of incest, both of which are instances of sexually assaulted females who may have to live with their rapists or assaulters, and serve their needs for an ongoing, indefinitely prolonged duration. Those who have worked with victims of incest and with women who have had battering spouses and boyfriends have commented that one of the most stressful aspects of these women's trauma is that they were forced to live with their assaulter and to be at his mercy on a daily basis. That work is highly instructive to those of us who are working with men and boys in penal facilities who are forced to live with their assaulters and to be at their mercy; this is the sort of traumatization which is an intrinsic part of the legal "punishment" meted out by our criminal "justice" system.

What motivates a man to commit rape in the prisons? What does a man hope to accomplish by it? Obviously, rape is intended to be a humiliating, shameful, dishonoring, traumatizing, and violent act. In the prisons, it is quite clear that the act of inflicting humiliation on the rape victim has to do with the transferring of the rapist's fears of personal and sexual inadequacy and impotence onto that of the rape victim, the one who is to be emasculated, reduced, undone, and "turned out"—recast into a "woman." Here again, the work of Wilbert Rideau is highly instructive. Rideau has written probably the closest thing we have to a definitive study of rape in prison. He says that

> The act of rape in the ultramasculine world of prison constitutes the ultimate humiliation visited upon a male, the forcing of him to assume the role of a woman. It is not sexual and not really regarded as "rape" in the same sense that society regards the term. In fact, it isn't even referred to as "rape." In the Louisiana penal system, both prisoners and personnel generally refer to the act as "turning out," a nonsexual description that reveals the nonsexual ritualistic nature of what is really an act of conquest and emasculation, stripping the male victim of his status as a "man." The act redefines him as a "female" in this perverse subculture, and he must assume that role as the "property" of his conqueror . . . [who] arranged his emasculation. He becomes a slave in the fullest sense of the term.[30]

One could spend a great deal of time working with this passage of Rideau's, especially if we bear in mind that the prisons are not only a laboratory for the study of violence, but a subterranean index of much of what is both expressed in our wider culture, and, at the same time, buried deep within the collective unconscious of patriarchal culture. Any reader of Rideau cannot fail to see both the deep misogyny and the misanthropy, which is the subtext of prison life, a text which invariably, inevitably accompanies the rampant fear on the part of these men (perhaps most men?) of being shamed by being seen as less than a "man." If for these men, to be "turned out," or turned "into" a "woman" is the ultimate denigration, consummated through an act of rape, then this may tell us something about the patriarchal legacy and making of "manhood" which is at the heart of "civilization" as we have known it, with all its violence between men; its class structure and racial prejudice; and its asymmetrical treatment of women and men.

Another account, this one by Colonel Walter Pence, chief of security at a State Penitentiary at Angola, picks up on the point I am making:

Rape in prison is rarely a sexual act, but one of violence, politics, and an acting out of power roles. Most of your homosexual rape is a macho thing. It's basically one guy saying to another: "I'm a better man than you and I'm gonna turn you out to prove it." I've investigated about a hundred cases personally, and I've not seen one that's just an act of passion. It's definitely a macho/power thing among the inmates. And it's the basically insecure prisoners who do it.[31]

But "insecure" in what way, about what? Wilbert Rideau answers:

Man's greatest pain, whether in life or in prison, is the sense of personal insignificance, of being helpless and of no real value as a person, an individual—a man. Imprisoned and left without any voice in or control over the things that affect him, his personal desires and feelings regarded with gracious indifference, and treated at best like a child and at worst like an animal by those having control of his life, a prisoner leads a life of acute deprivation and insignificance. The psychological pain involved in such an existence creates an urgent and terrible need for reinforcement of his sense of manhood and personal worth. Unfortunately, prison deprives those locked within of the normal avenues of pursuing gratification of their needs and leaves them no instruments but sex, violence, and conquest to validate their sense of manhood and individual worth.[32]

Or as C. Paul Phelps put it when he was secretary of the Louisiana Department of Corrections, "Sex and power go hand in hand in prison. Deprived of the normal avenues, there are very few ways in prison for a man to show how powerful he is—and the best way to do so is for one to have a slave, another who is in total submission to him."[33]

To understand the psychology and symbolism of punishment, and how it mirrors that of "crime," we need to ask: "What emotional gratification are people seeking when they advocate punishing other people harshly, as opposed to quarantining them in order to restrain them?" I am suggesting that the motives behind crime and punishment are identical: that the greatest fear in each instance is that of being shamed or laughed at; that the subsequent wish or need to dominate and humiliate others is in the service of gaining a swelled sense of pride and power by having dominion over others, including the power to inflict pain on them, punish them, and "give them what they deserve."

This is why the psychology and symbolism of punishment is a mirror of the psychology and symbolism of crime. How could it be otherwise, given that punishment has always been consciously intended to mirror crime ("an eye for an eye," etc.)? Namely, a defense against the fear of being shamed or laughed at, and the positive attainment of feelings of pride, even honor. For example, I vividly recall the comments of a prosecutor who expressed his outrage and chagrin at the fact that one defendant he had prosecuted had been found "not guilty by reason of insanity." The defendant had broken into a priest's house, tied him up, brutally tortured and mutilated him, and blinded him. The prosecutor was in no way appeased or relieved that the defendant was likely to spend the rest of his life in a prison mental hospital. Instead, what mattered to him was that this defendant might be "laughing up his sleeve" at all the legal authorities whom he had "fooled" (and thus "made a fool of") by "deceiving" the court into thinking that he was mad rather than bad.

Not long ago, an "op-ed" piece in the *New York Times*[34] revealed similar feelings—the use of punishment by prison as a defense against the fear of being laughed at and treated with contempt (that is to say, shamed). In this article, the author, Andrew Vachss, who also happened to be an attorney, asserted that "predatory sexual psychopaths" are "monsters" who "lack empathy for other people" and are "narcissistic; *they laugh behind their masks at our attempts* to understand and rehabilitate them. *We have earned their contempt* by our belief that they can change. . . ."—all of which was part of his argument as to why we should not waste time trying to understand them, or to facilitate their (nonexistent) capacity to change, but should instead lock them up and throw away the key.

I would agree with many of Vachss' points. These men are indeed "narcissistic," but I would stress that that is precisely why they feel the need to commit the very crimes that so appall us—they themselves are afraid of being laughed at and being treated with contempt. Those fears are precisely what motivate sadism—both the sexual psychopaths' sadism toward their victims, and the sadism of many of us toward sexual psychopaths, for whom "no punishment can possibly be too severe."

Two further comments: The ambiguity and imprecision of the word "narcissistic" often leads to confusion and misunderstanding, just as it did in this article, in which the author was unable to see that the criminal's tendency to "laugh" at other people and hold them in contempt was not based on feelings of superiority but rather on its opposite, on feelings of inferiority, of fearing that others would find him ridiculous and contemptible. Attitudes such as arrogance, superiority, and self-importance, to which the term "narcissism" is often attached, and which are so often misunderstood to be the genuine attitudes of the people who hold them, are actually defenses against, or attempts to ward off or undo, the opposite set of feelings: namely, underlying feelings of personal insignificance and worthlessness.

I would agree with the author that sadistic sexual psychopaths are "lacking in empathy" for other people, but I would also want to observe that that is no reason for us to lack empathy for them. A lack of empathy sets anyone on the path to violence. Finally, I would agree with the author of this article that some men (a few, but they do exist) are so badly damaged that it is unclear whether they can ever change, and are so dangerous to others that I too see no alternative but to "quarantine" them for the foreseeable future. But what is the emotion—the motive—that leads us to see other people as "monsters" rather than as damaged human beings, and to see the attempt to understand them rather than punish them as a waste of time? Interestingly, the motive behind such punitive attitudes turns out to be identical to the motive behind the very crimes that many of us are eager to punish—namely, the fear that one will be laughed at, held in contempt, or made a fool of (i.e., shamed), unless one is sufficiently sadistic. For the most direct way to prevent someone from laughing at you is to make them cry instead, and the most direct way to make them cry is to inflict pain upon them—and "pain," as I said, is what "punishment" means (for both derive from *poena*, the Latin word for pain).

What are the broader implications of this analysis of the symbolism of the violence that is inflicted in the name of justice, rationality, and the law? Punishment is a *form* of violence in its own right—albeit a legally sanctioned form—but it is also a *cause* of violence, as it stimulates the very same illegal violence that it is ostensibly intended to inhibit or prevent.

The importance of that fact would be hard to exaggerate. Punishment is almost universally rationalized as a means of preventing violence; elections to political office in America are increasingly becoming contests as to which of the candidates is "tougher" on crime. But the conclusion that my analysis leads to is that punishment does not inhibit or prevent crime and violence, it does not lower the rate or frequency of acts of violence. Punishment stimulates violence; punishment causes it. The more punitive our society has become, the higher our rate of violence (both criminal and noncriminal) has become. But if punishment increases the rate of crime and violence, rather than decreasing it, then why do people who say they want to "fight" crime, advocate increasing the amount of punishment that we impose on criminals? The

causes of violence are the same, whether the violence is legal punishment or illegal crime, and the symbolism of both forms of violence is
identical. Throughout history, the legal system has been as intent on
cutting out or otherwise destroying, damaging, despoiling, or dishonoring people's eyes, tongues, genitals, and other body parts—as have
criminals. The purpose of both forms of violence—crime and punishment—is the same: to restore justice to the world by replacing shame
with pride. And the means by which that is accomplished is the same.
The very same acts of violence and mutilation (by which one prevents
one's victim from shaming oneself further) serve to shame one's victim,
which accomplishes the purpose of transferring one's own shame onto
one's victim; for it is shameful to suffer violence (regardless of whether
it is called crime or punishment), just as it is a source of pride and
honor to be the one who dispenses violence to others.

Finally, I want to ask: What is it about our social class system that
holds in place a self-defeating policy of increasingly violent punishment, when we have clearly demonstrated that such policies stimulate
violence? A society's prisons serve as a key for understanding the larger
society as a whole. One can use the prison system as a magnifying glass
through which one might see what is otherwise less easily discernible in
the culture—underlying patterns of motivation, symbolization, and social structure that determine the life of the community as a whole.
From this perspective, it is worth noting that the rulers of any society,
just like the prison guards, have an interest in pursuing the strategies I
described earlier: "You scratch my back and I'll scratch yours" and "Divide and conquer." This is accomplished in the macrocosm of society
just as it is in the microcosm of the prison, by lulling the middle class
into accepting its subordination to, and exploitation by, the upper class,
by giving the middle class a class subordinate to itself (the lower class)
which it can exploit, and to whom it can feel superior, thus distracting
the middle class from the resentment it might otherwise feel and express toward the upper class. The subordinate classes (middle and
lower) are divided into predator and prey, respectively, and are more

likely to fight against each other than against the ruling class, which makes them easier for the ruling class to control. (E.g., middle class voters are angrier at "welfare queens" than they are at members of the Forbes 400—whom they rather tend to admire, and would like to emulate.)

But how are the members of the lower class set against each other, rather than against the two classes above them who reserve most of the wealth and privileges of society for themselves? In the same way the prison system is ruled, namely, by dividing the citizenry into predators and prey—by dividing the lower class into criminals and victims. It is not in the vested interests of the ruling class to pursue those social policies that would cut down on crime; on the contrary, it is in their interest to keep the crime rate as high as possible. The ruling class (all of whom are white, in America) is responsible, in large part, for the way in which we, as a community, have chosen to distribute our collective wealth (since they, or those who represent their interests, write the laws that constitute those choices), which is in turn responsible for the social inequities that lead to crime and violence. At the same time, it is the ruling class that wages the so-called "war on crime," which is really a war on the poor (as I will discuss in more depth in Chapter 8). Both the perpetrators and the victims of criminal violence are disproportionately the very poor. The kinds of assaults that the very poor suffer from the "criminals" among them (rape, murder, and assault and robbery) are so direct, palpable, and visible, so physically painful, so impossible to ignore, so life-threatening and lethal, that they inevitably distract the very poor from noticing or fighting the more hidden, disguised assaults they suffer from the class system itself. As Representative Charles Schumer recently pointed out, it is in the political interest of the party that represents the interests of the very rich to foster as high a rate of crime as possible; and even to exaggerate what the crime rate is, to foment fear and panic about violent crime far beyond what is realistically appropriate, and so on. For the more that people are worried about crime and violence, the more the middle class will focus its anger and fear on the poor and members of certain minority groups (for most of the violence that is labeled as "crime" is committed by people from those groups); the nonviolent and noncriminal poor will be angry at those other poor people who are violent criminals; and both those classes will be too distracted by their anger at the lower-class criminals to notice that they have much better reasons to be angry at the very rich, and the party that represents the interests of the rich, than at all the violent criminals put together. Ironically, when crime is at its maximum, the party of the rich can even represent itself as the savior of everybody, by promising to "get tough on crime" and by declaring its "war on crime" (which, as I said, is really a war on the poor—that social class which is seen, in this mystification, as being the ultimate source of most crime and violence), thus distracting attention from the fact that the ultimate source of most crime and violence is actually the upper class—or rather, the class system.

Thus, it is not surprising at all—indeed, it is only to be expected—that those who identify with the interests of the ruling class would be likely to pursue those policies that lead to an increase in the rate of what is legally defined as crime and violence. Such policies include the following:

1) Punishing more and more people (criminals) more and more harshly, by means of more and harsher prisons, capital punishment, and so on. Nothing stimulates crime as powerfully and as effectively as punishment does (since punishment stimulates shame and diminishes guilt, and shame stimulates violence, especially when it is not inhibited by guilt).

2) Outlawing those drugs that inhibit violence (such as marijuana and heroin), while legalizing and advertising those that stimulate violence and cause physical injury and death (such as alcohol and tobacco); and criminalizing those drugs that have no demonstrable direct (pharmacological) effect on violent behavior (such as cocaine), thus spending

billions of taxpayers' dollars to stimulate crime and violence by providing an enormous publicly funded subsidy for those organized crime groups who profit from the fact that the smaller the supply of these drugs, the higher their price; and then misinforming the public about the relationship between drugs, crime, and violence, as though crime and violence were caused by illicit drugs (which they are not) rather than by enormously profitable legal drugs such as alcohol (the one drug which has been shown to stimulate violence), all of which distracts the public from noticing that the real cause of violence is not drugs: The real cause of violence is the "war on drugs" (and the social and economic inequities which the "war on drugs" is designed to distract attention from).

3) Manipulating the tax laws and other economic policies so as to increase the disparity in income and wealth between the rich and the poor, for that also stimulates crime and violence, by maximizing the degree to which the poor are subjected to experiences and feelings of being shamed, humiliated, and made to feel inferior.

4) Depriving the poor of access to education (especially if they are in prison), for nothing decreases the rate of crime and violence as powerfully and effectively as does education. We know that the single most effective factor which reduces the rate of recidivism in the prison population is education, and yet education in the prisons is the first item to be cut when an administration "gets tough on crime." Educational achievement provides prisoners in need of rehabilitation with a nonviolent source of self-esteem or pride; it protects them against the vulnerability to shame, and the injuries of structural violence (poverty) that motivate criminal violence.

5) Perpetuating the caste divisions of society that usually fall along racial lines. The poor and members of minority racial and ethnic groups are regularly subjected to maximal degrees of shame, humiliation, and feelings of inferiority by being told that they are innately and inherently

stupid and intellectually inferior; that is then turned into a self-fulfilling prophecy by depriving them of the education they would need in order to develop their actual intellectual potential.

6) Exposing the public to entertainment that glorifies violence and holds it out as a source of pride, honor, and masculine self-esteem.

7) Making lethal weapons easily available to the general public.

8) Maximizing the polarization and asymmetry of the social roles of men and women. Nothing stimulates crime and violence more than the division of males and females into the roles of violence object and sex object, respectively.

9) Encouraging the prejudice against homosexuality, by striving to keep homosexuals out of the military, and from positions of leadership within religious institutions. Nothing stimulates violence more powerfully and effectively than homophobia, just as nothing would prevent it more effectively than a more relaxed, tolerant, and respectful attitude toward homosexuality (but what would the raison d'être of the military be without violence?).

10) Perpetuating and legitimizing the exposure of children and youth to violence such as corporal discipline in school and at home, injuries that would be considered assault and battery if inflicted on those who are more mature, and yet are regularly declared legitimate by our highest courts.

11) Regulating the economy so as to ensure that unemployment will never be abolished or even fall below a high enough minimum.

If these are the policies of the white ruling class—then what will we have achieved? We will have attained what we see all around us in America today—a society characterized by three complementary and mutually reinforcing characteristics: 1) the richest and most powerful, secure, and invulnerable upper class in the world; 2) a middle class in collusion with the upper class, yet itself exploited by the latter; and 3) an underclass that commits a higher degree of violence than exists in any other developed nation on earth, with violence committed primarily by the poor against the poor.

Isn't it remarkable how much the social structure of our society as a whole resembles the social structure of the prison, as this analysis of rape in prison reveals it?

These are among the things that the study of the prison system may have to teach us about society as a whole. By applying the patterns of manipulation and control that are easily visible in prisons to the corresponding but more skillfully disguised patterns that exist in the community at large, we can see things about our society that might not otherwise be as obvious.

CHAPTER 8

The Deadliest Form

of Violence

Is Poverty

YOU CANNOT WORK FOR ONE DAY WITH THE VIOLENT PEOPLE WHO FILL OUR prisons and mental hospitals for the criminally insane without being forcibly and constantly reminded of the extreme poverty and discrimination that characterize their lives. Hearing about their lives, and about their families and friends, you are forced to recognize the truth in Gandhi's observation that the deadliest form of violence is poverty. Not a day goes by without realizing that trying to understand them and their violent behavior in purely individual terms is impossible and wrongheaded.

Any theory of violence, especially a psychological theory, that evolves from the experience of men in maximum security prisons and hospitals for the criminally insane must begin with the recognition that these institutions are only microcosms. They are not where the major violence in our society takes place, and the perpetrators who fill them are far from being the main causes of most violent deaths. Any approach to a theory of violence needs to begin with a look at the structural violence in this country. Focusing merely on those relatively few men who commit what we define as murder could distract us from examining and learning from those structural causes of violent death that are far more significant from a numerical or public health, or human, standpoint.

By "structural violence" I mean the increased rates of death and disability suffered by those who occupy the bottom rungs of society, as contrasted with the relatively lower death rates experienced by those who are above them. Those excess deaths (or at least a demonstrably large proportion of them) are a function of class structure; and that structure is itself a product of society's collective human choices, concerning how to distribute the collective wealth of the society. These are not acts of God. I am contrasting "structural" with "behavioral violence," by which I mean the non-natural deaths and injuries that are caused by specific behavioral actions of individuals against individuals, such as the deaths we attribute to homicide, suicide, soldiers in warfare, capital punishment, and so on.

Structural violence differs from behavioral violence in at least three major respects.

* The lethal effects of structural violence operate continuously, rather than sporadically, whereas murders, suicides, executions, wars, and other forms of behavioral violence occur one at a time.
* Structural violence operates more or less independently of individual acts; independent of individuals and groups (politicians, political parties, voters) whose decisions may nevertheless have lethal consequences for others.
* Structural violence is normally invisible, because it may appear to have had other (natural or violent) causes.

Neither the existence, the scope and extent, nor the lethal power of structural violence can be discerned until we shift our focus from a clinical or psychological perspective, which looks at one individual at a time, to the epidemiological perspective of public health and preventive medicine. Examples are all around us.

In Boston, black babies in the inner city die before their first birth-days at three times the rate of white babies. This is nothing new; the poor have been dying at earlier ages than the rich ever since society was divided into rich and poor, when civilization was first invented. Medical professionals know how to prevent that high a rate of premature deaths. By applying the principles of preventive medicine to this problem, and treating it as a public health issue, it is possible to document the fact that these premature deaths are not caused primarily by the behavior of the individual mothers involved, but rather, by structural social and economic factors that are beyond the control of any individual mother.

A recent study conducted by epidemiologists at the Centers for Disease Control, of the U.S. Public Health Service, concluded that only about one-third of the "excess mortality" suffered by blacks (relative to whites) aged thirty-five to fifty-four was associated with any of the known health risks, such as smoking, hypertension, diabetes, obesity, alcohol consumption, and so forth. The remaining two-thirds could only be accounted for by the direct and indirect effects of low socio-economic status itself, i.e., the relative deprivation or poverty that blacks suffer from at vastly higher rates than whites: low family income, unequal access to health care, and the pathogenic (indeed, lethal) stresses caused by lower socioeconomic class position, racial discrimi-nation, social rejection, and unemployment.[1]

Another study,[2] conducted by faculty of the College of Physicians and Surgeons of Columbia University, found that death rates between the ages of five and sixty-five were higher in Harlem than in Ban-gladesh. The lethal effects of being a black in Harlem were especially strong for men, who were substantially less likely to reach the age of sixty-five (in fact, less likely to live beyond the age of forty) than were men in Bangladesh). Comparing the death rate in Harlem's almost entirely black population with that of the white population of the United States, they focused on the phenomenon called "excess mortal-ity"—that is, the number of blacks in Harlem who died, who would not have died if their death rate had been the same as that found among whites living elsewhere. Forty-five percent of the excess deaths in Harlem could be attributed to higher rates of homicides and accidents and substance abuse; the remaining 55 percent died from "natural" causes such as heart disease and cancer, but at rates two to three times higher than those experienced by the white population in this country. The authors of this article point out that in a similar study of Boston the number of excess deaths in the poorest areas of the city was considerably larger than the number of deaths in places that the U.S. government had designated as natural-disaster areas. They made the reasonable recommendation that the black inner-city ghettos with high rates of poverty and excess mortality be given "consideration analogous to that given to natural disaster areas."

H. A. Bulhan[3] has formulated another description of the mechanism of structural violence. He begins by referring to Brenner's[4] finding that a one percent increase in unemployment in the United States (based on 1970 census data) was regularly followed by an increased mortality of 37,000 deaths per year (both "natural," such as heart attacks, and "violent"), including almost two thousand more suicides and homicides than otherwise occur. To put it another way, every one percent rise in unemployment increases the mortality rate in this country by two percent, homicides and imprisonments by six percent, and the infant mortality rate by five percent. As if these findings are not grim enough, Bulhan then points out that "the unemployment rate of blacks has consistently remained at least twice that of whites in the postwar years".[5]

If we compare the death rates for blacks and whites (since 1960, when the U.S. Public Health Service began to calculate age-adjusted death rates separately for blacks and whites), blacks sustain about 280 more deaths per 100,000 than whites.[6] Now consider our national homicide rate, which is about 10 per 100,000. This is the national emergency, over which presidential elections are won and lost. These politicized discussions of violence overlook the true nature, location, and dimensions of violence in this country. When violence is defined as criminal, many people see it and care about it. When it is simply a by-product of our social and economic structure, many do not see it; and it is hard to care about something one cannot see.

Any doubt that the excess death rate among blacks is a function of the social and economic structure of our society is put to rest by epidemiological studies. Several investigations[7] have shown that high blood pressure, for example, is common among American, West Indian, South African, and other urbanized African blacks, but infrequent among rural Africans (that is, those least exposed to the social and economic structure of colonialism and white domination).

Since these discrepancies in the frequency of hypertension, homicide, and imprisonment vary with the social and economic structure in which the various populations are living, rather than with their race, and since varying the socioeconomic structure has similar effects on both whites and blacks (that is, exposing them to the class and caste structure of the United States increases the level of violence), the burden of proof would seem to be on those who do not consider the excess deaths to be a result of our socioeconomic structure.

The finding that structural violence causes far more deaths than behavioral violence does is not limited to this country. Kohler and Alcock[8] attempted to arrive at the number of excess deaths caused by socioeconomic inequities on a worldwide basis. Sweden was their model of the nation that had come closest to eliminating structural violence. It had the least inequity in income and living standards, and the lowest discrepancies in death rates and life expectancy; and the highest overall life expectancy in the world. When they compared the life expectancies of those living in the other socioeconomic systems against Sweden, they found that 18 million deaths a year could be attributed to the "structural violence" to which the citizens of all the other nations were being subjected. During the past decade, the discrepancies between the rich and poor nations have increased dramatically and alarmingly.[9]

The 14 to 18 million deaths a year caused by structural violence compare with about 100,000 deaths per year from armed conflict. Comparing this frequency of deaths from structural violence to the frequency of those caused by major military and political violence, such as World War II (an estimated 49 million military and civilian deaths, including those caused by genocide—or about eight million per year, 1939–1945), the Indonesian massacre of 1965–66 (perhaps 575,000 deaths), the Vietnam war (possibly two million, 1954–1973), and even a hypothetical nuclear exchange between the U.S. and the U.S.S.R. (232 million), it was clear that even war cannot begin to compare with structural violence, which continues year after year.

In other words, every fifteen years, on the average, as many people die because of relative poverty as would be killed in a nuclear war that caused 232 million deaths; and every single year, two to three times as many people die from poverty throughout the world as were killed by the Nazi genocide of the Jews over a six-year period. This is, in effect, the equivalent of an ongoing, unending, in fact accelerating, thermonuclear war, or genocide, perpetrated on the weak and poor every year of every decade, throughout the world.

Structural violence is also the main cause of behavioral violence on a socially and epidemiologically significant scale (from homicide and suicide to war and genocide). The question as to which of the two forms of violence—structural or behavioral—is more important, dangerous, or lethal is moot, for they are inextricably related to each other, as cause to effect.

Class and Caste:
The Sociology of Violence

Having looked at structural violence, or relative deprivation, as a form of violence, we now consider it as a cause of violence, and ask the question: What are the conditions, on a socially and epidemiologically significant scale, that lead people to feel so overwhelmed by shame as to resort to violent behavior?

There are several problems we face when we try to identify which groups are subjected to disproportionate degrees of shame or discrimination, or of being treated as inferior or of lower caste. One is that it could lead us to see that group only along the dimensions of its victimization, rather than also acknowledging its successes and strengths; and if we do that, we may only add one more insult to those to which the group has already been subjected. Also, it is rather absurdly ironic to discuss one group that is relevant here, the African-American community, as being one that suffers from an unusually high level of violent crime, when we reflect that blacks are, and always have been, subjected to far more violence from whites than they have themselves ever committed against whites—from the centuries of the slave trade, in which literally millions of kidnapped Africans were subjected to lethal conditions of transportation and labor, to their current decimation by what I referred to just above as the deadliest form of violence, namely, poverty. It is even more ironic when we remember that the most impressive and influential advocate and exemplar of nonviolence in this country was a black man, Martin Luther King, Jr. On the other hand, because more than ninety percent of the victims of black violence are other blacks, many leaders of the African-American community themselves have been among the most vocal in calling attention to the importance and dimensions of this problem, so I will proceed.

Even a brief analysis of the psychological situation of the different social classes in our society will illustrate the power of systematic shaming and humiliation as a cause of violence. The psychoanalyst Edith Jacobson observed that "people may feel ashamed of low financial or social or racial status."[10] The very fact that the words "low" and "status" are used to describe these differences—as in the term "lower class"— tells us which population groups in our society are more exposed to experiences of shaming. Who would not feel ashamed and inferior if described as "lower class" or of "lower status"?

John Adams, writing two centuries ago, noticed that the condition of poverty exposed the poor to shame, not guilt. As he described the situation, "The poor man's conscience is clear"—i.e., he does not feel guilty, and has no reason to—"yet he is ashamed." Why is this? Since Adams is also the man who felt that the "passion for distinction," the "desire not only to equal or resemble, but to excel [i.e., to attain pride and honor] . . . will forever be the great spring of human actions . . . next to self-preservation," it is perhaps not surprising that his explanation as to why the poor man is disproportionately exposed to shame was that "Mankind takes no notice of him. He rambles and wanders unheeded. In the midst of a crowd; at church; in the market . . . he is in as much obscurity as he would be in a garret or a cellar. He is not disapproved, censured, or reproached; he is only not seen. . . . To be wholly overlooked, and to know it, are intolerable."[11]

Lest all of this seem to contradict what I described earlier, that being seen and looked at can be one of the most powerful causes of shame, it is worth noticing that being seen and looked at are also necessary preconditions for the fullest augmentation of the feeling of pride. The only difference between the two is whether one's flaws, defects, and shortcomings, or one's achievements and distinctions are being seen. To have no one show interest in, pay attention to, or admire one's distinctive assets can deprive one of pride, as strongly as having others look too closely at one's personal liabilities can expose one to shame; but the net result, in the economy of self-esteem, is the same. Fame augments pride (which is why, in Adams's view, the obscurity in which the poor man lives, his deprivation of fame, deprives him of the opportunity to experience pride, and thus in effect exposes him to shame); just as infamy augments shame. The poor man tends to be ignored and disdained when he would like to be noticed, and exposed or attacked when he would like to have his privacy respected. Both constitute forms of slighting.

Commenting on Adams's remarks, Hannah Arendt[12] noted that he had accurately described the situation of the poor white man in America relative to the man of prominence and distinction, and that, like Marx a few decades later, he was among the few "in the literature of the modern age" to notice that "darkness [i.e., being socially "invisible," being treated as so insignificant that one is not even noticed] rather than want is the curse of poverty"; that to "injured lives" poverty adds "the insult of oblivion." But she added that the situation of the blacks (vis-à-vis all whites, rich and poor) was even more shame-inducing. As she put it, "The institution of slavery carries an obscurity even blacker than the obscurity of poverty; the slave, not the poor man, was 'wholly overlooked' "—even by Adams.[13] Many black authors have said the same thing about the experience of blacks in America, notably W.E.B. Du Bois, in a famous passage in *Dusk of Dawn*,[14] and Ralph Ellison, the title of whose novel, *The Invisible Man*,[15] expresses the same point.

One reason the class system in America has not been even more damaging and demoralizing to poor whites and never sparked a powerful, popular, socialist revolutionary movement is because the class system has always been buffered by an even more discriminatory caste system (of whites vs. blacks). Blacks have always been there to occupy a position lower in the social scale than even the poorest whites. This has created a vested interest on the part of both rich and poor whites to maintain the caste system of discrimination against blacks. For the rich, it has been a cheap way (both financially and morally) to continue to possess and control a disproportionate share of the national wealth and income. And poor American whites have let themselves be distracted from paying attention to how badly they are being discriminated against by the class system, by the fact that there is always a group they can look down upon in the caste system. For poor whites, discrimination against blacks has always been one of the few forms of self-esteem insurance that they are allowed. Keeping blacks below themselves has been for whites at the bottom of the white social ladder the only means available by which to rescue some pride. That in turn buys peace for the rich, who can continue to monopolize most of the nation's wealth and income without having to be bothered by any significant threats to their privileges from either of the two groups they are exploiting (all blacks, and poor and middle class whites), or from either of the nation's two political parties.

Class and Caste:
The Etiology of
Behavioral Violence

If people are lower status in class and caste, they are more prone to violence. How can we understand this? Sennett and Cobb[16] investigated the psychology of social class in America through a series of interviews of manual laborers and their families. They wrote: "The terrible thing about class in our society is that it sets up a contest for dignity,"[17] a contest that those on the bottom rung of the social ladder by definition lose. Lower-class people, they found, "felt that an educated, upper-middle-class person was in a position to judge them, and that the judgment rendered would be that working-class people could not be respected as equals. . . . The emotional impact of the class difference here is a matter of 'impudent snobbery,' of shaming, of put-down".[18] "Overlying these [class] distinctions" between the "mass" and the "elite," they concluded, "is a morality of shaming and self-doubt."[19] From the standpoint of the lower-class man, the system of social classes constitute "the social conditions that have made him feel open to shame, prey to feelings of inadequacy. [There is] no closure to [this] shame because, indeed, . . . the ascription of weakness the society forces on [lower class] men has no limits in time; the weakness is built into who they are."[20] For example, they refer to Ricca, a janitor: "He sees himself as receiving the ultimate form of contempt from those who stand above him in society: he is a function, 'Ricca the janitor,' he is part of the woodwork, even though he makes $10,000 a year. . . ."[21]

Throughout their interviews the same themes recur: "The sense of injured dignity" after one couple's car was repossessed by the bank, after the husband was laid off his job and they missed a few car loan payments.[22] "Over and over again," they found, "people expressed a great resentment against 'being treated like nothing,' 'being treated like you was dirt' " (which reminds us of the fact that "humus" is the root of "humiliation"), and " 'like you are part of the woodwork.' How is a man to make himself visible?"[23] One answer to that question (although Sennett and Cobb do not mention it) is by means of violence.

The "hidden injury" of class, then, to which the title of their book alludes, is shame. That is why they conclude that the only way "to stop the injuries of class" is to "do away with shaming"; and the only way to do that is to create a society characterized by "true classlessness."[24] I think they are profoundly correct in that conclusion. And since the only way to prevent violence is to stop shaming, the only way to prevent the hidden injury of class happens to correspond to the only way to prevent violence.

It should be emphasized that it is not poverty or deprivation in an absolute sense that causes shame—it is not lack of material things as such—but rather, relative deprivation, which really comes down to a form of psychological rather than material deprivation, of dignity, self-respect, and pride. In other words, it is the gap or disparity between the wealth and income of those at the top and those at the bottom of the social hierarchy that is a much more powerful cause of feelings of inferiority and shame than is absolute poverty. Even Marx saw that it was not poverty per se—it was not the fact of living in a hovel—that humiliated people, but living in a hovel next to a palace. It is for this reason that Marx referred to "shame" as the "emotion of revolution" (from the point of view—which was always Marx's point of view—of the poor).

This discussion may help us to see why a general rise in living standards or income does not necessarily reduce the feelings of inferiority experienced by the lowest of status groups. If the relative disparity between their situation and those of higher status groups remains the same, then their absolute rise in income will not diminish their vulnerability to shame. Shame is synonymous with feelings of inferiority; and inferiority is a relative concept based on an invidious comparison between one's self or group and other individuals or groups.

Another reason that an absolute or even a relative rise in income and living standards among the poor does not necessarily lead to a decrease in shame (and in violence) was discovered by Tocqueville,[25] when he noticed that the French Revolution (and others) may actually occur not when economic or other conditions are getting worse for the poor, but precisely when they are just beginning to get better. Something of the same sort happened in many of the Western nations, in both Europe and North America, during the 1960s and 1970s, when the situation of the poor—and, in America, that of blacks—improved both absolutely and relatively, and yet rates of criminal violence also increased.

The moment things begin to get better for the poor, the improvement itself sets off a "revolution of rising expectations," since change for the better proves that things can get better. Progress destroys fatalism and hopelessness by showing that relative deprivation is not necessary or eternal. So the level of aspiration increases—but much faster and higher than the actual level of achievement or attainment, since the aspiration is for equality. The net result is an increase in the gap between aspiration and achievement. And the intensity of shame that people experience is a function precisely of the size of that gap. So it is not surprising that the first improvements in even the relative position of the poor *vis-à-vis* the rich will lead to an increase both in feelings of shame and to violent actions. So the poor sit in front of their television sets watching "The Life Styles of the Rich and Famous," after first having been made aware that there is no natural law keeping them from living like the people on television. Add to that volatile mixture the "Horatio Alger" myth that has served for a hundred years to lead the poor in America to feel that their economic inferiority is caused by their own personal inferiority, and one can expect an inflammatory increase in feelings of shame, and acts of violence, just when things start to get better for them, because they will never get better enough—as long as the class system continues to exist.

Not surprisingly, if we compare blacks with whites in this country or other countries in which blacks have been victimized by racial discrimination, we find the same relative differences that we do when we compare upper and lower classes: relatively more inferiority feelings in the group with the inferior social status. Frantz Fanon, for example, the revolutionary black psychiatrist in North Africa, described his response to being black in a world dominated by whites: "Shame. Shame and self-contempt."[26] He quoted a black poet who wrote, "What a disgrace it is to be black in this world! . . . I rise burdened with the shame of my color,"[27] and another who wrote: "My Christian name: Humiliation!"[28] The situation is no different here. Grier and Cobbs, black psychiatrists, wrote in their book *Black Rage*[29] of "the endless circle of shame, humiliation, and the implied unacceptability of one's own person" that many blacks in this country experience. Kenneth Clark, the distinguished black psychologist, investigated the emotional situation blacks are in as they emerge from childhood experiences of being treated as inferior. He concluded: "The stigma remains; they have been forced to recognize themselves as inferior. Few if any Negroes ever fully lose that sense of shame."[30] The U.S. Supreme Court drew on Clark's research to support the desegregation decision, *Brown v. Board of Education* (1954): "To separate [black children] . . . solely because of their race generates a feeling of inferiority as to their status in the community that may affect their hearts and minds in a way unlikely ever to be undone."[31]

On the other hand, not all black leaders have supported integration. What is very clear, however, is that even those who advocated separation, such as the young Malcolm X, did so for exactly the same reason that Kenneth Clark supported integration: in order to protect blacks from the shame and humiliation that is implicit in either a racial segregation or a racial integration that was imposed on blacks by whites. As Malcolm wrote:

> Every time I mentioned "separation," some . . . would cry that we Muslims were standing for the same thing that white racists and demagogues stood for. I would explain the difference. "No! We reject segregation even more militantly than you say you do! We want separation, which is not the same! . . . Segregation is that which is forced upon inferiors by superiors. But separation is that which is done voluntarily, by two equals—for the good of both!"[32]

Malcolm's logic is just as understandable as Clark's—for, of course, both alternatives can be perceived and experienced as equally shameful: to be refused freedom to integrate if you want to, and to be refused freedom to separate if you want to. The problem with Malcolm's logic in this passage, however (as he himself came to see), is that the whites who resisted the integration of the races most adamantly were precisely those who were making the same argument—that they were being denied freedom to separate from blacks when they wanted to.

In fact, Malcolm X was one of the most eloquent and unflinchingly honest analysts of the psychology of racial discrimination (or caste stratification), and was as ready to bare his own soul as to lay bare the psychology of the oppressor. For example, speaking of his practice, as a young man, of straightening his hair so it would resemble a white man's (the nickname for which was "wearing a conk"), he wrote in later years that

> This was my first really big step toward self-degradation: . . . . I had joined that multitude of Negro men and women in America who are brainwashed into believing that the black people are "inferior"—and white people "superior". . . .[33]

. . . I don't see how . . . a black woman with any race pride could walk down the street with any black man wearing a conk— the emblem of his shame that he is black. To my own shame, when I say all of this I'm talking first of all about myself. . . .[34]

On the other hand, because his self-analysis had been so unsparing, he could also assert with confidence his diagnosis that "if you study closely any conked . . . Negro, . . . his hair lye-cooked to be 'white-looking' fairly shouts to everyone who looks at his head, 'I'm ashamed to be a Negro.' "[35]

At the end of his life, following his pilgrimage to Mecca, Malcolm transformed his earlier interpretation of American whites. He had come to realize, he said, that "it isn't the American white man who is a racist, but it's the American political, economic, and social atmosphere" [what I am calling "culture"] "that automatically nourishes a racist psychology in the white man. . . . The white man is not inherently evil, but America's racist society influences him to act evilly. The society has produced and nourishes a psychology which brings out the lowest, most base part of human beings."[36] It is remarkable that Malcolm could take that detached and even magnanimous a view toward American whites, when so many American whites still cannot do the same with respect to American blacks, but insist on blaming them, both as individuals and as a group, for whatever behaviors whites disapprove of—and often punishing them as well.

An intact culture can provide people with a powerful means by which to bolster their self-esteem and protect themselves from what could otherwise be overwhelming, soul-murdering intensities of shame and humiliation. While many minority groups, such as Jews and Asians, have been the subject of discrimination, their cultural traditions have remained intact and functioning, so that they have been successful in developing effective mechanisms for maintaining self-respect, and diminishing individual and group vulnerability. Among these cultural characteristics are a widely shared and collectively reinforced and rewarded positive value on education and achievement, together with the professional successes that naturally follow.

But when a group has been deliberately and systematically cut off from its cultural roots for five hundred years, as African-Americans have been, the value on education and achievement may appear to be a value of European-American culture alone, rather than being a value indigenous to one's own cultural identity. Thus, many African-American men in prison have made it clear to me that they feel they can maintain their psychological and social autonomy, and avoid the shame of feeling subservient to European-Americans and their cultural traditions and values, only by rejecting the value on education; for to them, doing well in school means becoming "like Whitey," which is perceived as rejecting one's own group and, indeed, one's own autonomous identity (which can only be defined in opposition to white culture and identity).

It would be a gross distortion and minimization of the social and economic discrimination that even the most gifted, hard-working, and successful blacks in America are still subjected to—another form of "blaming the victim"—to suggest that the attitude toward education of those black men to whom I just referred represents the main obstacle to black education and achievement in this country. On the contrary, the extraordinary growth of a black professional class in the single generation following the civil rights revolution of thirty years ago makes it very clear how much the relative absence of blacks from these fields of endeavor in the past was something imposed on those in the black community, not chosen by them. And those same discriminatory forces still exert an enormously inhibitory and destructive influence on the education of most blacks in America.

Why is inferior social status conducive not only to feelings of inferiority, but also to feelings of innocence? Because pain, punishment, and suffering not only intensify feelings of shame, they also relieve feelings of guilt and sinfulness. That emotional principle, as I said earlier, is the psychological mechanism that underlies both the religious practice of penance, in which self-inflicted pain or deprivation relieves the feeling of being sinful; and the legal practice of punishment, whose purpose is to remove or undo moral and legal guilt. And poverty *means* pain, punishment, and misery (both etymologically and psychologically).

I am not asserting any innate difference between rich and poor in the capacity for feelings of shame or guilt, or innate differences in sensitivity to those feelings. Rather, the objective conditions of life under conditions of class and caste stratification virtually guarantee that whites will be exposed more frequently and intensely to feelings of pride and guilt, and blacks to feelings of shame and innocence. For example, as Henry and Short[37] pointed out, in their analysis of the distribution of homicide versus suicide among lower and higher status groups, the greater the degree of advantage, power, and freedom a person has, the likelier he is to perceive himself as having only himself to blame when things go wrong (as they inevitably do for everyone, at one point or another); whereas those who cannot help but be aware how little control they have over the setbacks and disadvantages they suffer would virtually have to be out of touch with reality to blame themselves (and feel guilty) for most of their problems.

So those groups who are primarily exposed to feelings of shame and innocence would primarily blame and punish others, and would thus be more likely to commit homicide than suicide; whereas those who are statistically more likely to be exposed to feelings of guilt (and pride) would have a higher ratio of suicide to homicide (since they have only themselves to blame for their problems—given the power, advantages, and freedom that they enjoy). And that prediction is borne out by the vital statistics on those two forms of violence, and a score of studies which show that in societies (such as ours) that stratify people on the basis of class and caste, people in lower status groups are more likely to commit homicide, and those in higher status groups are more likely to commit suicide.[38]

Finally, it is important to remember that in discussing the relative vulnerability to shame and violence that is suffered by blacks in this country, we are talking about a social phenomenon, namely caste, not a biological phenomenon, namely race. In the next chapter, I will turn to the question: Are there biological factors that predispose individuals or groups to higher rates of violence?

The

Biology of

Violence

IN THE HISTORY OF HUMAN VIOLENCE, BIOLOGICAL CONCEPTS HAVE BEEN among the most potent stimulants of violent behavior. For example, racism itself is a "biological" concept—or rather, a pseudo-biological one. The widespread belief in the inherent biological inferiority of different individuals and groups has often been used to justify and even obligate violence toward them. That is why an analysis of biological concepts is itself an intrinsic part of any thorough investigation of the causes and prevention of violence.

What relationships exist between biology and culture? Is violence caused by instinct, heredity, or race? Is violence caused by lesions in the brain? Is violence caused by drugs and alcohol? Do male hormones lead to violence? These are the sorts of questions I will explore in this chapter.

Is Violence Instinctual?

One of the most popular theories of violence over the past century or more has suggested that impulses toward violent behavior are part of our instinctual endowment, inherited from our animal ancestors. By "instinct" I mean a spontaneously occurring impulse to engage in violent behavior that builds up in intensity until it is discharged, so that the individual can obtain relief from tension only by acting out the inherited, innately preprogrammed pattern of action. Freud is perhaps the most influential thinker who has proposed such a theory. But students of animal behavior, like Konrad Lorenz and other ethologists, and E.O. Wilson's "sociobiology," have also promulgated one version or another of the idea that violence is determined by inborn instinctual or biologically determined drives. I hope to show, in what follows, that there are so many problems with this explanation of violence that it is valueless, and dangerously unhelpful as a theory.

In recent years, one of Lorenz's fellow ethologists, N. Tinbergen, who has probably done more than anyone to clarify the concept of instinct,[1] has concluded that that term is "used in too many different senses to be of further use in the present stage of the behavioral sciences."[2] Tinbergen, in fact, has recommended that the term "instinct" be replaced by the notion of a "fixed-action pattern," to reflect the specificity and rigidity of the innate, unlearned, preprogrammed behaviors that can be observed in many animal species (unlike the high degree of plasticity and flexibility characteristic of human behavior). Even in animals, suggests Tinbergen, such behavior occurs only when it is elicited by a highly specific environmental "trigger," rather than being spontaneously emitted after a buildup of internal tension. Elaborating on this point, L. Bernard Luther[3] has pointed out that

> . . . such terms as fighting, gregariousness, self-assertion . . . and the like are not single and definite behavior patterns. They are class terms for hundreds and thousands of concrete behavior mechanisms which are grouped together in action or in conceptual thinking because of their general similarity of function. The whole list of activities having a common conceptual or classificatory name never occur in action together, that is, they never func-

tion as a unit behavior process, as would be necessary if they were
true instincts. . . . An instinct is a biological fact and it is a unit
character, or it does not exist. It is structural. It is not possible to
inherit an abstraction.

In fact, leading investigators of aggressive behavior in animals, such
as J. P. Scott,[4] have long since rejected "the concept of an aggressive
instinct as an innate or independent motivational force analogous to
hunger. That is, there is no predictable periodicity, no measurable
changes in internal parameters (such as glucose concentrations in the
blood), and no evidence of a 'need' to attack in the absence of provocative stimuli."

The theoretical assumption that violence is instinctual is often argued as if it were more "scientific" than the assumptions derived from
the "softer" behavioral sciences, such as psychology and the social sciences (despite the fact that these concepts can be tested against empirical data). Today, in fact, such "biological" notions as "violent instincts"
are seen as pseudo-biology by biologists themselves.

I emphasize the need to retire the concept of instinct because it is
dangerous, for several reasons. The first is that the very notion that
violence is instinctive tends to lead to an attitude of pessimism about
the possibility of preventing violence. If, by definition, we cannot eradicate "instincts" because they are inherited, then what is the point in
ever thinking that we can do something substantial toward preventing
violence? Such notions can easily lead to self-fulfilling prophecies by
blinding us to the fact that the most important and powerful causes of
violence are not at all inevitable. If violence is the product of human
social arrangements and individual decisions, then violence is quite
susceptible to change. We just need to be genuinely committed to
preventing it and willing to take the necessary steps to do so.

A second reason this concept is dangerous is that it leads us to
believe that violent impulses need to be discharged periodically or they
will build up to the point where they explode spontaneously and uncon-

trollably. One corollary of these notions is the idea that one way to prevent violence is to expose people to aggressive (but nonlethal) alternatives to criminal or military violence, such as violent sports, competitive economic arrangements, and so on, to provide an "outlet" for men's "innate violent drives," on the mistaken assumption that that will diminish the incidence and destructiveness of crime and war. The anthropologist R. G. Sipes[5] decided to test this "hostility-catharsis, drive-discharge" model of violence empirically, which he did by comparing the practice of athletics in ten pacific, nonviolent cultures and ten highly belligerent, warlike ones. He found that the societies that played the most combative, physically violent games also engaged in the most warfare, concluding that far from serving as mutually exclusive alternatives to one another, the two forms of violence only reinforced each other. In other words, if a culture places a positive value on violence, it is only to be expected that that cultural value would lead them to engage both in violent contact sports and in warfare. But the cause of the violence is clearly a cultural value that stimulates violence in every sphere, not an "instinct" that can be diminished in intensity by being discharged in aggressive athletic contests.

Why then, given the dubious nature of the concept that violence is instinctual, and the lack of empirical scientific data to prove it, would this idea have gained so wide a following? One reason may be that it justifies political conservatism, the support of the status quo. If violence is innate and instinctual, then clearly there is no point in trying to change our social and economic system (for we cannot undo the cause of violence). If the assumption is that violence is an inextricable part of our inborn "human nature," then clearly the only way to keep the problem under control is to emphasize just that: control, meaning the control of some people (whose violence is "bad") by other people (whose violence is "good"). The fact that that "solution" simply constitutes a perpetuation of violence, a "recycling" of it, so to speak, among different victims, rather than the elimination or prevention of it, can always be regarded as unavoidable, if violence is "instinctual." Thus, for example, in beginning their discussion of *Crime and Human Nature*, the conservative social theorists James Q. Wilson and Richard Herrnstein state as their underlying assumption that "the problem of social order is fundamental: How can mankind live together in reasonable order?"[6] Why should the problem of order be more fundamental than, say, the problem of establishing mutual, universal respect for each other's human dignity? Or of establishing and implementing the principle of universal, mutual care, the principle that "we are all responsible for all," as Dostoevsky's Father Zossima put it? Or the problem of eliminating the gross and rapidly escalating inequities in the distribution of the world's wealth and power which cause the feelings of shame and humiliation that stimulate the violence that threatens to destroy civilization and, indeed, our whole species, from within?

But while it is easy to see how the belief that violence is instinctual can be pressed into the service of authoritarianism, social Darwinism, and anti-democratic politics, I do not mean to imply that that is the only interest that this idea can serve. Freud had to rely on "instinct" as his explanation for violence, because he had no theory of shame with which to understand and explain it. One has to explain aggression somehow, if one is to have any theory of behavior. But if we can see more clearly how misleading this concept is, perhaps we can retire it as an explanation of violence, and turn to human emotions—specific emotions, such as love, hate, shame, guilt, and so on, emotions which act as motives, or causes, of behavior. This is compatible with the valid and useful aspects of psychoanalytic theory.

But before we relinquish the idea of "instinct" entirely as a theoretical explanation which accounts for violent behavior, we may have to come to terms with one remaining interest that may be served by "instinct theory." It enables some men (especially violent men) to hide their most shameful secret, namely, that violence is not an innate, authentic part of men's inborn human nature, but serves instead as a smoke screen that hides the unacceptable, "unmanly" desire to be taken care of—wishes, which, if gratified, would make many a man feel that he was passive, dependent, infantile, and weak, that is to say, "not a man." Violent men's deepest fear is that they will go out not with a bang but a whimper; which is why they try so hard to create the biggest and loudest bang they can, in an effort to drown out their shame-inducing whimper. If the world does end with a bang, it will not be because of an "aggressive instinct" but because of the precise opposite: the fear that someone might hear the whimper of the wish to be loved and taken care of. Violent men would like nothing better than to be thought of as filled with "aggressive instincts"; nothing is more flattering to the shaky self-esteem of a man who fears that he is "really" a "wimp" than to be told, and to believe, that he is actually carrying within himself very dangerous instincts. But challenging that defense will not work unless we can change our attitudes toward taking care of each other, instead of regarding it as shameful if men have a need to be helped by each other (and, more shameful yet, by women).

Is Violence Hereditary?

Another popular theory about violence is that it is inherited. This theory about human violence has a certain prima facie scientific plausibility, since animal studies show that aggressive and nonaggressive strains of rodents demonstrate significant heritability of aggression. But according to a review of this study by a National Academy of Sciences Panel on the Understanding and Prevention of Violence, these "animal studies . . . [also] show that tendencies toward aggression can be modified by experience, contextual cues, and the social environment."[7]

More important, the most carefully designed tests of this hypothesis to date among humans have been unanimous in failing to confirm the view that violence is hereditary. Studies involving identical twins have so far included too few subjects to be able to test hypotheses concerning the heritability of violent behavior. For a variety of reasons, however, adoption studies are even more useful in the effort to separate environmental from genetic determinants of behavior than twin studies are. We are fortunate to have three large studies of that sort from Scandinavia. Moffitt, Mednick, and Gabrielli,[8] taking advantage of the unusually complete vital statistics kept in Denmark, examined the criminal records of all 14,427 men adopted into unrelated families from 1924 to 1947 and compared them with those of their biological parents. If the tendency to engage in violent behavior were inherited, they should have found that the biological sons of parents convicted of violent crimes had a significantly increased rate of convictions for such crimes themselves. Instead, they found "no significant relationship for violent offenses" (p. 27). Two large adoption studies conducted in Sweden showed exactly the same results.[9]

Ironically, both studies found that property crimes correlated with heredity! That finding is irrelevant to the question of whether violent behavioral tendencies are inherited. But it is an excellent example of how important it is not to confuse "violence" with "crime." Most crime is not violent, it is property crime, and the differences between the two are—literally—vitally important! In their review of research on biological determinants of violence for the National Academy of Sciences, Siegel and Mirsky[10] concluded that the finding "that biological parent-child relationships predicted property convictions, but not violent offenses . . . supports the view that the circumstances leading to the commission of violent acts are more likely due to nongenetic (i.e., environmental) than genetic determinants."

The same considerations apply to several studies that claim to have found that antisocial (or sociopathic) personality disorders are inherited. Since a history of committing acts of violence can be one (though it is not a necessary one) of the criteria by which this diagnosis is made, it would be easy to conclude, mistakenly, that these studies have provided evidence that violence is hereditary. In fact, when the criterion of violence has been specifically isolated from the several other diagnostic criteria, violence has turned out not to correlate with heredity.

In the 1960s, several investigators claimed that men who had an extra "Y" chromosome were significantly more likely to commit violent crimes. Further study of this subject, however, disproved that hypothesis, and it is no longer regarded as plausible. (Even if it had turned out to be valid, of course, the condition is rare enough that it would have explained only a tiny minority of all the violent crimes that are committed, anyway.)

The National Academy of Sciences report does caution that "in view of the general difficulties of establishing genetic relationships to rare behaviors that are also subject to environmental influences, . . . it would be premature to rule out the possibility that some complex interaction involving multiple genes and life experiences may account for some instances of sexual violence."[11] However, the consensus up to this point is that, so far, no clear genetically transmitted inheritability of tendencies to engage in violent behavior has been demonstrated.

The one exception to this discussion concerns the issue of violence against the self—suicide. Although some studies have reported no significant correlation between suicide and heredity, others have found a weak tendency for suicides to cluster in families. Suicides are more common in people who suffer from certain psychiatric conditions (chiefly depression, schizophrenia, and alcoholism), and people who suffer from these conditions seem to possess some degree of hereditary predisposition. Thus, those illnesses correlate with heredity, and suicide correlates with those illnesses, and the result is a weak but statistically significant correlation between suicide and heredity. In other words, unless a person is among the fraction of persons who happen to inherit from a parent or parents the particular combination of genes that predispose them to major depression—(if, in fact, there is such a combination of genes)—and then is part of the fraction of those persons (say, 50 to 60 percent, according to identical twin studies) who actually become clinically depressed; he or she might then become among the fraction of those suffering from depression who go on to commit suicide. But clearly, even in those who have a family history of depression followed by suicide, we are still talking about a fraction of a fraction of a fraction. And since not all those who commit suicide are believed to have shown signs of symptoms of any of the psychiatric illnesses for which there is some hereditary predisposition, there is really no reliable evidence to date that many suicides are caused even in part by an hereditary predisposition to suicide.

The evidence suggests that environment and experience are stronger determinants of both depression and suicidal behavior than heredity is, so that a healthy environment and upbringing can render whatever suicidal "predisposition" a person inherited effectively harmless. If our goal is to prevent suicide, then, we should concentrate our efforts on social and psychological factors; while at the same time, of course, providing the best possible treatments for those individuals who do suffer from one of the diagnosed mental illnesses that predispose a person to suicide.

Do Brain Lesions or Epilepsy Cause Violence?

Violent criminals and other prison inmates show evidence of a wide and miscellaneous variety of brain injuries and of different types of epilepsy, at rates that are significantly higher than those found in the public at large. This has naturally raised the question whether damage or illness of the brain can cause violence, and if so, how large a contribution this makes to the overall rates of violent behaviors. After reviewing the evidence, the National Academy of Sciences panel quoted earlier concluded that "to date, no known neurobiologic patterns [of brain damage, lesions or disease] are precise and specific enough to be considered reliable markers for violent behavior, whether sexually related or not."[12] In other words, no specific, identifiable, diagnosable brain lesion, abnormality, or syndrome has yet been identified which can clearly be shown to cause violent behavior. With respect specifically to epilepsy, the only conclusion that can be reached on the basis of the studies that have been done is that nothing has been finally proven either way: "The question remains unanswered as to whether patients with seizure disorders have greater or smaller potentials for violence than the general population."[13]

Why, then, do violent criminals show a higher incidence of these types of problems than does the general public? The National Academy panel concluded that "some individuals' dysfunctions may well be a result rather than a cause of aggressive behavior: they may originate in head injuries inflicted by others in retaliation."[14] In other words, if a person is habitually getting into barroom brawls, there is a pretty good chance that he will get his head injured sooner or later; such brain lesions can then serve as "epileptogenic foci" that cause epilepsy.

There is a second potential source of brain damage, however, that may well precede a person's developing a violent style of life—child abuse. Many children who suffer violent abuse at the hands of a parent later become violent themselves, as a result of the emotional trauma which their physical abuse causes, independently of whether or not they suffer brain damage or any other lasting physical injury. If they also have brain damage when they are examined in adulthood, that lesion may be merely a coincidental finding, which is itself an effect of the real cause of their violent behavior, namely, the beatings the child received years before.

Another means by which brain lesions or malfunctions may indirectly contribute to the onset of violent behavior, without themselves being the active etiological agents, is by subjecting the child to social handicaps which are so frustrating or humiliating that it is those handicaps, rather than the organic damage per se, that precipitate the violence, either at the time or in later years.

In twenty-five years of evaluating men brought before the courts or sent to prisons or mental hospitals because of their violent behavior, I have been most impressed by the extreme rarity with which there was any evidence that such a person's brain lesion could be found to be a causal factor in his violent behavior.

Do Drugs and Alcohol Cause Violence?

Alcohol use has repeatedly been found to be correlated with violent behavior; for example, more than 50 percent of the perpetrators or victims of murder and other serious violence (as well as of lethal automobile accidents) have alcohol in their bloodstreams at the time; diagnosed alcoholics commit violent crimes at a much higher rate than do their nonalcoholic peers; a large percentage of violent criminals are alcoholics (although an equally large percentage of nonviolent criminals, i.e., property offenders, are also).

There is, however, no simple, one-to-one relationship between alcohol use and violent behavior. Studies on the psychopharmacology of alcohol use and violence suggest that the relationship between the two is a complicated interaction among biological, psychological, social and cultural factors. For example, there is some evidence that small amounts of alcohol taken quickly temporarily increase, and high doses temporarily decrease, aggressive behavior in many animal species, including primates and humans.[15] Nevertheless, there is nothing inevitable about this in humans, and "ethnographic research on alcohol use suggests . . . that its role in violence depends on drinkers' expectations and on cultural norms—even binge drinking is commonly observed in some non-European cultures without violent aftermaths."[16] A self-fulfilling prophecy has been observed here in a variety of settings: When an individual or a culture expects alcohol use to be followed by violence, it more often is. When violence is not the expectation, or when it is not accepted or approved of, it tends not to follow alcohol use.

What about other drugs? The National Academy study says: "Taking marijuana and opiates [including heroin and other narcotics] in moderate doses temporarily inhibits aggressive and violent behavior; withdrawal from opiate addiction, however, may lead to heightened aggressive and defensive reactions."[17] So the assumption that a "war on violence" requires the prevention of marijuana and heroin use is simply mistaken, looking at the pharmacological effects on violence alone, without considering other factors. In fact, the most effective way to prevent violence from heroin use would be to make sure that heroin is available to the withdrawing addict—from a purely pharmacological standpoint.

The same appears to be true, for the most part, of the other psychoactive drugs:

> Long-term frequent use of amphetamines, LSD, and PCP has changed a few individuals' neurochemical functioning in ways that induced violent outbursts, but examples are extremely rare except among users with preexisting psychopathology. No evidence has yet established direct neurobiologic links between violent behavior and acute or chronic use of powdered cocaine. However, more research is urgently needed on the pharmacological effects of smoked cocaine or "crack," which enters the brain more directly.[18]

In short—and this is by far the most important finding of all that is known on this subject: *"For illegal psychoactive drugs, the illegal market itself accounts for far more violence than pharmacological effects."*[19] Thus, the "war on drugs" appears to be a self-generating war. Outlawing drugs, with the consequent decrease in their supply, followed by the increase in their cost, generates the illegal market—and all the violence that follows from that.

Since the war on drugs victimizes mostly those who are young, poor and/or black, and benefits mostly organized crime, it might be said to be a war on the young, the poor, and on blacks, a method of stimulating violence, and a very expensive means of subsidizing organized crime, boosting the employment of police and correction officers and border guards, and subsidizing the construction industry by promoting the building of more and more prisons. One could also wonder whether it is not, wittingly or unwittingly, a means of distracting the white middle class voting public from recognizing and ameliorating the real poverty and misery that are endemic in the central-city ghettoes.

Young Men Are the Most Violent: Is This Biological?

The only two innate biological variables that do appear to be among the determinants of violent behavior are youth and maleness. These patterns are universal across cultures, historical epochs, and social circumstances. So it is difficult to assume that they result purely from cultural, social, or individual psychological causes. This pattern is also seen across a wide variety of species, including our closest primate "relatives." For example, in all mammalian species (including the human), males are reported to be the more aggressive sex. Among chimpanzees, who are the most closely related to us of all other primates in the evolutionary branch from which we evolved—for example, 99 percent of the DNA of humans and chimpanzees is identical—males have been described as significantly more aggressive than females.

It is the positive correlation with male sex hormones or androgens, especially testosterone, and the negative correlation with female sex hormones, that appear to correlate most closely with the greater levels of violence observed among males, compared with females, and with youth. Testosterone facilitates and stimulates aggressive responses to environmental stimuli, just as estrogens and progestogens inhibit them.

If one compares a chart of the average level of circulating testosterone, with another chart plotting the average rate of committing murder, as they each vary with age over the life cycle, the two charts are astonishingly similar: relatively low amounts of each before puberty, then a sudden dramatic increase in each at puberty, with the levels of both remaining high throughout adolescence and young adulthood, then diminishing gradually but steadily together from middle age onwards. It strains the imagination to believe that this similarity is simply a coincidence, given the wide variety of collateral data that indicates that androgens stimulate aggressiveness. The opposite appears to be true of female sex hormones, according to both clinical experience with humans, and animal studies involving chimpanzees and other mammalian species. There is an increasing amount of evidence that the neurotransmitter serotonin is another biological inhibitor of violent behavior, both homicidal and suicidal. It may be relevant to the sex differences in the frequency of both of these types of violence that men on average appear to have lower levels of serotonin than women do.

Thus, men would seem to have larger amounts of the male sex hormones that stimulate aggression, and smaller amounts of two classes of inhibitors of aggression. However, while these findings do suggest a biological cause of sex differences in violent behavior, we should not forget that psychological and social factors are also determinants of whether or not a given individual or group will engage in violent acts; in fact, these latter determinants can be even more powerful than the biological ones. For example, Marvin Wolfgang's detailed study of criminal homicide rates among black and white men and women in Philadelphia found that while men in each racial group committed several times more homicides than did women of the same race, black *women* committed three times more homicides than did white *men*. In other words, the *social* determinants of violence were far more powerful than were the *biological* determinants. This suggests that even women, if they are exposed to more shaming than men, can become more homicidal than men; and as the evidence reviewed in the previous chapter shows, there is good reason to think that blacks as a group are subjected to substantially more frequent and intense humiliations, slurs, slights, and insults than are whites as a group.

On the whole, I think we would have to conclude that biology does not cause violence except to say that there are higher indices of violence among young men than there are among males of other ages and females of all ages, a matter which has far more to do with the cultural construction of manhood than it does with the hormonal substrates of biology.

If we replace the outmoded concept that violence is "instinctual," we must remember that violent behavior, like all behavior, can only occur in a psychophysiological and anatomical matrix that creates the potential to engage in violent behavior. Bringing our understanding of this psychophysiological matrix into line with the more recent ethological thinking, we could say that the potential to engage in violent behavior is built into the very structure and functioning of our central nervous system, which can be "triggered" by the social environment. Unless it is triggered, this potential will remain dormant and quiescent. I believe that the most effective and powerful stimulus of violence in the human species is the experience of shame and humiliation, and that feelings of guilt, where the capacity for them and sensitivity to them exists, can further alter the resulting psychophysiological situation, transforming it from one primarily oriented toward the destruction of others into one focusing on the destruction of one's own body.

But the fact that human violence only erupts when there are triggers from the social environment, which act on a personality that has been sensitized to shame, can be illustrated most simply, perhaps, as follows. If we were to maintain that the causes of violence were biological factors such as instinct, heredity, or brain damage, then we would have to assume that during the century between 1815 and July 1914 the young male population of Europe was blessedly free of those instincts, genes, or brain lesions; but that in August 1914 they suffered a sudden epidemic of one or all of them, which lasted without pause until November 1918, when they were suddenly cured because a physician finally discovered the right prescription to write for them—called a peace treaty!

Culture,

Gender, and

Violence:

"We Are Not Women"

IN THE PREVIOUS CHAPTER, I SUMMARIZED SOME OF THE REASONS FOR concluding that even those biological factors that do correlate with increased rates of murder, such as age and sex, are not primary determinants or independent causes of violent behavior. They do not spontaneously, in and of themselves, create violent impulses; they act only to increase the predisposition to engage in violence, when the individual is exposed to the social and psychological stimuli that do stimulate violent impulses. In the absence of those stimuli, these biological factors acting alone do not seem to stimulate or cause violence spontaneously or independently.

That is good news; for while we cannot alter or eliminate the biological realities of age and sex, which are made by God, we can bring about fundamental changes in the social and cultural conditions that expose people to increased rates and intensities of shame and humiliation, since culture and society are made by us. In this chapter I will analyze some of the cultural patterns, values, and practices that stimulate violence, and how they might be altered to prevent violence.

When these conditions are altered the exposure of human populations to shame is dramatically reduced—and so is violence. Those economically developed democracies all over the world that have evolved into "welfare states" since the end of the Second World War, including all of Western Europe, Japan, Canada, Australia, and New Zealand, offer universal and free health care, generous public housing, unemployment and family leave policies, and so on. Every one of those countries has a more equitable (and hence less shame-inducing) socio-economic system than the United States does. There is a much greater sharing of the collective wealth of the society as measured, for example, by the smaller gap between the income and wealth of the most and least affluent segments of their populations. Our rate of violent crime (murder, rape) is from two to twenty times as high as it is in any of the other economically developed democracies. This is precisely what the theory presented in this book would predict.

Other cultures have also altered their social conditions so as to protect their members from exposure to overwhelming degrees of shame and humiliation, and have experienced the dramatic diminution in rates of violence that the theory espoused in this book would lead us to expect. They demonstrate the degree to which rates of violence are determined by social, cultural, and economic conditions. One example would be those societies that practice what has been called "primitive Christian communism," and are truly classless societies whose economic systems are based on communal sharing—Anabaptist sects such as the Hutterites, Mennonites, and Amish. One remarkable feature of these societies is that the incidence of violence in them is virtually zero. The Hutterites, for example, do not appear to have had a single confirmed case of murder, rape, aggravated assault, or armed robbery since they arrived in America more than a hundred years ago. They also practice a strict and absolute pacifism, which is why they had to emigrate to America from Europe in the last century—to escape becoming victims of genocide at the hands of governments there which were persecuting them. While that aspect of their experience is one reason why I do not propose them as a model for our own society to emulate in any concrete, literal way, they do demonstrate that violence does not have to be universal; and that altering social, cultural, and economic conditions can dramatically reduce, and for all practical purposes eliminate, human violence from the face of the earth.

One apparent exception to the generalizations I am making here is Japan, which has often been cited as a "shame culture." If frequent exposure and intense sensitivity to shame (in the absence of a correspondingly powerful exposure to guilt) stimulates violence toward others, then why does Japan have a relatively low homicide and high suicide rate—the same pattern that characterizes those societies that have sometimes been called "guilt cultures," namely, the European and other economically developed "welfare state" democracies? There are two answers to that question, one that refers to the period before World War II, and the other, the time since then.

During both periods, Japan has been described by those who know it best as an intensely homogeneous and conformist society, with strong pressures against individual deviations from group norms and behaviors. That social pattern had, and still has, a powerful influence on the patterns of Japanese violence. Until the end of the Second World War, Japan was an extremely violent society—indeed, one of the most violent in the history of the world; they have been described, both by themselves and by their neighbors, as "a nation of warriors" since they first emerged as an independent nation two to three thousand years ago. However, that violence was directed almost entirely toward non-Japanese. Some cultures, such as Japan's, have been more successful than others in channeling the homicidal behavior of their members toward members of other cultures, so that it is labeled warfare or genocide, rather than toward members of their own culture, which is called murder. Thus, the Japanese engaged in a degree of violence toward their Asian neighbors from 1930 to 1945 that was just as genocidal as what the Germans perpetrated in Europe. When compared to the number of suicides that Japanese citizens committed during the first half of this century, the number of homicides that they committed (in the form of warfare) during that same period was astronomical—exactly as the theory proposed in this book would predict.

However, since 1945 the social and economic conditions in Japan have changed remarkably. Japan today has the lowest degree of economic inequity among its citizens in the world (as judged by the World Bank's measures of relative income and wealth). So it is not surprising that Japan also has a remarkably low frequency both of violent crime and of structural violence. For if socioeconomic inequities expose those at the bottom of the ladder to intense feelings of inferiority; if relative equality protects people from those feelings; and if inferiority feelings stimulate violent impulses, then it is not surprising that Japan's current socioeconomic structure would be marked by a low level of violence toward others, as indeed it is—even if the Japanese are unusually sensitive to feelings and experiences of shame, and even if (as some observers have claimed) they are not especially sensitive to or likely to experience guilt feelings. For their socioeconomic system, even if it does revolve primarily around sensitivity to shame rather than guilt, actively protects most individuals from being exposed to overwhelming degrees of shame, and also provides them with nonviolent (e.g., economic) means by which to prevent or undo any "loss of face" that is experienced.

If the main causes of violence are these social and psychological variables (shame versus honor), an apparent anomaly lies in the fact that men are and always have been more violent than women, throughout history and throughout the world. If shame stimulates violence; if being treated as inferior stimulates shame; and if women have been treated throughout history as inferior to men, then why are women less violent than men? (And they are indeed vastly less likely than men are to commit homicide, suicide, warfare, and assault, in every culture and every period of history.)

The Making of "Manhood"
and the Violence of Men

To understand this apparent anomaly, we must examine the cultural construction of masculinity and femininity, and the contrasting conditions under which the two sexes, once they have been cast into patriarchally defined "gender roles," are exposed to feelings of private shame or public dishonor. To understand physical violence we must understand male violence, since most violence is committed by males, and on other males. And we can only understand male violence if we understand the sex roles, or gender roles, into which males are socialized by the gender codes of their particular cultures. Moreover, we can only understand male gender roles if we understand how those are reciprocally related to the contrasting but complementary sex or gender roles into which females are socialized in that same culture, so that the male and female roles require and reinforce each other.

Gender codes reinforce the socialization of girls and women, socializing them to acquiesce in, support, defend, and cling to the traditional set of social roles, and to enforce conformity on other females as well. Restrictions on their freedom to engage in sexual as well as aggressive behavior is the price women pay for their relative freedom from the risk of lethal and life-threatening violence to which men and boys are much more frequently exposed (a dubious bribe, at best, and one which shortchanges women, as more and more women realize).

The outpouring of scholarship across disciplines on the asymmetrical social roles assigned to males and females by the various cultures and civilizations of the world, including our own, has included works in history, economics, literary theory, philosophy, sociology, anthropology, psychology, science, law, religious studies, ethnic studies, and women's studies. One thing all this work has made clear to me (and to many others) is that listening to women (for the first time), and opening up a dialogue between men and women, rather than merely continuing what has throughout most of the history of civilization been primarily a male monologue, is a necessary prerequisite for learning how to transform our civilization into a culture that is compatible with life. And to do that requires that men and women both learn to interact in ways that have simply not been permitted by the gender codes of the past.

My work has focused on the ways in which male gender codes reinforce the socialization of boys and men, teaching them to acquiesce in (and support, defend, and cling to) their own set of social roles, and a code of honor that defines and obligates these roles. Boys and men are exposed thereby to substantially greater frequencies of physical injury, pain, mutilation, disability, and premature death. This code of honor requires men to inflict these same violent injuries on others of both sexes, but most frequently and severely on themselves and other males, whether or not they want to be violent toward anyone of either sex.

Among the most interesting findings reported by social scientists is the fact that men and women stand in a markedly different relationship to the whole system of allotting honor in "cultures of honor." For example, one observation that has been made recurrently is that men are the only possible sources, or active generators (agents), of honor. The only active effect that women can have on honor, in those cultures in which this is a central value, is to destroy it. But women do have that power: They can destroy the honor of the males in their household. The culturally defined symbol system through which women in patriarchies bring honor or dishonor to men is the world of sex—that is, female sexual behavior. In this value system, which is both absurd from any rational standpoint and highly dangerous to the continued survival of our species given its effect of stimulating male violence, men delegate to women the power to bring dishonor on men. That is, men put their honor in the hands of "their" women. The most emotionally powerful means by which women can dishonor men (in this male construction) is by engaging in nonmarital sex, i.e., by being too sexually active or aggressive ("unchaste" or "unfaithful") before, during, or even after marriage.

These themes are prominent in one well-known "culture of honor," for example, the American South. Bertram Wyatt-Brown illustrated this by quoting from a letter Lucius Quintus Cincinnatus Lamar wrote to Mary Chesnut in 1861, in which he compares the men of the South to Homer's heroes, who "fought like brave men, long and well," and then went on to say "We are men, not women." The real tragedy for Lamar, as Wyatt-Brown saw, was that "for him, as for many, the Civil War was reduced to a simple test of manhood."

And women can adopt those same views of manhood, as Mary Chesnut recounts in her diary: " 'Are you like Aunt Mary? Would you be happier if all the men in the family were killed?' To our amazement, quiet Miss C. took up the cudgels—nobly: 'Yes, if their life disgraced them. There are worse things than death.' "[1] These attitudes are exactly the same as those of the men I have known in maximum-security prisons.

That the same relative differences between the two gender roles can be found in many civilizations throughout history and throughout the world emphasizes the importance of understanding that it is men who are expected to be violent, and who are honored for doing so and dishonored for being unwilling to be violent. A woman's worthiness to be honored or shamed is judged by how well she fills her roles in sexually related activities, especially the roles of actual or potential wife and mother. Men are honored for activity (ultimately, violent activity); and they are dishonored for passivity (or pacifism), which renders them vulnerable to the charge of being a non-man ("a wimp, a punk, and a pussy," to quote the phrase that was so central to the identity of the murderer I analyzed in Chapter Three). Women are honored for inactivity or passivity, for not engaging in forbidden activities. They are shamed or dishonored if they are active where they should not be— sexually or in realms that are forbidden (professional ambition, aggres-

siveness, competitiveness and success; or violent activity, such as warfare or other forms of murder). Lady Macbeth, for example, realized
that to commit murder she would have to be "unsex'd," i.e., freed from
the restraints on violence that were imposed on her by virtue of her
belonging to the female sex; and even then, she was unable to commit
murder herself, but had to shame her husband into committing murder
for her, so that she could only participate in violent behavior vicariously
(just as she could only gain honor vicariously, through the honor she
would obtain through being his queen when he became king).

Further evidence that men are violence objects and women, sex
objects, can be found by examining the kinds of crimes that are committed against each sex. Men constitute, on the average, 75 percent or
more of the victims of lethal physical violence in the United States—
homicide, suicide, so-called unintentional injuries (from working in
hazardous occupations, engaging in violent athletic contests, and participating in other high-risk activities), deaths in military combat, and so
on. And throughout the world, men die from all these same forms of
violence from two to five times as often as women do, as the World
Health Organization documents each year. Women, on the other hand,
according to the best available evidence, seem to be the victims of sex
crimes (such as rape and incest) more often than men are. Both men
and women seem to feel that men are more acceptable as objects of
physical violence than women are, for both sexes kill men several times
more often than they kill women. Even in experimental studies conducted by psychologists, both men and women exhibit greater readiness
and willingness to inflict pain on men than on women, under otherwise
identical conditions. Studies of child abuse in those countries in which
reasonably accurate statistics are available find that boys are more often
victims of lethal or life-threatening violent child abuse (being treated as
violence objects), whereas girls are more often victims of sexual abuse
(being treated as sex objects)—with few exceptions. Virtually every nation that has had a military draft has decided either that only men
should be drafted, or that only men should be sent into combat. Again,

none of this should surprise us, given the competition between men for status, valor, bravery, heroism—and honor—in patriarchal societies.

We cannot think about preventing violence without a radical change in the gender roles to which men and women are subjected. The male gender role generates violence by exposing men to shame if they are not violent, and rewarding them with honor when they are. The female gender role also stimulates male violence at the same time that it inhibits female violence. It does this by restricting women to the role of highly unfree sex objects, and honoring them to the degree that they submit to those roles or shaming them when they rebel. This encourages men to treat women as sex objects, and encourages women to conform to that sex role; but it also encourages women (and men) to treat men as violence objects. It also encourages a man to become violent if the woman to whom he is related or married "dishonors" him by acting in ways that transgress her prescribed sexual role.

Since culture is itself constructed, by all of us, if we want to take steps to diminish the amount of violence in our society, both physical and sexual, we can take those steps. To speak of eliminating the sexual asymmetry that casts men and women into opposing sex roles is to speak of liberating both men and women from arbitrary and destructive stereotypes, and to begin treating both women and men as individuals, responding to their individual goals and abilities, rather than to the group (male or female) to which they belong.

There is a deep and tragic paradox about civilization. On the one hand, it has been, up to now, the most life-enhancing innovation the human species has created. The sciences have made it possible for more people to live, and to live longer lives, and to live better lives, freer of pain and illness, cold and hunger, than was ever possible before civilization was invented; and the many forms of art that could not and did not exist except under conditions of civilization are among the main things that make life worth living. But the paradox is that civilization has also increased both the level of human violence, and the scale of the human potential for violence, far beyond anything that any precivilized human culture had done. In the past, the primary threat to human survival was nature, now it is culture. Human suffering before civilization was mainly pathos; since the creation of civilization, it has become, increasingly, tragedy. In fact, it would not be going too far to say that violence is the tragic flaw of civilization. The task confronting us now is to see whether we can end the tragic (violent) element of civilization while maintaining its life-enhancing aspects.

Why has civilization resulted in the most enormous augmentation of human violence since the human species first evolved from its primate forebears? I believe that that question can only be answered by taking into account the psychology of shame. Shame not only motivates destructive behavior, it also motivates constructive behavior. It is the emotion that motivates the ambition and the need for achievement that in turn motivates the invention of civilization.

But—and this is the crux of the matter—this same emotion, shame, that motivates the ambition, activity, and need for achievement that is necessary for the creation of civilization also motivates violence. And when the enormous increase in technological power that civilization brings with it is joined to the enormous increase in violent impulses that shame brings with it, the stage is set for exactly the drama that the history (that is, the civilization) of the world shows us—namely, human social life as an almost uninterrupted, and almost uninterruptedly escalating, series of mass slaughters, "total" and increasingly genocidal wars, and an unprecedented threat to the very continuation not only of civilization itself (which brought this situation about, it cannot be emphasized too strongly) but much more importantly, of the human species for the sake of whose survival civilization was invented in the first place.

Through my clinical work with violent men and my analysis of the psychodynamics of shame and guilt, I have come to view the relationship between civilization and violence in a way that is the diametrical opposite of Freud's. Freud saw violence as an inevitable, spontaneously occurring, natural, innate, instinctual impulse, and civilization and morality as attempts at "taming," neutralizing, inhibiting or controlling that

violent impulse. I see violence, in contrast, as defensive, caused, inter-
pretable, and therefore preventable; and I see civilization, as it has
existed up to now (because of class, caste and age stratification, and
sexual asymmetry), as among the most potent causes of violence.

One of the puzzles of this century is the phenomenon of Nazism:
how could one of the most civilized nations on earth have been capable
of such uncivilized, barbaric behavior? (One could ask the same question about Japan's record in World War II.) But from the perspective
being elaborated here, genocide is not a regression or an aberration
from civilization, or a repudiation of it. It is the inner destiny of civilization, its core tendency—its tragic flaw. Genocide has characterized the
behavior of most of the great world civilizations, from ancient Mesopo-
tamia to Rome, to medieval Europe, to the African slave trade and the
conquest of the Americas, to the Holocaust and atomic weapons.

How to deal with violence, then? The moral value system (which I
will call "shame-ethics") that underlies the code of honor of those patriarchal cultures and subcultures in which behavioral norms are enforced
primarily by the sanctions of shame versus honor, such as the Mafia,
urban street gangs, and much of the rest of American culture, rational-
izes, legitimates, encourages, and even commands violence: it does not
prohibit or inhibit it.

The kind of morality that I am calling guilt-ethics (that says "Thou
shalt not kill") is an attempt at a kind of therapy, an attempt to cure the
human propensity to engage in violence, which is stimulated by shame-
ethics. And that was a noble attempt, which one can only wish had
been successful. Why has it not worked? I think that the analysis of
violence presented in this book can enable us to see the answer to that
question. The reason that guilt-ethics has not solved and cannot solve
the problem of violence is because it does not dismantle the motivational structure that causes violence in the first place (namely, shame,
and the shame-ethics that it motivates). Guilt, and guilt-ethics, merely
changes the direction of the violence that shame has generated, it does
not prevent the violence in the first place. It primarily redirects, onto

the self, the violent impulses that shame generates toward other people. But it does not prevent violence, or even inhibit it. Suicide is no solution to the problem of homicide; both forms of violence are equally lethal. Masochism is no solution to the problem of sadism; both forms of pathology are equally destructive and painful.

Neither shame nor guilt, then, can solve the problem of violence; shame causes hate, which becomes violence (usually toward other people), and guilt merely redirects it (usually onto the self). But to say simply that we need more love, and less shame and guilt, is vacuous. What we really need is to be able to specify the conditions that can enable love to grow without being inhibited by either shame or guilt. And it is clear that shame and guilt do inhibit love. Shame inhibits people from loving others, because shame consists of a deficiency of self-love, and thus it motivates people to withdraw love from others and ration it for the self. Guilt, on the other hand, inhibits self-love, or pride, which the Christian guilt-ethic calls the deadliest of the seven deadly sins. Guilt motivates people to hate themselves, not love themselves, because the feeling of guilt is the feeling that one is guilty and therefore deserves punishment (pain, hate), not reward (pleasure, love).

If we approach violence as a problem in public health and preventive medicine then we need to ask: What are the conditions that stimulate shame and guilt on a socially and epidemiologically significant scale? The conditions that are most important are relative poverty, race and age discrimination, and sexual asymmetry. If we wish to prevent violence, then, our agenda is political and economic reform.

The social policies that would be most effective in preventing violence are those that would reduce the amount of shame. To reduce the amount of shame, we need to reduce the intensity of the passive, dependent regressive wishes that stimulate shame. And to reduce the intensity of those wishes, we must gratify those wishes, by taking better care of each other, especially the neediest among us—particularly beginning in childhood, when the needs for love and care are most intense and peremptory. To quote again the phrase that Dostoevsky put in the mouth of Father Zossima, we then would recognize that "all are responsible for all."

We have a horror of dependency in this country—particularly dependency on the part of men. No wonder we have so much violence—especially male violence. For the horror of dependency is what causes violence. The emotion that causes the horror of dependency is shame. Men, much more than women, are taught that to want love or care from others is to be passive, dependent, unaggressive and unambitious or, in short, unmanly; and that they will be subjected to shaming, ridicule, and disrespect if they appear unmanly in the eyes of others. Women, by contrast, have traditionally been taught that they will be honored if, and only if, they accept a role that restricts them to the relatively passive aim of arranging to be loved by men and to depend on men for their social and economic status, foregoing or severely limiting or disguising activity, ambition, independence, and initiative of their own. This set of injunctions decreases women's vulnerability to behaving violently, but it also inhibits women from participating actively or directly in the building of civilization, in part by reducing them to the role of men's sex objects.

We Americans, as a society, appear to be horrified by the thought that a man could be dependent on anyone (other than himself), and that a woman could be dependent on anyone (other than "her man," that is, her father or husband). The extent of our horror of dependency can be seen in our horror of what is somewhat misleadingly called "welfare dependency"—whether it is the "dependency" on society of an unemployed or disabled man, of an unmarried mother, or of a child without a father. This conceals, or rather reveals, that we as a nation do less for our own citizens than does any other democracy on earth; less health care, child care, housing, support to families, and so on. So that we end up shaming and blaming those whose needs are exposed. Therefore it is not surprising that we also have more violence

than does any other democracy on earth, as well as more imprisonment—since we shame some people for having needs that all people
have.

For needs that are repressed do not get met, nor do they just disappear. The return of repressed needs, in unconscious, disguised form, is
what the various symptoms of psychopathology consist of. One form in
which repressed needs for care return is chronic institutionalization—
that is, long-term imprisonment or mental hospitalization—which allows us as a society to punish massively, while we gratify grudgingly,
those needs of which we are so intolerant.

In fact, the violence of our society reveals our shame at being less
"independent" than we "declared" ourselves to be two centuries ago. In
contemporary America, to want love, to depend on others, to be less
than completely self-sufficient, is to be shamed by all the institutions of
our society, from welfare offices to mental hospitals to prisons. One can
pretend that one is in an institution only because one is so tough and
dangerous and scary, so active and aggressive, and so independent of
the community's standards, that the courts insisted on locking one up
against one's own wishes. But nevertheless, it is true that for many men
in our society it is only in prison that one is given three meals a day, a
warm bed to sleep in at night, a roof over one's head, and people who
care enough about one to make sure that one is there every night.

Those are among the reasons why the most effective way to increase
the amount of violence and crime is to do exactly what we have been
doing increasingly over the past decades, namely, to permit—or rather,
to force—more and more of our children and adults to be poor, ne-
glected, hungry, homeless, uneducated, and sick. What is particularly
effective in increasing the amount of violence in the world is to widen
the gap between the rich and the poor. We have not restricted that
strategy to this country, but are practicing it on a worldwide scale,
among the increasingly impoverished nations of the third world; and we
can well expect it to culminate in increasing levels of violence, all over
the world.

Relative poverty—poverty for some groups coexisting with wealth for others—is much more effective in stimulating shame, and hence violence, than is a level of poverty that is higher in absolute terms but is universally shared. Shame exists in the eye of the beholder—though it is more likely to exist there if the beheld is perceived as richer and more powerful than oneself. In that archaic, prescientific language called morality, this gap is called injustice; but most people throughout the world still think in moral terms, and the perception that one is a victim of injustice is what causes shame, which in turn causes violence.

From the standpoint of public health, then, the social psychology of shame, discrimination, and violence becomes central to any preventive psychiatry. The causes and consequences of the feelings of shame as well as their psychodynamic parameters have become more urgently compelling as a focus of investigation, given the potential ultimacy of violence in a nuclear age, as well as the continuing high rate of violence in American society. In my analysis of the psychological consequences of the feelings of shame, I have set out to show how such seemingly trivial events as personal experiences of chagrin or embarrassment can explode into epidemics of violence, just as the physical consequences of organisms as insignificant as microbes can have the gravest implications for public health. As Rudolph Virchow, who helped to lay the foundations of preventive medicine and public health more than a century ago, put it, "Medicine is a social science, and politics is simply medicine on a larger scale."

If cleaning up sewer systems could prevent more deaths than all the physicians in the world, then perhaps reforming the social, economic, and legal institutions that systematically humiliate people can do more to prevent violence than all the preaching and punishing in the world. The task before us now is to integrate the psychodynamic understanding of shame and guilt with the broader social and economic factors that intensify those feelings to murderous and suicidal extremes on a mass scale.

Civilization

and Its

Malcontents

"On my father's farm there are many acres," thought the boy, gallop-
ing his horse over rolling green pastures in the Missouri River valley to a
hilltop below which the land spread out before him beyond the horizon,
across Nebraska into Kansas, Iowa, Missouri: fecund, rich breasts of land
from which flowed real milk and real honey. "Yes, this is the Promised
Land that Moses only dreamed of," he thought, as he rested in the shade of
a tree to rest his sweating horse and refresh himself. As his fingers idly
played in the rich earth under the tree, he found just below the surface an
Indian arrowhead—unmistakable, beautifully chiseled—and thought, "We
are living on their land! They were here only a lifetime ago. I have seen
their pictures in a history painting on the landing of the great pillared
mansion, Arbor Lodge, celebrating their signing away their land to us. But
we made them do it! It was 'Sign or die!'—and die they did, whether they
signed or not. So we stole their land and murdered them. How strange—
they say to me in church 'Thou shalt not kill or steal,' but that does not
stop us from owning, farming, even loving this beautiful land that they
loved too, so much that they refused to let anyone own it, lest they rape it;
and which we got by stealing and killing. So we fertilized it with their

blood and bones," just as the armies of Hitler he saw rolling across the movie screen on the March of Time *every week did the same thing: raping the green pastures of Belgium, France, Poland, Russia—landscapes of Europe so much like our own. And then he thought, "Why are my friends' fathers and older brothers dying in Europe to stop Hitler? It is because we know what he would do if he won, because he is already doing it even before he has won. He would kill everyone he didn't like, and then he would make Slavs slaves. That is what their name means, and to him 'nomen est omen,' a name is a thing—and so are people. He can't distinguish between words and things and people, just like our neighbor, 'the old crazy woman,' who lives on my street, who chases us off her sidewalk because we might make it dirty; and who sweeps the dirt off it all day, because that is how she sweeps the dirty thoughts out of her mind that torment her. She thinks dirty thoughts are dirty things, and vice versa, so we walk in the street instead of the sidewalk when we go past her house. So no wonder Hitler is cruel: he treats words like things, and people like words, Slavs like slaves. So of course he ends up treating people like things. And yes, he is more dangerous by far than she is—but she is no crazier than he is! We also know there are other people he wants to kill, not just enslave. He hates the Jews and Gypsies, the halt and the lame. The ones he would kill are the ones who cannot defend themselves. Like any bully he wants to kill those who are weaker than he is. So why does he feel so weak he has to do that?*

"And then we think what it would be like if he won. A hundred years from now, the descendants of his soldiers would be sitting under a tree on the plains of Bohemia or Moldavia, just as I am here, enjoying the beauty of the land. And would they notice, would they care, that it had been purchased with the blood of the people they had displaced, whose survivors were now herded like cattle onto reservations, or enslaved, or simply all killed? And just as he invaded the East for Lebensraum, *so my ancestors invaded the West for Lebensraum. And just as he enslaved millions, so my ancestors enslaved millions. And just as he killed whole races of people, so*

my ancestors exterminated entire tribes of Indians—every man, woman, and child. 'The only good injun is a dead injun,' goes the old motto of the West. So the authentic voice of genocide runs like a bloody thread throughout the whole tapestry of our history, just as much as it does through our enemies', the Germans and the Japs. And here I am, finding arrowheads beneath a tree on my father's farm, just as some German child a hundred years from now would find a Star of David in the same location in the plains of eastern Europe—and with the same significance and meaning."

When I first realized that I, and all other Americans, were living on and enjoying land that we had stolen from other people, by the simple expedient of killing any who resisted, and that this had happened no more than one long lifetime ago on the land my family owned, it set in motion a skepticism about the received, conventional notions of crime and punishment, justice and injustice, property and theft, legal and illegal, that I finally found expressed in Tolstoy's great novel about nine-teenth-century Russian prisons, *Resurrection.* In that book he puts into the mouth of an old, half-crazy prisoner a speech that perfectly sums up how I felt about myself and my ancestors, in relation to those who were native to the American plains. The old man mutters semicoherently, when some visitors enter the room he is in, that his jailers were Antichrist, and when an English visitor to the prison asks the narrator what he said, he tells him that

the old man was blaming the superintendent for keeping men in prison. "Ask him what he thinks ought to be done with those who refuse to obey the law," said the Englishman. The old man broke into an odd laugh, displaying two rows of sound teeth. "The Law!" he repeated contemptuously. "First he robbed everybody, taking for himself all the land and all the wealth that belonged to the

people—converted it all to his own use—killed all those who resisted him, and then wrote laws forbidding men to rob and kill.
He should have made the laws first."[1]

I do not say all this in the spirit of feeling that I have any solutions to
the moral inheritance we were bequeathed by our ancestors. But I
would hope that some reflection on that tragic inheritance would temper our American tendency to be self-righteous and punitive. It could
remind us that a spirit of generosity and giving is not inappropriate,
given that we have what we have not because it was given to us, but
because we stole it. Perhaps it would remind us that the death of God
is such a tragedy not because we no longer have anyone to uphold the
moral law but because we have no one who is capable of forgiving us.

No one, of course, can be held morally responsible for what his or
her ancestors did, but we are morally responsible, and therefore criminally responsible, for continuing to live on and enjoy the advantages of
land that was obtained through armed robbery and mass murder. And
yet that way of formulating the American condition runs the risk of
oversimplifying the moral complexity of our history. To begin with, one
cannot equate all Americans with all other Americans. The slaves from
Africa were brought here against their will, for example, and many new
immigrants to America are refugees who fled here to save their lives,
after undergoing atrocities themselves that were so appalling that they
certainly have no (rational) reason to feel any personal guilt. Many of
these new immigrants' own land was stolen, and they themselves are
refugees from attempted murder. And the same is true of the original
immigrant ancestors of most of those whose families have lived here for
generations, including my own. Nobody's ancestors left other countries
to come here because things were going so well for them in their home-
land. Most people came here because they knew they were in danger of
starvation, pogrom, warfare, or genocide. They came here to save their
lives, leaving behind friends and relatives many of whom did perish by
virtue of staying where they were. So most of the ancestors of ours who

murdered and robbed the native Americans were themselves victims of theft and attempted murder in the countries from which they came.

But that same moral complexity and ambiguity applies to the violent men, and occasional women, who murder and rob the "native Americans" of today—who murder and rob us, or our friends and relatives. In other words, the people who murder and rob today, whom we call "criminals," are just as desperate, for the most part, just as traumatized, just as much victims of robbery and attempted murder themselves, as my own ancestors, pioneers and cowboys, were when they went about killing earlier generations of native Americans, or Indians, in order to have a piece of land to live on.

History is a tragedy, not a morality play; American history, which like all history is largely a story of violence,[2] is a tragedy, not a morality play. It cannot—except at the cost of a moral oversimplification which itself does violence to reality—be reduced to a tale of good Indians versus bad cowboys (or vice versa), or of good Indians and bad Puritans (or vice versa), or of good cops and bad robbers (or vice versa). Violence is a tragedy, in which everyone involved is exposed and vulnerable to the risk of moral corruption and physical destruction. But violence also reveals the tragic flaw of civilization.

It is remarkable to me how seldom people recognize the extent to which many of the criminals of today are contemporary versions of our own ancestors. For example, in my current home state, Massachusetts, I vary between being amused and bemused by the moral indignation with which some politicians who happen to be Boston Brahmins denounce the scandalous behavior of young male drug dealers. These young men are, of course, classic examples of capitalist entrepreneurs, whom one would think would be extolled by these Bostonians as role models for their peers. They are, after all, making fortunes by their business activities, with tremendous returns on relatively small investments, and they often manage to save and invest their considerable earnings as conscientiously as did the Brahmins' own ancestors. The fact is that the ancestors of the latter group made the fortunes on which their descendants are now living (comfortably enough that they do not need to deal drugs) by means of the seventeenth- and eighteenth-century equivalents of drug-dealing, such as slave-trafficking, opium-smuggling, rum-running, and killing. If they had not engaged in it, their descendants would certainly not be wealthy enough to have the moral luxury of denouncing the "criminality" of the young African-American, Latino, and Asian-American men who are busy accumulating their own fortunes in equivalent ways today.

What I have said about today's drug dealers is not meant to minimize or trivialize the devastation that the epidemic of drug abuse causes in the inner-city ghettoes. These illegal drugs do almost as much damage to health as alcohol and tobacco, the legal drugs, do. On the other hand, they do not do nearly as much harm as another legal commodity does—namely, guns. So I do not mean to minimize the harm the drug dealers do. I simply want to point out that the harm the early white settlers of New England and other regions of America did to their neighbors was certainly at least as devastating as anything the street gangs of today are doing.

What is the nature of our tragic flaw as a nation, the flaw that has resulted in our uniquely high levels of criminal violence? I think it is the same as Captain Ahab's, which is why he is my model of our flawed American character. I would describe the flaw as a Puritanical kind of moralism and punitiveness, which is generated by the illusion that "we" have a monopoly on the knowledge of good and evil (conveniently forgetting what happened to the last couple who ate the fruit of the tree of that name), and that we know that "we" are good and "they" are evil. And lest it be thought that since Ahab was a man he represents only the male minority in the population, it is worth remembering that unless the female majority voted as it did, the Captain Ahabs of this country would never attain power.

I was reminded of the tragedy of Captain Ahab when I had occasion to talk with a young man whose own tragic story took place in the world from which Melville came. It seemed to exemplify and synthesize many of the themes I have been developing in this book. It is a story about a young man—a boy, really—that unfolds in a prosperous and historic New England fishing village from which, according to Melville, some of the crew members of the *Pequod* came; a lovely town of trees and gardens whose streets are lined by the Greek-revival mansions of whaling-ship captains. In fact, the contrast between the loveliness of the setting and the tragedy of this young man and his family added, for me, to the sadness of what happened.

This young man, the protagonist of our story, exemplifies the most central theme in my discussion of violence, the importance of shame in the etiology of violent behavior. Indeed, he illustrates the predictive power of that theory of violence. Matthew T. was the nineteen-year-old son of a clergyman who presided over an affluent and socially prominent parish in this pleasant and peaceful town. A few years before, Matthew's father had fallen in love with one of his parishioners, and eventually he and she both divorced their respective spouses and married each other. Matthew felt that his mother was deeply distressed and hurt by this, stricken and humiliated. As he saw it, her sense of abandonment and aloneness, of feeling that everyone wanted to discard her, to make her simply disappear, was only exacerbated when she was visited by two of his father's fellow clergymen, who told her that her husband's behavior was God's will and even that his love for someone else might be considered holy—after all, God commanded us to love one another—so she should be a good Christian and accept his need to begin a new life without her. Eventually, as it happened, higher authorities in the church took a more serious view of the matter and barred Matthew's father from serving as a clergyman. Nevertheless, he continued to live in this small town with his new wife, not far from where Matthew and his mother and siblings continued to live, as a result of which, Matthew felt, his mother's humiliation was made complete by the fact that she inevitably saw his father and his new wife together frequently and publicly.

Since childhood, Matthew had been the problem child in the family.

Socially and physically awkward, he was less popular and did less well
in school than his better-adjusted siblings. In fact, he was something of
a loner and generally felt unable to keep up with his classmates as they
progressed from one social task to another, from athletics to dating. In
his unhappiness and loneliness, he became involved with drugs and
alcohol, got in minor scrapes with the law, and was visibly depressed.
Actually, this was not always the case. Although he found that his
family's frequent moves from one parish to another made it more difficult to be accepted by his classmates, he had actually found a sense of
belonging in the town where they had lived before moving to the sea-
coast village in which this tragedy occurred. It was after this move that
Matthew felt he could not keep up with the "faster" crowd in his new
high school. His life, and the life of his whole family, spiraled helplessly
downward.

His father left his mother a year or two after their move to the new
town, during Matthew's adolescence. This left Matthew with a bitter
question in his mind: If his father had valued his career so much more
highly than he did Matthew's need to stay in one place, then why was
he so ready to sacrifice that same career the moment he wanted to live
with a different woman? Matthew began to develop the feeling that his
father simply wanted him to disappear, and wanted his mother to do
the same. As Freud saw, a child's perception that he is not loved generates feelings of inferiority, or shame; and if he has not yet matured to
the point where he has internal or relatively autonomous sources of
self-respect and self-love, he may be dangerously vulnerable to experiences or incidents that leave him feeling unloved by others, especially
by a parent.

It was in the context of his turmoil that he was admitted to one of
the university teaching hospitals, in the nearest large city, where they
concluded: "He feels as if he has not lived up to parental expectations;
however, he is confused about what these may be. . . . His shame
over failing is overwhelming to him. He feels that he must conceal
these internal realities, by wearing masks. His present feelings of de-

pression appear to be binding his anger for him. In the examiner's judgment, this patient's potential for suicide is moderate, and his potential for physical violence is not significant."

In the light of what I have said earlier in this book, that psychological assessment—that his shame over failing was overwhelming to him—can now be recognized as a red flag warning us that his potential for physical violence was highly significant. If the solid, undifferentiated black nuclei in cells under the microscope are markers for carcinoma, so shame is the marker in a psychological test report of the presence of the potential for violence.

After he left the hospital, Matthew's emotional and behavior problems worsened. One night in a suicide attempt, he got drunk and drove the family car over a sand dune onto an ocean beach. He was hospitalized again, this time at a small unlocked public mental health center located nearer his home. Not long after arriving there, he "escaped" from this facility (that is, he opened an unlocked door and walked out, realizing that they did not even care enough about his life to lock the door) and returned to his home town, where he presented himself that evening at the door of his father's new house and said he needed to talk with him. His father, who knew that Matthew had recently made a suicide attempt, had been hospitalized for it, was officially on "escape" status from the hospital, and wanted (or needed) to talk with him, told Matthew that he and his new wife were going to the movies and would not postpone that, so that Matthew would have to wait until they returned to talk with him. Matthew felt rejected, humiliated, and angry. He felt he had revealed his wish to be close to his father, his need for his father, and had been rebuffed.

In a state of rage and despair, he took out a shotgun that his father kept in the house, loaded both barrels, and waited for his father to return, sitting in a chair directly facing the door through which his father would enter the house. As soon as his father returned, Matthew shot him with the first barrel. His father was knocked over by the blow, and Matthew then walked over and shot him with the other one. Still alive, his father managed to make it down the street and crawl into the reception hall of a stately old whaling-captain's mansion that had been turned into an elegant hotel, with exquisite art and antiques shops flanking the entrance. Matthew in the meantime reloaded the shotgun and pursued his father. When he saw him lying on the floor inside the front door of the mansion, he shot directly through the glass door-panes to kill him with two final blasts. He then waited for the police to arrive, and after he was arrested and arraigned in court, he was sent to the hospital for violent mentally ill men that I directed.

There I was ordered by the court to perform a psychiatric evaluation of Matthew in order to assist the judge in deciding what had been going on in his mind at the time he had allegedly shot his father to death—for "guilt resides in the intention," as Edmund Burke put it in the eighteenth century, so the question of his legal guilt, or "criminal responsibility," hinged on the issue of whether or not he had killed his father with an "evil mind," or in other words, with "evil intentions"; or whether he "lacked the substantial capacity to appreciate the wrongfulness (criminality) of his conduct, or to conform his conduct to the requirements of the law." If either of the latter two conditions were the case, the court would have to find him not guilty by reason of insanity, and he could be committed to the hospital (rather than being sent to prison), but only for as long as the court continued to find that he was a danger to himself or others by reason of mental illness, at the end of which time he could be released to return to the community.

The most extraordinary thing about Matthew was how ordinary he appeared. He was not someone anyone would ever pick out of a crowd, as either a raving maniac, a dangerous criminal, a rebellious adolescent, a fanatic, or, at the other extreme, a young man with any extraordinary personal assets either. He was of medium height and build, seemed rather shy and diffident, and in no way presented a threatening or belligerent appearance, nor one that was at all unusual.

But the moment I began talking to him it quickly became apparent how sad, lonely, and lost he was, and how confused and inadequate he felt. There was a winsome quality to him, and it seemed to me that he was still looking for a father to attach himself to. I could understand why the psychologist who had evaluated him the year before had been struck by his relative immaturity; he acted and appeared younger than nineteen, did not show much self-confidence, seemed naive for his age, and even he mentioned how hard he had found it to "keep up with" his peers. He spoke of them as being "faster" than he was, more socially sophisticated. For example—and he felt painfully lonely and inadequate because of this—he had never had a satisfying ongoing romantic relationship with a girlfriend. I spent several hours listening to Matthew tell me the story of his life, and his father's death.

Some eight or nine months after I submitted my report to the court, Matthew went on trial for murder. The courthouse was the most prominent building in the same town in which Matthew and his family had been living when he killed his father. It was located a few blocks from their house on the main street in a large, impressive edifice whose classical columns and pediment symbolized the continuity of Western law and justice since the time of ancient Greece and Rome. This building represented intellectual and moral structure; it was the embodiment not only of justice, but of the whole historical tradition of justice since the Greeks.

I thought of all this as I walked up the steps to testify at Matthew's trial as to whether or not he had an "evil mind," a *mens rea*—or at least, whether he had had such a mind at the time he pulled the trigger of his father's shotgun. Unless he did, the law decreed it would be an injustice to hold him responsible for what he had done, and he could not be found guilty of murder. And naturally, the whole community, so stunned by the first murder in that town in thirty years, wondered the same thing—what had been going on in his mind when he killed his father?—in order to find some way to begin to make sense of what had happened. For until they could understand it, they could not heal the wounds this had inflicted on them all, not just on their sense of trust in their neighbors but of a moral order in the universe.

Did it make sense to think of the outrage this young man had committed, not only against his father but against the sensibilities of the whole community, as a product of evil, or an evil mind? Should our response to it attempt to replace injustice with justice? Thinking in those ancient moral and legal terms at least had the virtue of redeeming the faith that what happened in the world was not simply random or meaningless. Evil and injustice as concepts make everything else understandable as well, promising a moral order to the universe. People had a need to understand what had happened, I felt, and why it had happened, that went far deeper than just their need to be reassured that "justice would be done." They also needed to find a way to understand why an injustice had been done and to find a way to think not only about the murder but about the whole sequence of events that led up to it, and make sense of it.

The wholeness and integrity of a community is violated when one of its members commits an act of serious violence against another. Participating in this elaborate communal legal ritual, I came to understand as I never had before the important function a criminal trial performs for a community rent asunder by such an act of violence. What I discovered as one of the actors in this trial was how similar it was to what I imagine a Greek tragedy must have been for the citizens of ancient Athens, when the entire populace crowded into a hillside amphitheater to see their deepest fears dramatized on stage, their deepest pity elicited.

Everyone knew this family (I should say, both families); many had been parishioners of the dead father. And the offense itself constituted what to many since the rise of patriarchy has seemed the most shocking crime of all, parricide. But in this case the father also had transgressed communal norms and expectations, had violated his own role as husband and father. In the eyes of Matthew and of the community, he had also violated his role as a man of God, repeating the commandment against adultery from the pulpit while pursuing a woman who was not only a member of his parish but who was married to another of his parishioners. Then he added insult to injury by publicly divorcing his

wife and marrying the other man's wife—all while continuing to live in
the same small town, and even presiding over the same parish.

To gauge the strength of feelings in the culture of New England
about this kind of behavior, one need only think of Melville's friend
Nathaniel Hawthorne, and his account of the adulterous relationship
between Reverend Dimmesdale and Hester Prynne. In that version of
the same story, the pastor was aware that he would certainly suffer
social death, if not physical death as well, if the community ever
learned what he had done, so he did not dare reveal it—especially after
he saw the public humiliation to which his lover was subjected, the
least of which was her being forced to wear the scarlet letter "A." He
may have felt guilty toward her, ashamed of his own cowardice, and
tormented by the frustration of his love for her, but none of those
feelings, alone or in combination, was powerful enough to induce him
openly to break the multiple taboos he had violated. Even today, one
does not lightly break those taboos in the towns and villages of New
England.

Every seat in the courtroom, this modern-day Graeco-Roman amphitheater, was filled by a cross-section of the whole community, who
came perhaps to witness what would be the last act of this tragedy;
perhaps to experience a catharsis of the pity and terror that Matthew's
outrageous act had aroused in them. But even more than that, I felt,
they came in the hope of finding some explanation that would make
sense of what seemed like such a senseless waste of human life, such a
senseless infliction of suffering. Matthew was there, impassive, seated
next to his lawyer. Just behind them were members of the clergy, colleagues of the dead father, identified by their white collars. Both griev-
ing wives were there: Matthew's mother, dressed modestly in a plain
blue dress and simple flat shoes, the second wife wearing sunglasses
and an elegant print dress with a smart straw hat, a matching handbag,
and tastefully designed shoes. And then the town: teachers and former
classmates who had known Matthew in high school until a year or two
before; members of the dead man's former parish, some weeping; po-

licemen who would be called as witnesses, journalists who were taking
it all down, friends of the families, shopkeepers and store clerks who
knew them all; and, entering one by one, when their names were called,
a "pool" of more than forty candidates for the jury, drawn at random
from the entire township, but none of them strangers to anyone in the
room. In fact, most of the prospective jurors had to be eliminated,
because they knew the defendant and his family too well. Eventually,
however, they selected a group that the judge and lawyers agreed could
be as objective as human beings can be—and the trial proceeded.

I had been accepted by the prosecuting attorney, the defense attorney, and the judge as the person who would try to help them decide
what Matthew's mental state had been at the time he killed his father.
What I was first struck by, however, when I rose to testify, was the
prominent presence of the clergymen in the courtroom, Matthew's late
father's colleagues. Given the central concepts and symbols of the
Christian religion, could the irony have been any more complete? For
this trial, like the religion they represented, and in which a major con-
tributing factor was the father's exercise of, and subsequent betrayal of,
his religious vocation, centered on a Father and a Son, the Son and the
Father, and the relationship between them. In the religious version, the
Father sacrifices the Son (or gives the Son as a sacrifice) for the sake of
the human community. In the version involving Matthew and his father, however, something had gone awry. The son did feel that his
father had sacrificed him (his mother as well), but in the father's own
interest, not for the sake of the community; Matthew felt sacrificed first
for the sake of his father's career, and then for the sake of gratifying his
wish to share his bed with a new wife. So this son responded by sacrificing his father. But in doing so he felt that he was, ironically, hewing
more closely to the original religious model. For he was also, in a sense,
sacrificing his victim for the sake of the human community, not merely
for himself: for his mother, whose humiliation he was avenging and
attempting to undo; for his whole family, whose honor and integrity he

was standing up for; and for the community at large, whose trust in each other had been shaken by Matthew's father's behavior.

But of course this formulation of the killing—which derives directly from Matthew's comments about the meaning of his father's behavior and his own—constitutes a role reversal; Matthew sacrifices the Father, and his father becomes the sacrificed Son. This fact is the crucial key in unlocking the mystery, which is simultaneously, equally, psychological, moral, legal, and religious: Why did this son feel that he needed to kill this father at this time—and not just needed to, but felt that he had a right to, and even an obligation to? What was the full meaning of this act to him?

The first to testify were the policemen who had first arrived at the scene where the shooting culminated, where Matthew was still holding his smoking shotgun over the bloody corpse of his father, in front of the shattered glass of the old whaling mansion, as impassive as if he had merely been out shooting squirrels. I realize that the older you get, the younger everyone else looks, but even for me, a man in his forties as I was then, the policemen looked remarkably young—even innocent, as though they had stumbled by sheer accident onto one of the outer reaches of human behavior, for which they were not prepared. They described their total bafflement, their amazement and incomprehension, at Matthew's utter calm; he betrayed neither rage nor fear, shame nor guilt, grief nor sadness—no feelings at all. They had the hardest time making sense of this fact.

At the hospital, Matthew had told me that he had been completely without feelings, except, perhaps, for a sense of relief. The policemen's testimony raised a question that was in everyone's mind: Did this emotional numbness, which Matthew's demeanor in the courtroom seemed to confirm, mean that he was heartless and unfeeling, an evil monster, a zombie, or what? He did not look like a monster either, but how could someone do what he did and then feel nothing about it? and how could one even begin to think about this and understand it?

When my turn came to testify, I began by describing the sequence of events leading up to the shooting, the essentials of which I have already mentioned. I tried to explain how people who feel so overwhelmed by shame as to be capable of killing someone else can feel emotionally dead and numb themselves, and how that can even be one reason they commit homicide. It also explains why they can then be without feelings over behavior that would fill most people with grief and remorse. And I described something Matthew had said some months earlier, about his state of mind at the time he killed his father. He described a delusional belief he had developed during the weeks before the killing, when he was in a state of acute emotional turmoil over his father's treatment of him and his mother. It seemed to me to express, in a symbolic, indirect, but understandable manner how he saw the problem between him and his father. Matthew believed that each day his father lived subtracted one day from his (Matthew's) life and added one to his father's. His father was in effect stealing his life from him, a day at a time, a year at a time, a decade at a time, and the only way he could survive, and reclaim his own life, was to kill his father.

When I thought about it, I realized that what that delusion was "saying" was that Matthew saw his father as exchanging roles and ages with him; for his father was getting younger (in time, he would reach Matthew's age), and Matthew was getting older, that is, closer to death, so that in time he would reach his father's age. And that was what Matthew felt his father had done by getting married, and leaving Matthew to take care of his mother and siblings. Matthew felt that he himself was the one who was at an age to be getting on with the business of finding a mate, that that was appropriate for a young man; whereas his father should have been at home, with Matthew's mother. Instead, his father was getting married again, as if he were the young man, and Matthew was the one left with the responsibility to meet his mother's needs. So the delusion summed up Matthew's sense that his father had walked out on his role as the father and was acting like the adolescent in the family, an impression that was powerfully reinforced when his father would not even postpone seeing a movie with his new wife when his son had just escaped from the mental hospital to which he had been committed following a suicide attempt. So there was method in his "madness."

Let me reflect for a moment about the implications of understanding Matthew and his parricidal behavior in this way. The law allows three possible responses to someone in Matthew's position: bad (guilty), not-bad (innocent: he did not do it, or doing it was justifiable), or mad (not guilty by reason of insanity). These choices may be adequate for the court's purpose, insofar as it is a purely legal one. But if we are approaching violence as a problem in public health and preventive medicine, in which our purpose is to understand the causes and prevention of violence, these choices are limited. At Matthew's trial, the first two of those choices, it seemed to me, would have restricted us to an oversimplified view of the world: either he was all-good or all-bad. The third choice, however, was equally unsatisfactory, for it seemed to me to restrict us to seeing Matthew as just a sick brain, saying that he had inherited twisted genes or contracted a brain disease. We would not have to listen closely to what he tells us, take his thoughts seriously on their own terms, or make an effort to understand the meaning of his behavior to him: what he meant to accomplish by it, why he wanted to accomplish it; and why that behavior seemed to him to be the best way to attain his goals. When internists or surgeons treat only their patients' diseased organs, rather than treating them (the whole human beings whom their patients actually are), they are rightly criticized as being poor physicians. It is especially important, then, for psychiatrists (who are physicians of the soul, meaning the mind and personality, the whole human being, not just a physical organ like the brain) to avoid doing this.

All of the ways of talking about and labeling Matthew—the moral/legal, bad/not-bad, and the forensic psychiatric, mad/not-mad—constituted ways of not listening to Matthew, of not hearing what he was saying to us by his parricidal behavior and through his delusional beliefs. For what more is there to say about someone as a person, what more is there to understand about him as a human being, once we have labeled him as simply evil or insane, monstrous or crazy, inhuman or maniacal? If someone's crime was a product of his evil mind, what can his thoughts about his crime be but evil thoughts? Conversely, if it was a product of his crazy, irrational mind, what can his thoughts about it be except crazy and irrational? And how can one take either evil or crazy thoughts seriously?

Labels like bad or mad, "guilty" or "insane," may or may not serve a useful function for legal purposes. But if our purpose is to learn about the causes and prevention of violence, then the labels simply enable us to close the door on someone, lock him away and never have to listen to him, understand him, or think further about him. In fact, these labels serve as substitutes for psychological understanding.

Both moral value judgments and psychiatric diagnoses can serve as excuses with which to justify the unwillingness to listen to, and take seriously on its own terms, what another person says, to think what it means to that person, and to do the difficult and often emotionally painful work that genuine understanding requires.

Calling Matthew evil, calling him mad, or even calling him innocent (after he has just killed his father), help us to avoid listening to him and letting him tell us the meaning to him of his behavior. And the only way I knew of to follow him into the world he had entered, so he would not be all alone there, was to make the attempt to understand both his lethal behavior and his so-called "delusion" as meaningful statements which in fact made an understandable comment about realities in his life. That seemed to me the only way to respond to his situation as one of tragedy, rather than melodrama or pathos. In fact, what I am describing here is what I would call a psychoanalytic as opposed to either a moralistic (bad guys vs. good guys) or a psychiatric (mad guys vs. bad guys) approach to both his violent behavior and his psychotic "symptoms." And perhaps that may clarify why I referred to psychoanalysis as the only modern approach to the human psyche and human life that I knew of that was capable of responding to and understanding its tragic dimension.

But in saying this, I am taking psychoanalysis into a place that it has not gone before. Just as most psychoanalysts have not gone near prisons, most of analytic theory has not gone near violence. Only when you go into violence and its logic can you see the heart of darkness at the center of the psychology of civilization.

I have detailed this at such length because it would be terrible for us not to listen to Matthew, for at least three reasons. The first was because he had already said, as clearly as he could, that the main reason he killed his father when he did—the immediate precipitant, or proximate cause, of his decision to take his father's shotgun out of the gun closet and shoot him when he returned—was precisely because his father had not been willing to listen to him, to hear out what he had to say. So we would only be repeating his exposure to the very pathogen that had precipitated his lethal (psycho)pathology in the first place. Second, because the people in Matthew's town, including his own family, would learn nothing that would enable them to make sense of an irreparable tear in the fabric of the family and the community, so they could heal their wounds (or at least be able to live with them)—for what is incomprehensible is incurable. And third, because if we did not hear what he was trying to say, we could never learn anything from him that might eventually help us to understand the causes of violence well enough to improve our ability to anticipate and prevent it.

After considering all the testimony, mine and the other participants', and the questioning and cross-examining, the jury of his peers found Matthew not guilty of the murder of his father by reason of insanity, and he was ordered by the court to remain at the maximum-security hospital until such time as he was determined no longer to be dangerous to himself or others by reason of his mental illness.

At the conclusion of the trial, Matthew, his mother, and his siblings each came up to me, separately, and thanked me—Matthew's mother, for making it possible for the people of the community to understand

Matthew, even with his terrible violence. She could now understand
how the same pressures, despair, and desperation that had led him to
try to end his own life by driving his car over a cliff could have led him
to shoot his father to death—not because he was "evil," or because he
had inherited some bad gene or twisted molecule, but because such an
act made a twisted kind of sense to him, and in fact represented the
only possible way he knew of to act in accordance with the sense he
had made of his life. If we could understand the sense that his delusion
and his act made to him, no matter how twisted the thought or how
horrifying the act, Matthew was no longer some weird and incomprehensible monster who had no recognizable connection with the rest of
us and deserved only to be anathematized, damned to hell, expelled
from membership in humanity. He was a severely troubled and desperately unhappy boy, some of the sources of whose desperation and unhappiness anyone could understand, who could now be reincluded in
the human race, even if he did have to stay in a mental hospital for the
indefinite future. But Matthew's siblings spoke in even more personal
terms; they said that what I had explained in the courtroom had enabled them to understand their brother for the first time—not just since
the murder, but even before the murder—and to see what he had been
going through. Matthew himself simply said that he was grateful that I
had enabled all those other people—his siblings and the community at
large—to grasp why he had felt he had to do what he did.

Much is written about "community psychiatry," by people interested
in social and preventive psychiatry. This trial exemplified for me how
central a role nonpsychiatric institutions, such as the criminal justice
system, can play in accomplishing tasks that help a whole population
recover from its collectively experienced trauma, and to find nonpatho-
logical and nondestructive ways to cope with it. Not all trials perform
that function; some, in fact, may only exacerbate the pathology and
destructiveness, by turning into exercises in collective punitiveness, sadism, and further violence. But this time the judge and both the prosecuting and the defense attorneys were all in agreement that no useful

social purpose would be served by emphasizing punishment, revenge, further violence, or the demonization of the defendant. They agreed that everyone would benefit by trying to find alternative ways to understand and respond to what had happened. I felt, or at least I hoped, that this trial had enabled them all not merely to attend to collective wounds that had not yet had time to heal but to experience a catharsis of the feelings those wounds had aroused in them. It might have helped to transform their understanding of those events—from the realm of the incomprehensible and unpredictable, from the evil, or inhuman, to be able instead to see why this tragedy had occurred, and how to respond to it in ways that would not simply add to everyone's suffering. We might be able to learn from this tragedy so as to be better able to anticipate and prevent such tragedies, if only by recognizing more clearly just how vulnerable we all are; how much our needs for love and care and respect are not just luxuries or negotiable options, but absolute life-and-death necessities. If we can recognize the danger signals when they occur and take them seriously, from suicide attempts to psychological test results, from escaping from mental hospitals to requesting attention, then we can intervene more promptly, vigorously, and appropriately.

There is, of course, much more that can be said about Matthew, and more than I have yet understood myself. I would now like to discuss how one of the themes that I discussed in the last chapter may apply to Matthew, namely, the special obligations that are placed on men, by the "code of honor" of patriarchal societies, to defend the honor of the family, usually by means of violence, especially when the women in the family (especially the mother) have been sexually dishonored. Did this ancient value system play a role in Matthew's parricide? Did Matthew kill his father in order to fulfill the obligation that the code of honor imposes on men to avenge any slurs on the honor of the women in the family?

I have no evidence that the code of honor was a direct or conscious influence on Matthew's decision to kill his father. For example, his capacity for empathy with anyone else's suffering, including his mother's, seems to me to have been severely compromised and limited by the degree to which he was preoccupied with his own suffering. His parricidal act seems to have been more a response to his feeling that he was being shamed and unloved than that his mother was being treated the same way.

Nevertheless, cultures are complicated bundles of moral, cognitive, emotional, and social forces, which can exert their influences in a surprising number of ways; and people are complicated enough that we should not dismiss too lightly the influence of a value system that is so fundamental and pervasive in shaping the most basic assumptions and institutions of a social order that is organized along patriarchal lines. So let us examine the issue in more detail.

Honor. That word is rarely used these days, at least in modern industrialized societies, rendered outmoded and irrelevant by a whole series of related historical changes. Among these are the hegemony of the impersonal rule of law (and the associated decline in duels, feuds, vigilante actions, and lynch mobs); the anonymity of mass society; the political egalitarianism of democracy; the measurement of personal worth in terms of impersonal criteria of financial "net worth," rather than of personal physical courage; the increased fluidity of social mobility; the rise of "possessive individualism" and the corresponding decline in importance of the family, including the extended family, or clan; and the ideology of sexual freedom, equality, and permissiveness.

How can the concept of "family honor" have any meaning, how could it not have died out, when the family, as an institution, seems to be dying out? In fact, the only groups in society in which the concepts of honor, family, and family honor appear still to be taken seriously—at least on the surface—are those that exist on the margins of society, from the underworld to the underclass—such as the Mafia, which calls itself both a "family" and a "society of honor"; and urban street gangs, which serve as surrogate families for adolescents whose own families have often disintegrated. Both groups specialize in taking the law into their own hands, especially to avenge slights to their honor.

People need families. And it is precisely when families disintegrate that people's need for families becomes most intense, and their impulse is to create substitutes for them. So they recreate some previous or more archaic version of family, some image of family order and coherence. Urban street gangs are one of the most visible examples of this phenomenon. They become more salient in their communities as the family structure in those communities dissolves—and the "families" they create are precisely those that are ruled by the most rigid codes of honor and the most rigorous obligations to enforce that code by means of violence (so that to be "dis'ed" is literally a mortal insult). This includes the enforcement of the asymmetry in the social roles assigned to the two sexes. (That is, no culture or subculture is more patriarchal and "macho" than that of the urban street gangs—as I have seen them reconstitute themselves inside the world of the prison.)

Matthew was a "loner," and his kind of community did not include street gangs. But since his family was breaking apart, his need to consolidate or reconstitute his family was correspondingly intensified, and his personal mental functioning, in response to the stress he was experiencing, was becoming more and more regressed, even psychotic.

If people who are seriously disturbed, mentally, emotionally, and behaviorally, such as Matthew, really are like "broken crystals" who reveal the hidden structure of even normal personalities (to quote a metaphor of Freud's), then perhaps Matthew's act of extreme violence can also be seen as a broken crystal that reveals the hidden structure of important aspects of American mores, social structure, and national character, and indeed of all civilizations characterized as "patriarchal."

For example, Matthew's act of parricide, given the particular familial context in which it occurred, in which his father was humiliating and dishonoring his mother (not to mention the whole family) raises the question: Could it be that this young man, precisely because he was so

"regressed," so lacking in the normal inhibitions against saying and doing the forbidden, has revealed aspects of the structure of marriage, of
relations between the sexes, of the social roles to which each of the
sexes are assigned, and of the definitions of masculinity and femininity,
that are normally deeply hidden and subterranean? I think this is true,
and that the power and vitality of the supposedly archaic code of honor
are far greater than one would ever guess from either the rhetoric or the
surface behavior that is characteristic of Matthew's culture. If the code
of honor were really dead, as dead as listening to cocktail party chatter
and the sneers or laughter that would greet anyone who suggested
taking the concept of "honor" seriously would conclude, how could it
continue to be so deadly? Matthew's parricidal act constituted a form of
acting out a sacrificial ritual by means of which he could wipe out the
affront to his mother's honor (and his own, and his whole family's), and
vicariously gratify for the other members of his family their shared need
to attain that goal by means of sacrificing his father (even though they
themselves never overtly or consciously expressed such a wish, and
would have repudiated it unequivocally if it had ever been put to them).
That Matthew perceived himself as being under an obligation to perform this ritual for his family, and to sacrifice himself as well, in the
process, is not something he needed to pick up from them. That obligation is an undercurrent, part of the subterranean foundation and the
underlying logic, of the structure of patriarchal society and the patriarchal family, founded as it is on the differentiation of the two sexes into
violence objects and sex objects, with criteria of personal and family
honor that differ correspondingly for men and women.

Many cultures assign to the young, unmarried man in the family the
responsibility to avenge slurs on the family's honor, especially the
mother's. This responsibility is given to the male member of the family
who does not yet have a family of his own to protect. This is important
because slurs on a family's honor can only be wiped clean, or avenged,
by means of violence. And committing violent acts is dangerous—often

the one who is violent gets either killed himself, or imprisoned. One aspect of this father's behavior that was most prominent in this family's collective turmoil was the public humiliation to the mother in a small community where her nose was rubbed in her shame every day.

Of course, Matthew, as the most emotionally disturbed member of the family, was the one most likely to act out impulses that the healthier members would inhibit or repress—if they had them. But given that the role of the young unmarried man as the avenger of the family's honor is assigned by parents in traditional societies, is it absurd to wonder if Matthew felt that he had at last accomplished the task he had previously failed to do: He had finally, to quote his original psychological evaluation, "lived up to parental expectations"—the very task he had failed to accomplish at the time of his first hospitalization, as a result of which he had felt "overwhelmed by shame"? And I have already discussed the notion that when people cannot ward off shame by nonviolent means, and it is overwhelming to them, there is always a strong pressure to do so by violent acts.

On the other hand, violence directed against another person always risks that the cost of replacing the shame and dishonor with a restored pride may be prohibitively high. For the original feeling, in this case that Matthew and his mother were both the innocent victims of his father's shaming, was replaced by the new feeling that he was guilty toward his father. Can there be any heavier burden for a young man than to feel called upon to uphold his family's honor when his mother has been dishonored—at the expense of his father's life?

The culmination and completion of this tragedy, its last act, had not yet occurred. In killing his father, Matthew had passed the point of no return. Although he talked bravely about the new life he could imagine for himself, once he was well enough to leave the hospital in a few years' time, he was actually unable to imagine in any realistic way how to go on living after committing this act. Like Cain, like Judas, he felt unable to live among men or women; and, just as importantly, and

painfully, unable to live with himself. Like Sophocles' Oedipus, he felt
a need to punish himself far more severely than the State did for killing
his father.

The more he reflected on his feelings about his father, the more he
became aware that he also had feelings of love, remorse, sadness, guilt
and regret, which he found impossible to live with. He would talk about
eventually leaving the hospital, but it was clear that he could do little
more than pay lip service to the idea. He remained at the hospital
during the remainder of my tenure there, and although he, like all
patients, had his own individual and group therapists, I remained a sort
of father figure to him. A month after I had resigned as the medical
director, Matthew went into a normally well-traveled basement work-
shop area at a time when it was empty, and hanged himself. In retro-
spect, I think my presence as the one who had helped him be seen as
an understandable human being by the people who made up his world
had kept him alive. He and I had talked about my leaving the hospital
and also about his future, his eventual leaving as well. Perhaps my
leaving underscored his realization that he would, in a deep sense,
never be able to leave behind what he had done. Perhaps in the end,
despite all the others who were there for him, my leaving reawakened in
him the feelings of abandonment he had felt when he felt left by his
real father—except this time, having already killed his father, he
hanged himself.

One final irony in this tragedy is that I had resigned in part because I
had come to feel that I was neglecting my own three sons by exhausting
myself trying to save all the lost souls who came to the hospital. It is
presumptuous to think that anyone can "save" another person; the most
one can do is to be present for them and encourage their ability and
their motivation to live. Perhaps I did not do enough in that way; or
perhaps it may simply have been too late for Matthew, no matter what
anyone did—I will never know. But one conclusion this whole tragedy
reinforced for me was that, where violence is concerned, attempting to
repair the damage, whether by means of punishment or of therapy, after

irrevocable violence has already occurred, is too little too late, not only for the primary victim but also for the perpetrator. The overwhelming emphasis needs to be on prevention—which is exactly why nothing is more important than to learn everything we can about why people become violent, toward others or toward themselves, so that we can be more successful in preventing such destructiveness in the future, before it reaches the point of no return.

Just as Matthew was the violent problem child in his family, so violence itself is the problem child for civilization. Civilization, one of the greatest blessings humanity has yet created for itself, also has a tragic flaw—the violence that it stimulates. For civilization has also brought with it the greatest increase in the scale and frequency of human violence. I have tried to indicate how the increased propensity toward violence that civilization has brought with it is inextricably tied to its patriarchal structure, in which men and women are each assigned radically different social roles, each of which is governed by a code of honor in terms of which the members of each sex are accorded honor or dishonor, pride or shame, depending on whether or not they behave according to the moral obligations of their code.

The fundamental challenge for our time, I believe, is to break the link between civilization and patriarchy so that we can continue to receive the benefits of the former without having to pay the costs of the latter. If humanity is to evolve beyond the propensity toward violence that now threatens our very survival as a species, then it can only do so by recognizing the extent to which the patriarchal code of honor and shame generates and obligates male violence. If we wish to bring this violence under control, we need to begin by reconstituting what we mean by both masculinity and femininity.

N O T E S

Prologue (pp. 1–26)

1. BOSWELL: "I think Dr. Franklin's definition of Man a good one—'A tool-making animal.'" JOHNSON: "But many a man never made a tool; and suppose a man without arms, he could not make a tool." Quoted in James Boswell, *Life of Samuel Johnson* (1791; Chicago: Encyclopaedia Britannica, Inc., *Great Books of the Western World, 1953*), Vol. 44, p. 377.

2. For a tabulation of the sex-ratios of the victims of violent deaths in the United States from 1900–1984, see Paul C. Holinger, *Violent Deaths in the United States: An Epidemiologic Study of Suicide, Homicide, and Accidents* (New York: Guilford Press, 1987). These figures are updated each year in the annual volumes of *Vital Statistics of the United States* published by the U.S. Department of Health and Human Services (Public Health Service, National Center for Health Statistics), Hyattsville, MD. Comparable statistics from nations around the world are tabulated yearly in the *Demographic Yearbook*, edited and published by the Statistical Office, Department of International Economic and Social Affairs, United Nations, New York. Current and cumulative statistics on deaths by capital punishment in the United States are updated each year in two annual publications put out by the Bureau of Justice Statistics of the U. S. Department of Justice (Washington,

D.C.: U.S. Govt. Printing Office), the *Sourcebook of Criminal Justice Statistics*, and the B.J.S. Bulletin entitled *Capital Punishment* (published annually since 1973).

Lewis F. Richardson, *Statistics of Deadly Quarrels*, ed. Quincy Wright and C. C. Lienau (London, 1960), is a compendium of statistics about wars and war-related deaths, 1820–1949. Cf. also *The Twentieth Century Book of the Dead*, by Gil Elliot (New York: C. Scribner, 1972), and David Singer and Melvin Small, *The Wages of War, 1816–1965: A Statistical Handbook* (New York: Wiley, 1972), for summaries of the sex-ratios of the war-related fatalities during the first half of this century. What all these sources document is the overwhelming predominance of males among the victims of every form of lethal violence (homicide, suicide, warfare, capital punishment, hazardous occupations and working conditions, violent child abuse, "unintentional" injuries caused by recklessness and risk-taking bravado, etc.) in every nation, every year, and every age group, for which statistics are available. The only major exception to this pattern is the apparent excess of girls among the victims of infanticide in certain developing nations in Asia, especially India and China, and in some hunting-and-gathering cultures.

3. George Steiner, *The Death of Tragedy* (1961: New York: Oxford Univ. Press, 1980), pp. 8, 4 and 8; emphases added. This can be compared with Wittgenstein's comment, "You get tragedy where the tree, instead of bending, breaks." [Die Tragödie besteht darin, dass sich der Baum nicht biegt, sondern bricht.] (Ludwig Wittgenstein, *Culture and Value*, Chicago: University of Chicago Press, 1984, pp. 1–1e; the remark is from unpublished manuscripts dated 1929).

4. Elliott Currie, *Confronting Crime: An American Challenge* (New York: Pantheon, 1985), p. 19.

5. *Prison Conditions in the United States: A Human Rights Watch Report* (New York: Human Rights Watch, 1993). On this same subject, see: Nils Christie, *Crime Control as Industry: Toward GULAGS, Western Style?* (New York: Routledge, 1993), and David J. Rothman, "The crime of punishment," *New York Review*, Feb. 17, 1994, pp. 34–38.

Chapter 1 (pp. 29–43)

1. Dante Alighieri, *The Inferno* (London: J.M. Dent & Sons, 1900/1932/1970). Translated by J. A. Carlyle, revised by H. Oelsner, III.56–57: ". . . *io non avrei mai creduto, che morte tanta n'avesse disfatta.*"

2. I am alluding here primarily to the remarkable and detailed report that Chekhov wrote, the lengthiest of all his published works, summarizing his impressions of the penal colony on Sakhalin, a large island off the east coast of Siberia, which he visited in 1890: *A Journey to Sakhalin* (1893; Cambridge, England: Ian Faulkner Publishing, 1993).

3. Dante, *Inferno*, III.9.

4. Many other researchers have noted this about the most violent people. James Alan Fox, Professor of Criminal Justice at Northeastern University, and co-author, with Jack Levin, of *Mass Murder: America's Growing Menace* (New York: Plenum Press, 1985), has commented that "the typical mass murderer is extraordinarily ordinary. He does not stand out in the crowd. He is not a glassy-eyed lunatic." (*New York Times*, n.d.)

5. Dr. Helen Morrison, a Chicago psychiatrist who has spent hundreds of hours interviewing multiple murderers, was struck by the fact that one of them, a well-known serial killer who gained notoriety as the "Mad Biter" for bite marks he left on the flesh of young women he killed in Illinois and Wisconsin in the 1970s, once told her a dream in which he imagined attacking a person: "Picked up the person, slammed them into wall, beating until death, lifeless, or unconscious." Dr. Morrison concluded that "he doesn't know the difference between those three states. That's striking because to us death and lifeless are the same thing but to him [they're] not." (*New York Times*, n.d.)

6. James M. Reinhardt, *The Murderous Trail of Charles Starkweather* (Springfield, Ill.: Charles C. Thomas, 1960), p. 98.

7. Ibid., pp. 49–50.

8. Ibid., p. 23.

9. Ibid., p. 51.

10. Ibid., p. 32.

11. David Berkowitz (1981), "Prison Diary." In Lawrence D. Klausner, *Son of Sam* (New York: McGraw-Hill, 1981), pp. 141–142. Other publications I have found helpful and have drawn on in this discussion include a psychoanalytic study of Berkowitz, *Confessions of Son of Sam* (New York: Columbia

University Press, 1985), by David Abrahamsen, M.D., a psychiatrist who interviewed him repeatedly over a prolonged period and performed a lengthy and detailed evaluation of his life history and his social and psychological functioning. Also the chapter on Berkowitz in the anthropologist Elliott Leyton's *Compulsive Killers: The Story of Modern Multiple Murder* (New York: New York University Press, 1986), an attempt to explain the recent epidemic of serial and mass murders by means of an original and thoughtful sociological theory.

12. There are powerful empirical, clinical, and theoretical grounds for concluding that the practice of executing murderers stimulates more murders than it deters. This is true not only because capital punishment gratifies the suicidal wishes of those who are prone to committing murders in the first place but also because the State's example gives legitimacy to the notion that killing people is an acceptable means of attaining ends that are widely if not universally sought, such as solving interpersonal conflicts, teaching moral lessons, disciplining rule-breakers, taking revenge, punishing (indeed, eliminating) those whom one does not like, and so on. As Justice Brandeis said, the state, whether we like it or not, is *in loco parentis* and serves as one of the most powerful moral teachers we have; and it teaches by example, such as by the example it sets by the laws it passes and—sometimes literally— executes.

As Brandeis put it: "Our government is the potent, the omnipresent teacher. For good or ill, it teaches the whole people by its example. Crime is contagious. If the government becomes a lawbreaker, it breeds contempt for laws; it invites every man to become a law unto himself; it invites anarchy. . . ." Quoted in Charles E. Silberman, *Criminal Violence, Criminal Justice* (New York: Random House, 1978), p. 47. To paraphrase the last two sentences: "Violence is contagious. If the government commits cold-blooded murder, i.e., capital punishment, it breeds contempt for life; it invites every man to become a murderer; it invites universal violence. . . ."

Anyone who doubts the validity of Brandeis's observation might reflect on the power and influence the Nazi state demonstrated to bring about the moral corruption of so much of the population of an otherwise highly civilized nation, to the point where millions of people became either the actual perpetrators of, or the accomplices to, mass murder. Violence is as contagious as many other deadly diseases because it can so easily be taught; it differs from the others only in that the vector of transmission is not micro-organisms but teaching by example (whether by means of child-rearing methods, educational practices, the criminal justice system and the wider legal and political system of which it is a part, or any other means of accul-turation and socialization). And the most powerful teaching tool—compared with which words hardly matter—is example, or in other words, behavior.

Chapter 2 (pp. 45–55)

1. Stuart Palmer, *A Study of Murder* (New York: Crowell, 1960).
2. As Father Zossima put it, in Dostoevsky's *The Brothers Karamazov* (I.VI.3.i): "What is hell? . . . it is the suffering of being unable to love."
3. "To enjoy something," as St. Augustine put it, "is to cling to it with love for its own sake"—that is, as an end in itself. In *On Christian Doctrine*, I.3 (New York: Liberal Arts Press, 1958), p. 9. Aquinas also saw that ". . . none takes pleasure save in that which is loved in some way." In *Summa Theologica*, Part I of 2nd Part, Q. 27, Art. 4. Translated by Fathers of the English Dominican Province, revised by Daniel J. Sullivan, Chicago: Encyclopaedia Britannica, Inc., *Great Books of the Western World*, Vol. 19, p. 739. Or, as Spinoza said, "Love is nothing but joy accompanied with the idea of an external cause," i.e., the thought of the beloved person or thing. In *Ethics*, Part III, Prop. 13, Schol.. Translated by W. H. White, revised by A. H. Stirling, Chicago: Encyclopaedia Britannica, Inc., *Great Books of the Western World*, Vol. 31, p. 400.

In other words, to love something or someone is to enjoy it, or him, or her. And to enjoy someone is to love her or him. Where there is love, there is joy; and where there is joy, there is love. Conversely, where there is no love, there is no joy (this is the condition called hell, in theological language). And the cause of lovelessness (the incapacity for love) is joylessness (the incapac-ity for joy); and vice versa. The chief causes of the incapacity for love and joy are *shame* (the lack of self-love, which inhibits love of others, and stimulates hatred toward them, and fear of them, instead); and *guilt* (the presence of self-hate, which inhibits self-love, and stimulates fear and condemnation of one's own hostile and destructive impulses and wishes). Among the clinical and behavioral syndromes caused by shame are paranoia, narcissism, soci-opathy, selfishness, sadism, and revenge; whereas guilt causes, among other things, depression, penance, self-punishment, self-sacrifice, martyrdom, and masochism.

Chapter 3 (pp. 57–85)

1. Primo Levi, *The Drowned and the Saved* (New York: Summit Books, 1988), p. 53.
2. Goethe, *Faust,* Part One, Faust's Study (ii), Line 1237 (Baltimore, MD: Penguin Classics, 1949). Translated by Philip Wayne: *"Im Anfang war die Tat!"* See also, on this passage, Harry Redner's *In the Beginning was the Deed: Reflections on the Passage of Faust* (Berkeley, CA: University of California Press, 1982).
3. Kenneth Burke, *Language as Symbolic Action* (Berkeley: University of California Press, 1966).
4. This is one reason why it is appropriate to think of people with the most violence-producing character disorders as "borderline" psychotic.
5. Cf. the Oxford English Dictionary; Ernest Klein, *A Comprehensive Etymological Dictionary of the English Language* (Amsterdam and New York: Elsevier, 1971); Eric Partridge, *Origins: A Short Etymological Dictionary of the English Language* (1958; New York: Greenwich House, 1983); Carl Schneider, *Shame, Exposure and Privacy* (Boston: Beacon Press, 1977), pp. 29–30.
6. Charles Darwin, *The Expression of the Emotions in Man and Animals* (1872; Chicago: University of Chicago Press, 1965), pp. 320–321.
7. Erik H. Erikson, *Childhood and Society.* 2nd ed. (New York: W. W. Norton, 1963), pp. 252–53 (emphasis added).
8. ". . . to en ophthalmois einai aido," the eyes are the abode of shame. And, he added, "For this reason we feel most shame before those who will always be with us and those who notice what we do, since in both cases eyes are upon us." Aristotle, *Rhetoric,* II.vi.18–20 (1384a). Translated and edited by W.D. Ross (Oxford: Oxford University Press, 1954). The proverb he refers to, "aidos en ophthalmoisi gignetai teknon," can be found in a fragment remaining from Euripides' lost play, *Cresphontes* (T.G.F. frag. 457).
9. For example, in 1344 a man who insulted the City of Florence by kicking the Great Seal of the City with his muddy boot was sentenced by the Captain of Florence to have his foot cut off. In Samuel Edgerton, *Pictures and Punishment: Art and Criminal Prosecution During the Florentine Renais-*

sance (Ithaca: Cornell Univ. Press, 1985), p. 132. In that case, the organ that committed the insult was the foot, so, according to the laws of what Freud called "magical thinking," the shame could be removed only by having the foot removed. Lest we imagine that we have evolved beyond such barbarism, it is worth remembering that within very recent decades, in both Denmark and many of the United States, the punishment for sex crimes (rape, incest, pedophilia), among the most humiliating and shame-inducing acts a man can inflict on another person, consisted of castration; again, the offender is punished, or in other words, is humiliated himself, in the (sexual) organ with which he commits the (sexual) insult/assault. Thus, the shame of the rape victim is magically removed, by being transferred onto the rapist instead; her shame, in this construction, can only be removed by having his penis removed, since his penis was the vehicle by which she was shamed.

10. For years before he came to power, Hitler repeatedly referred to the Versailles treaty as "a *shame* and a *disgrace*" and "this instrument of . . . *abject humiliation*" which should arouse the German people to "a common sense of *shame* and a common *hatred*" (notice the explicit link between shame and hatred). It was the failure of the Germans to respond in that spirit, Hitler said, that "has been drowning the very last remnant of *respect* for us on the part of the rest of the world" and had brought "the nation [to] its time of deepest *humiliation* and *disgrace*." (Adolf Hitler, *Mein Kampf* [1925], Boston: Houghton Mifflin, 1962, pp. 632 and 231; emphases added.)

11. Seymour Martin Lipset, *Political Man: The Social Bases of Politics* (1960) (New York: Anchor Books, 1963), pp. 138–152. In *Political Man*, Lipset shows how it was the lower middle class, when threatened with becoming lower class, that turned massively toward the extreme right, i.e., Nazism. This analysis is supported also by Thomas Childers, *The Nazi Voter: The Social Foundations of Fascism in Germany, 1919–1933* (Univ. of North Carolina Press, 1983), who describes how Nazism became the "long-sought party of the middle-class concentration" (p. 262).

Incidentally, exactly the same dynamic (qualitatively, but not quantitatively, that is, not on the same scale) has been at work in American society over the past twenty years or so. As the most vulnerable members of the middle class have been increasingly threatened with losing their jobs and their homes, as their incomes have stagnated or actually retrogressed, their unions have lost power, and their job security and overall financial security have diminished, and they have been faced with the threat of losing status and suffering the shame and inferiority of falling into the lower class, or underclass (the unemployed, the working poor, the homeless, those who live on welfare, etc.), there has been a massive move to the right politically. Fortunately, the economic debacle this group has suffered does not begin to approach what happened in Germany in the 1930s, and the degree of political reaction has not reached the same dimensions either, for a variety of reasons. Nevertheless, the move is in the same direction, and will give cause for increasing alarm if it continues unabated. For all such movements increase the frequency and the probability of violence (both legal and illegal). Indeed, the political movements that such economic catastrophes spawn overtly glorify violence—as can be seen in the degree of mass support in this country over the past two decades for increasing the number of guns in circulation, the frequency of capital punishment, the bombing of abortion clinics, the support for a militaristic police state (by diverting more and more money into the military, the police, and the prison system, weakening the laws protecting civil liberties), and so on.

The more impotent (and thus vulnerable to shame) people feel, the more they turn to violence, individual or collective, as the quickest way to regain the feeling of power—even if that feeling is an illusion. The weaker the members of the lower middle class have become over the past two decades, relative to the upper class, and the more inferior they have become, economically and socially, to the very wealthy, the stronger has their temptation become to direct their violence toward those who are even weaker and more vulnerable than they are, namely, the lower class (the poor, the underclass, immigrants, minority groups, single mothers, the unemployed, the sick, and so on). For to direct the violent impulses that are generated by feelings of inferiority toward those of superior power would only result in defeat and punishment, and thus, increased feelings of inferiority, loss of status, and shame. But the poor, the sick, the starving, the children, the unemployed, the homeless, the hospitalized, the imprisoned, the refugees from other countries are all almost defenseless scapegoats on whom to discharge the homicidal impulses that are generated by the status anxieties—the feelings of shame and envy—created by our social and economic system.

12. Leonard W. Moss and Stephen C. Cappannari, "Mal' occhio, Ayin ha ra, Oculus fascinus, Judenblick: The Evil Eye Hovers Above," chapter 1 (pp. 1–16) in *The Evil Eye* (Clarence Maloney, ed.), New York: Columbia University Press, 1976, p. 8.

13. Helmut Schoeck, "The evil eye: Forms and dynamics of a universal superstition," pp. 192–200 in Alan Dundes (ed.), *The Evil Eye: A Folklore Casebook*, New York: Garland, 1981, p. 194.

14. *The Origins of Totalitarianism* [1951] (New York: Meridian Books, 1958), p. 241.

15. "I'm thinking of the wife of Consul Scharrer. She had hands laden with rings which were so big that she couldn't move her fingers. She was the sort of Jewess one sees in caricatures. . . . One day Werlin showed me Scharrer's car. Its radiator was plated, not in nickel, but in gold. It furthermore contained a thousand little articles of everyday use, starting with a lavatory, all in gold. I can still see Consul Scharrer when he used to arrive in a top hat, with his cheeks . . . puffed out . . . , for the Sunday concert on the avenue. On their property at Bernried they had white peacocks. . . . he received Prussian princes in his house. . . ." (*Hitler's Table-Talk, 1941–44*, Oxford: Oxford University Press, 1988, p. 325, entry for 21 February 1942.)

The day after he recalled this memory, his reminiscences began with a description of how "I was so poor, during the Viennese period of my life. . . .", a theme that he continued a month later on the same note: "I experienced such poverty in Vienna. I spent long months without ever having the smallest hot meal. I lived on milk and dry bread."

16. Charles Darwin, *The Expression of the Emotions in Man and Animals* (1872; Chicago: University of Chicago Press, 1965).

17. Sir Julian Huxley, *Proc. Zool. Soc.*, 1914, pp. 511–515, an interpretation of the elaborate courtship "ceremonies" of the Great Crested Grebe.

18. The quotations, in the order cited, can be found in the *New York Times*, Dec. 1, 1988; Dec. 3, 1988, p. 30; Dec. 2, 1988, p. B5; Dec. 6, 1988, pp. B1 and B9.

19. Jack Katz, *Seductions of Crime: Moral and Sensual Attractions in Doing Evil* (N.Y.: Basic Books, 1988). From a review of the criminological literature, this author anticipated many of the same conclusions to which I was led by my clinical work with violent people. For example:

One feature of the typical homicide, then, is its character as a self-righteous act undertaken within the form of defending communal values. . . . What the . . . assailant is attempting to do is more accurately captured by the concept of sacrifice: the marking of a victim in ways that will reconsecrate the assailant as Good. . . . Thus, I arrive at a definition of the problem to be explained as "righteously enraged slaughter," or an impassioned attack through which the assailant attempts to embody in his victim marks that will eternally attest to the assailant's embrace of a primordial Good. . . . The project is the honoring of the offense that he suffered through a marking violently drawn into the body of the victim. Death . . . comes as a sacrificial slaughter. (p. 18)

Would-be killers create their homicidal rage only through a precisely articulated leap to . . . righteousness. . . . Righteousness shares with rage a blindness to the temporal boundaries of existence. . . . [R]ighteousness, concerned only with what always has been and always will be right, is justly indifferent to the historical moment. In this way, the Good serves as the springboard for the leap into blind rage. (p. 30)

Cursing sets up violence to be a sacrifice to honor the attacker as a priest representing the collective moral being. If the priest is stained by the blood of the sacrifice, by contact with the polluting profane material, that is a measure of the priest's devotion to society.

. . . to attempt to stomp someone [to death, or to "kick your eyes out of your head"] specifically seeks to leave the normal universe of routine behavior, with its multiple, morally inconsequential motives, and to enter a battlefield, where the stakes are incomparably higher—where Good and Evil fight for a final victory with a passion that understands the nature of the stakes.

. . . although impassioned homicides are extreme attacks on perhaps the most fundamental communal taboo [i.e., "Thou shalt not kill"], to the killers they are efforts to defend what they, often idiosyncratically, take to be eternal, collectively shared values. (p. 37)

The closer one looks at crime, . . . the more vividly relevant become the moral emotions. (p. 312)

20. Walter Burkert, *Homo Necans: The Anthropology of Ancient Greek Sacrificial Ritual and Myth* (1972; Berkeley: Univ. of California Press, 1983), p. 23.

Chapter 4 (pp. 89–102)

1. As summarized by Charles Silberman, *Criminal Violence, Criminal Justice* (N.Y.: Random House, 1978), p. 163, quoting from James Q. Wilson, *Thinking About Crime* (N.Y.: Basic Books, 1975), p. xv:

> The lesson Wilson draws is that if our aim is to reduce street crime, we should forget about measures designed to eliminate its underlying causes. "I have yet to see a 'root cause,' " . . . Wilson writes. More important, "The demand for causal solutions is, whether intended or not, a way of deferring any action and criticizing any policy. It is a cast of mind that inevitably detracts attention from those few things that governments can do reasonably well and draws attention toward those many things it cannot do at all." In Wilson's view, what government can do is reduce crime by sending more convicted felons to jail. . . . What government cannot do at all, according to Wilson, is turn lower-class criminals into law-abiding citizens through measures to reduce poverty and discrimination.

2. Carol Smart, "Feminist approaches to criminology or postmodern woman meets atavistic man." In *Feminist Perspectives in Criminology*, eds. Loraine Gelsthorpe and Allison Morris (Milton Keynes: Open University Press, 1990).

3. *Understanding and Preventing Violence*, eds. Albert J. Reiss and Jeffrey A. Roth (Washington, D.C.: National Academy Press, 1993), pp. 21 and 39.

4. I have been unable to locate the source of this quotation, which I am quoting from memory, but there is an essentially identical passage in Molière's play *The Doctor in Spite of Himself* (Act II, scene 4), in which Sganarelle, the eponymous hero, has been summoned to treat Geronte's daughter, who has become mute: "*Sganarelle:* . . . your daughter is dumb. *Geronte.* Yes; but I wish you could tell me what it comes from. *Sganarelle.* Nothing easier: it comes from the fact that she has lost her speech. *Geronte.* Very good; but the reason, please, why she has lost her speech. *Sganarelle.* All our best authors will tell you that it's the stoppage of the action of her

tongue." In Molière, *The Misanthrope and Other Plays*. Translated Donald
M. Frame (New York: New American Library, 1968), p. 112.
5. Fyodor Dostoevsky, *Notes From Underground* (1864). In *The Short Novels
.of Dostoevsky* (New York: Dial Press, 1951), p. 148.
6. J.P. Scott, *Aggression* (Chicago: Univ. of Chicago Press, 1958).

Chapter 5 (pp. 103–136)

1. Julian Pitt-Rivers, "Honor," *International Encyclopaedia of Social Science*,
pp. 503–511, 1968; pp. 503–4.
2. Frantz Fanon, *The Wretched of the Earth* (1961; New York: Grove Press,
1968), p. 208.
3. Charles Silberman, *Criminal Violence, Criminal Justice* (N.Y.: Random
House, 1978), p. 85.
4. *Ibid.*, pp. 85–86.
5. *Ibid.*, p. 78.
6. That statistic was found repeatedly and consistently in every kind of
study performed, from the most careful, detailed, and thorough studies
done, one city at a time, by criminologists such as Marvin Wolfgang, *Patterns
in Criminal Homicide* (1958; New York: John Wiley & Sons [Science Edi-
tions], 1966); or the National Commission on the Causes and Prevention of
Violence, *Crimes of Violence: A Staff Report Submitted to the National Commission on the Causes & Prevention of Violence* (Washington, D.C., U.S.
Govt. Printing Office, 1969, Vol. 11, pp. 207–258), to the most general and
large-scale national statistics reported by police forces throughout the country to the F.B.I. and published every year in their Uniform Crime Reports.
As the National Commission summarized these findings:

"In the mate killings half of the offenders were husbands and half were
wives." (p. 218)

". . . while our data reflect a ten percent sample of all big city
murders in 1967, the F.B.I. tabulated the same information for all the
1967 criminal homicides. The results were about the same. The F.B.I.
found 45 percent of all cases had wives as offenders and 55 percent
had husbands (*Uniform Crime Reports 1967*, p. 8). The data are consistent with those found by Wolfgang: in 53 percent of all Philadelphia

husband-wife homicides, the husband was the offender and in 47
percent the wife was. . . ." (Footnote 50, p. 248)

7. One author who was very perceptive about this aspect of shame (although she did not discuss its relevance to violence) was Helen Merrell
Lynd, in her book *On Shame and the Search for Identity* (New York: Harcourt, Brace, 1958). As she put it, "It is peculiarly characteristic of these
situations . . . that evoke shame that they are often occasioned by what
seems a 'ridiculously' slight incident. An ostensibly trivial incident has precipitated intense emotion" (p. 40). I would add that this makes complete
sense if we remember that shame is precisely the feeling that one is, either
actually or potentially, ridiculous (in one's own eyes and/or the eyes of others), ridiculed, slight (i.e., unimportant, trivial, small, or weak), or slighted
(by other people). In other words, the more slight one feels oneself to be, the
more easily one will feel slighted. Thus,

> What has occurred is harmless in itself and has no evil pragmatic
> outcome. It is the very triviality of the cause— . . . a gaucherie in
> dress or table manners, . . . a gift or witticism that falls flat, . . . a
> mispronounced word . . . —that helps to give shame its unbearable
> character (p. 40).
>
> Because of the outwardly small occasion that has precipitated
> shame, the intense emotion seems inappropriate, incongruous, dispro-
> portionate to the incident that has aroused it. Hence a double shame
> is involved; we are ashamed because of the original episode and
> ashamed because we feel so deeply about something so slight that a
> sensible person would not pay any attention to it (p. 42).

Tolstoy and Dostoevsky also both recognized the same psychological fact
and illustrated it repeatedly. In *Anna Karenina,* for example, Tolstoy says of
Levin: "There had been in his past, as in every man's, actions recognized by
him as bad, for which his conscience ought to have tormented him; but the
memory of these evil actions was far from causing him so much suffering as
these *trivial* but *humiliating* reminiscences. These wounds never healed."
(*Anna Karenina,* New York: Modern Library, 1953, pp. 178–9, emphasis
added). I would add only that those wounds were so humiliating precisely
because they were so trivial.

8. Shervert Frazier (in conversation).

Chapter 6 (pp. 139-161)

1. Karl Menninger, *The Crime of Punishment* (1966; New York: The Viking Press) 1969.

2. Sigmund Freud, *Civilization and Its Discontents* (1930 [1929]; standard edition (London: Hogarth Press, 1964), Vol. 21, p. 142.

3. Julio Caro Baroja, "Honour and shame: A historical account of several conflicts," pp. 79–137 in J.G. Peristiany (ed.), *Honour and Shame: The Values of Mediterranean Society* (Chicago: The University of Chicago Press, 1966), p. 85.

4. Samuel Edgerton, *Pictures and Punishment: Art and Criminal Prosecution During the Florentine Renaissance* (Ithaca: Cornell University Press, 1985), p. 132.

5. Richard van Dulmen, *Theatre of Horror: Crime and Punishment in Early Modern Germany* (1985) (Cambridge, England: Polity Press, 1990), p. 130.

6. Michel Foucault, *Discipline and Punish: The Birth of the Prison* (1975; New York: Pantheon, 1977), p. 16.

7. *Ibid.*

8. Gustave de Beaumont and Alexis de Tocqueville, *On the Penitentiary System in the United States and Its Application in France* (1833; reprint ed. [Carbondale: Southern Illinois University Press, 1964], p. 65. In Lawrence M. Friedman, *Crime and Punishment in American History* (New York: Basic Books, 1993), p. 79.

9. Friedman, *ibid.*

10. Charles Dickens, *American Notes* (1842; New York: Penguin, 1972), pp. 146, 148. In Friedman, *ibid.*

11. Friedman, *ibid.*

12. Thorkil Vanggaard (1969; *Phallos: A Symbol and Its History in the Male World*, N.Y.: International Universities Press, 1972), pp. 72–75.

13. "Man is the only animal that blushes. Or needs to." (Mark Twain, *Following the Equator: A Journey Around the World*, 1897, chap. 27), New York: AMS Press, 1971.

14. Harold Garfinkel, "Conditions of successful degradation ceremonies," *American Journal of Sociology*, 61:420–424, 1956.

15. Erving Goffman, *Asylums: Essays on the Social Situation of Mental Patients and Other Inmates* (N.Y.: Anchor Books, 1961).

16. Goffman, *ibid.*

17. Samuel Y. Edgerton, *Pictures and Punishment: Art and Criminal Prosecution during the Florentine Renaissance* (Ithaca: Cornell Univ. Press, 1985).
18. *Ibid.*, p. 27.
19. *Ibid.*, p. 66.
20. *Ibid.*, p. 52.
21. *Ibid.*, p. 134.

Chapter 7 (pp. 163–190)

1. I am not alone in reaching this conclusion. Gresham Sykes, in his classic monograph, *The Society of Captives: A Study of a Maximum Security Prison* (Princeton: Princeton University Press, 1958, pp. 70–72), has commented that "the inmate . . . is figuratively castrated by his involuntary celibacy. . . . the psychological problems created by the lack of heterosexual relationships can be even more serious" than the physiological ones associated with castration. For "a society composed exclusively of men tends to generate anxieties in its members concerning their masculinity regardless of whether or not they are coerced, bribed, or seduced into an overt homosexual liaison. . . . an essential component of a man's self conception—his status of male—is called into question." And if the foundation upon which a prisoner's self-concept and self-esteem is built includes as a central component his sense of heterosexuality (as the great majority of men's does, from about the age of three onwards), and they do go on to experience homosexual acts, whether voluntarily or involuntarily, "the psychological onslaughts on his ego image will be particularly acute." But even when sex with men is not part of the prisoner's experience, "the deprivation of heterosexual relationships carries with it another threat to the prisoner's image of himself. . . . The inmate is shut off from the world of women. . . . Like most men, the inmate must search for his identity not simply within himself but also in the picture of himself which he finds reflected in the eyes of others; and since a significant half of his audience is denied him [i.e., the female half], the inmate's self image is in danger of becoming half complete, fractured. . . ." That is, his sense of himself as a man, and a sexually adequate one at that, cannot be reinforced, under conditions of heterosexual deprivation, by its reflection in the eyes of a woman with whom he is sexually involved; so it is no wonder that men in that condition are vulnerable to

feelings of having been functionally and symbolically castrated, or emasculated, or transformed into homosexuals.

Since men who are predisposed to committing violence are those who doubt their sexual adequacy in the first place (violence being the ultimate last-resort defense against feelings of masculine sexual inadequacy, when all else fails—the ultimate way to "prove," both to others and to oneself, that one is a man, and not "a wimp, a punk, or a pussy"), the effect of this symbolic castration on the population of violent men is to intensify their violence even further—with effects that are catastrophic, both in prison and after these men return to the community. Thus, to the list of the many ways in which prisons and punishment only endanger the public rather than making it safer, and only stimulate violent crime rather than inhibiting or preventing it, must be added the almost universal American policy of refusing to allow prisoners to have conjugal visits from their wives or lovers.

2. I do not mean to suggest, of course, that all men in prison share a heterosexual orientation. But even gay men are not immune to prison violence; in fact, if they are perceived to be homosexual, they are likely to be even more at risk.

3. Haywood Patterson and Earl Conrad, *Scottsboro Boy* (Garden City, N.Y.: Doubleday, 1950). In Wilbert Rideau and Ron Wikberg, *Life Sentences: Rage and Survival Behind Bars* (New York, N.Y.: Times Books, 1992), pp. 89–90.

4. Rideau, *ibid.,* p. 90.

5. Anthony M. Scacco, Jr., *Rape in Prison* (Springfield, IL: Charles C. Thomas), 1975.

6. Allan J. Davis, "Sexual assaults in the Philadelphia prison system and sheriff's vans," *TransAction,* Dec. 1968, pp. 8–16.

7. C. Bartollas, S. J. Miller, and S. Dinitz, *Juvenile Victimization: The Institutional Paradox* (Beverly Hills: Sage Publications) 1976.

8. C. Paul Phelps. In Rideau, op. cit., p. 86.

9. Rideau, op. cit., p. 86.

10. Much of this evidence is summarized in Robert W. Dumond, "The sexual assault of male inmates in incarcerated settings," *International Journal of the Sociology of Law,* 20:135–157, 1992, pp. 146–47. S. F. Sylvester, J. H. Reed, and D. Nelson, in their study of *Prison Homicides* (N.Y.: Spectrum Publications, 1977), concluded that sexual assault was the leading motive of inmate murders in American prisons. When E. Herrick analyzed prison vio-

lence for *Corrections Compendium* ("The Surprising Direction of Violence in Prison," *14* (6):1–17, 1989), he found that the state of Arkansas reported the highest number of assaults on staff by inmates of any correctional system in the United States (1,113 in 1988); and they identified conflicts over sexual relations as the single biggest cause of violence. Hans Toch, in *Police, Prisons and the Problems of Violence* (Washington, D.C.: National Institute of Mental Health, U.S. Government Printing Office, 1977), also concluded that conflicts over sex and sexual assault in prison are a major cause of inmate violence.

11. Rideau, op. cit., p. 88.

12. Rideau, op. cit., p. 88.

13. *Uniform Crime Reports 1988: Crime in the United States* (Washington, D.C.: Federal Bureau of Investigation, U.S. Department of Justice, U.S. Government Printing Office, 1989), p. 15.

14. Davis, op. cit.

15. *Ruiz* v. *Estelle,* 503 F. Supp. 1265, U.S. District Court.

16. Lerner, Steven, "Rule of the cruel," *Corrections,* Vol. 3, Article No 38, 1987, Boca Raton, FL: Social Issues Resources Series. In Robert W. Dumond, op. cit., p. 136.

17. Loretta Tofani, "Rape in the county jail," *The Washington Post* (Sept. 26–28, 1982). In Dumond, op. cit.

18. All the quotations in this paragraph are from Rideau, op. cit., p. 85.

19. Testimony of Dr. Carl C. Bell, Chairman of the National Commission on Correctional Health Care, before the Appropriations Committee of the U.S. House of Representatives, Subcommittee on Labor, Health and Human Services, Education, and Related Agencies, Washington, D.C., April 28, 1992. In *CorrectCare,* 6(2):1, 1992.

20. Steven Donaldson, "Rape of males: A preliminary look at the scope of the problem," unpublished dissertation, 1984. In Dumond, op. cit.

21. Peter L. Nacci and Thomas Kane, for example, found that *36 percent* of the sexual assaults in prison that their informants described were *gang rapes* (multiple perpetrators against a single victim); see "Sex and sexual aggression in federal prisons," *Progress Reports* (Washington, D.C., U.S. Department of Justice, Federal Bureau of Prisons, June 1982), p. 10.

22. Donald Cotton and Nicholas Groth, "Inmate rape: prevention and intervention," *Journal of Prison and Jail Health,* 2(1):47–57, 1984.

23. Daniel Lockwood, *Sexual Aggression Among Male Prisoners* (Ann Arbor, MI: University Microfilms), 1978.

24. Peter L. Nacci and Thomas Kane, "The Incidence of sex and sexual aggression in federal prisons," *Federal Probation*, 47(4):31–36, 1983.

25. Clemens Bartollos and Christopher Sieveides, "The sexual victim in a coeducational juvenile correctional institution," *The Prison Journal*, 58(1):80–90, 1983.

26. Rideau, op. cit., p. 90.

27. Dr. Anthony Scacco, Jr., op. cit. In Rideau, op. cit., pp. 91–2.

28. Rideau, *ibid.*, p. 77.

29. *Ibid.*, p. 75.

30. *Ibid.*, p. 75.

31. *Ibid.*, p. 75.

32. *Ibid.*, p. 74.

33. *Ibid.*, p. 75.

34. Andrew Vachss, "Sex predators can't be saved," *New York Times*, Jan. 5, 1993. (Emphases added.)

Chapter 8 (pp. 191–208)

1. Mac W. Otten, Jr., Steven M. Teutsch, David F. Williamson, and James S. Marks, "The effect of known risk factors on the excess mortality of black adults in the United States," *Journal of the American Medical Association*, 263(6):845–850.

2. Colin McCord and Harold P. Freeman, "Excess mortality in Harlem," *New England Journal of Medicine*, 322(3):173–177.

3. Hussein Abdilahi Bulhan, *Frantz Fanon and the Psychology of Oppression* (New York: Plenum Press), 1985.

4. M. H. Brenner, *Mental Illness and the Economy* (Cambridge, MA: Harvard University Press) 1973. M. H. Brenner, "Personal stability and economic security," *Social Policy*, 8:2–4, 1977.

5. Bulhan, op. cit., p. 158.

6. *Vital Statistics of the United States 1987*, Volume II—Mortality, Part A (Hyattsville, MD: National Center for Health Statistics, Centers for Disease Control, Public Health Service, U.S. Department of Health and Human Services, 1990). See especially Table 1-3, "Age-Adjusted Death Rates by Race and Sex: Death-Registration States, 1900–1932, and United States,

1933–87," Section 1—General Mortality—Page 5. Separate age-adjusted death rates for blacks and whites, permitting a comparison between the two castes in this country, were not calculated (or at least not recorded and published) until 1960 and thereafter.

7. *Hypertension in Africa,* eds. O. S. Akinkugbe and E. Bertrand (Lagos: Literamed, 1976). Y. K. Seedat, M. A. Seedat, and M. N. Nkomo, "The prevalence of hypertension in the urban Zulu," *South African Medical Journal,* 53:923–927, 1978. J. P. Vaughn and W. E. Miall, "A comparison of cardiovascular measurements in Gambia, Jamaica, and the United Republic of Tanzania," *Bulletin of the World Health Organization,* 57:281–289, 1979.

8. Gernot Kohler and Norman Alcock, "An empirical table of structural violence," *Journal of Peace Research,* 13:343–356, 1976. Reprinted in Anita Kemp, ed., *Peace and Violence: Quantitative Studies in International and Civil Conflict* (New Haven, CT: Human Relations Area Files [Cross-Cultural Research Series], 1980).

9. In fact, during the thirty years since Kohler and Alcock's study was done, the gap between the rich nations and the poor ones has doubled. For example, James Speth, administrator of the United Nations Development Program (and the highest-ranking American in the United Nations system) recently reported that "the income gap between the world's richest 20 percent and poorest 20 percent has not narrowed over the last 30 years. . . . Rather, *that gap has doubled.* This widening gulf breeds despair and instability. It imperils our world. One hundred and fifty years ago the world launched a crusade against slavery. Today we must launch a world crusade against mass poverty." (*New York Times,* 7 March 1995, p. A6) That does not mean, of course, that the gap itself, between the richest and poorest quintiles, is merely double now; it means that the gap between the rich and the poor, which was already enormous thirty years ago, high enough to produce 18 million excess deaths per year among the poor, is now twice as high as it was even then. According to data presented to the United Nations World Summit for Social Development, meeting in Copenhagen in March 1995, the number of people on earth today who meet agreed-on criteria to be described as "absolutely destitute" (literally not having enough food to eat to meet daily caloric requirements, not having access to a regular supply of sanitary water, to medical care, or to adequate shelter, and not possessing any realistic means of being able to alter their situation, through education

or employment, so as to obtain any of those goods) numbers approximately one billion, three hundred million—or somewhat more than 20 percent of the entire human population.

Given how easily the masses of people who are this desperate and hopeless can be persuaded to join whatever crackpot religious, political, racial, or ethnic movement makes them utopian promises, in exchange for robbing, and engaging in the genocidal slaughter, of whichever of their neighbors belongs to a different religious, political, racial or ethnic group, the only surprise is not how much violence there is in the world, but how little. From this perspective, the tragedies that have befallen Rwanda, Cambodia, Somalia, the Sudan, and a few years before that, Biafra, Bangladesh, and Indonesia, and a few years before that, and on a larger scale, Russia and China, seem less like inexplicable anomalies than like exactly what one would expect, considering the condition in which hundreds of millions of people are living—or rather, dying.

10. Edith Jacobson, *The Self and the Object World* (New York: International Universities Press, 1964), pp. 144–45.

11. John Adams, *Discourses on Davila, Works* (Boston: Little Brown, 1851), Vol. VI, pp. 239–49.

12. Hannah Arendt, *On Revolution* (New York: Viking, 1963), p. 64.

13. *Ibid.*, p. 66.

14. W.E.B. Du Bois, *Dusk of Dawn* (New York: Harcourt Brace & Co., 1940), pp. 130–131:

> It is as though one, looking out from a dark cave in a side of an impending mountain, sees the world passing and speaks to it; speaks courteously and persuasively, . . . but notices that the passing throng does not even turn its head. . . . It gradually penetrates the minds of the prisoners that the people passing do not hear; that some thick sheet of invisible but horribly tangible plate glass is between them and the world. They get excited; they talk louder; they gesticulate. Some of the passing world stop in curiosity; these gesticulations seem to be pointless; they laugh and pass on. They still either do not hear at all, or hear but dimly, and even when they do hear, they do not understand. Then the people within may become hysterical. They may scream and hurl themselves against the barriers, hardly realizing in their bewilder-

ment that they are screaming in a vacuum unheard and that their antics may actually seem funny to those outside looking in. . . .

15. Ralph Ellison, *The Invisible Man* (New York: Random House, 1952).
16. Richard Sennett and Jonathan Cobb, *The Hidden Injuries of Class* (1972; New York: Vintage, 1973). (In all the quotations from this book that follow, emphases have been added.)
17. *Ibid.*, p. 147.
18. *Ibid.*, p. 38.
19. *Ibid.*, p. 74.
20. *Ibid.*, p. 128.
21. *Ibid.*, p. 50.
22. *Ibid.*, p. 32.
23. *Ibid.*, p. 139.
24. *Ibid.*, pp. 259–261.
25. Alexis de Tocqueville, *The Old Regime and the French Revolution* (Garden City, New York: Doubleday, 1955). Tocqueville's original and profoundly perceptive but still somewhat intuitive insight has been supported by empirical research sponsored by the National Commission on the Causes and Prevention of Violence. See Davies, "The J-Curve of rising and declining satisfactions as a cause of some great revolutions and a contained rebellion," in *Violence in America*, the Report of the Commission's Task Force on Historical and Comparative Perspectives (Washington, D.C.: Government Printing Office, 1969). As summarized in the Commission's final report, published as *Violent Crime: Homicide, Assault, Rape, Robbery* (New York: Braziller, 1969), p. 65:

We have in this country what has been referred to as a "revolution of rising expectations". . . . But . . . a rapid increase in human expectations followed by obvious failure to meet those expectations has been and continues to be a prescription for violence. Disappointment has manifested itself not only in riots . . . but may also be reflected in the increasing levels of violent crime.

This diagnosis has been proved even more strongly than at the time it was made, as there has been a marked widening over the past two decades of the two crucial gaps that increase the level of violence: namely, the gap between the wealth and income of the rich and the poor; and the gap between

aspiration and achievement on the part of the poor themselves, as their
socioeconomic status has declined both relatively and absolutely, but without any corresponding lowering of their sense of being entitled to a more
equitable share of the nation's opportunities and wealth. Indeed, with the
spread of mass communication, they may be even more aware than ever of
how inferior their opportunity structure is compared to those whose lives of
affluence and luxury they can observe daily on their omnipresent television
sets. So it is not surprising that there has also been a marked increase in the
rate of violent crime during that same period. What I have tried to elucidate
in my analysis in this book is the psychological mechanism that causes this
relationship between aspiration, frustration, and violence—namely, that violence is a function of shame, and shame is a function of the size of the gap
between aspiration and achievement.

26. Frantz Fanon, *Black Skin, White Masks* (1952; New York: Grove Press,
1967) p. 116.

27. *Ibid.*, p. 214.

28. Frantz Fanon, *The Wretched of the Earth* (1961; New York: Grove Press,
1968), p. 86.

29. William H. Grier and Price M. Cobbs, *Black Rage* (1968; New York:
Bantam Books, 1969), p. 37.

30. Kenneth Clark, *Dark Ghetto: Dilemmas of Social Power* (New York:
Harper & Row, 1965), p. 65.

31. U. S. Supreme Court. Quoted in Clark, *op. cit.*, p. 76.

32. *The Autobiography of Malcolm X* (1964; New York: Grove Press, 1966),
p. 246; emphases added.

33. *Ibid.*, p. 54.

34. *Ibid.*, p. 55.

35. *Ibid.*, p. 259.

36. *Ibid.*, p. 371.

37. Andrew F. Henry and James F. Short, Jr., *Suicide and Homicide: Some
Economic, Sociological, and Psychological Aspects of Aggression* (New York:
The Free Press, 1954).

38. For example, Andrew Henry and James Short, in the classic study of this
subject, *Suicide and Homicide: Some Economic, Sociological, and Psychological Aspects of Aggression* (New York: The Free Press, 1954), reported that for
blacks in this country the ratio of homicides to suicides (7.2 to 1) was 36

times higher than the corresponding ratio among whites (0.2 to 1). The homicide rate alone among blacks in this country was 11 times as high as the rate among whites, and even higher in some of the larger cities. Marvin E. Wolfgang, *Patterns in Criminal Homicide* (1958; New York: John Wiley & Sons [Science Editions], 1966), found the black homicide rate in Philadelphia to be 14 times higher than the white rate. These findings, which were first reported in the 1950s, have been consistently repeated in every study of this subject that has been made since then. Marc Riedel and Margaret Zahn, *The Nature and Patterns of American Homicide* (Washington, D.C.: National Institute of Justice, U.S. Department of Justice, 1985), for example, reported detailed analyses of homicide rates in eight American cities over the eleven-year period 1968–78, and found that the black homicide rate was from six to fifteen times higher than the white rate in each of them.

Studies of a number of native African populations with intact (non-Westernized) cultures, as reported in the anthropologist Paul Bohannan's *African Homicide and Suicide* (Princeton, N.J.: Princeton University Press, 1960) have shown homicide rates that are far below those among blacks in this country; in fact, many populations of whites in this country (e.g., in the Southern states) have higher homicide rates than are seen in many native African communities. These kinds of data are important, for they indicate that the elevated black homicide rate in this country is not a function of race, biology, or heredity, but of the conditions to which blacks are subjected in the United States. There is every reason to think that black violence in the United States has been caused by white racism (past and present). And, I would add, the intervening variable is shame.

Comparing lower- with upper-class homicide/suicide ratios, we find the same inversion, though not quite as extreme: The lower-class homicide/suicide ratio is 10 to 20 times higher than the upper-class ratio (depending on the study, and how "upper" the class is). Wolfgang, judging social class by occupation, concluded that "90 to 95 percent of [those who committed murder] of either race [black or white] were in the lower end of the occupational scale, or from the category of skilled workers down through the unemployed. See Wolfgang, op. cit., p. 37. For other studies that document the stability and replicability of this same inverse correlation between socioeconomic status and the homicide/suicide ratio throughout this entire century, see Henry and Short, op. cit.; Paul C. Holinger, *Violent Deaths in the United*

States: An Epidemiologic Study of Suicide, Homicide, and Accidents (New York: The Guilford Press, 1987); Albert P. Iskrant and Paul V. Joliet, *Accidents and Homicide*, Vital and Health Statistics Monographs, American Public Health Association (Cambridge, Mass.: Harvard University Press, 1968); Morton Kramer, et al., *Mental Disorders/Suicide*, Vital and Health Statistics Monographs, American Public Health Association (Cambridge, Mass.: Harvard University Press, 1972).

The rate of interpersonal homicide alone is many times higher among the poor than among the rich in every nation in which it has been studied; and the suicide rate, while it is sometimes elevated among the poorest and most miserable, desperate, and helpless of the poor, such as those who are sick and elderly, homeless, or "skid row" alcoholics, is consistently so overshadowed by the much higher homicide rate among the poor that the homicide-suicide ratio is significantly higher among the poor than among the rich in every nation in which reliable statistics are available.

Chapter 9 (pp. 209–223)

1. See his classic exposition of this concept, *The Study of Instinct* (New York: Oxford Univ. Press, 1969).

2. *The Harper Dictionary of Modern Thought*, eds. Alan Bullock and Stephen Trombley (New York: Harper & Row, 1977), p. 426.

3. "The Misuse of the Concept of Instinct." In *Instinct*, ed. Birney-Teevan (Princeton: Van Nostrand, 1961), pp. 16–17.

4. J.P. Scott, *Aggression* (Chicago: Univ. of Chicago Press, 1958).

5. R.G. Sipes, "War, sport and aggression: An empirical test of two rival theories," *Amer. Anthropolog.*, 75:64–86, 1975.

6. James Q. Wilson and Richard Herrnstein, *Crime and Human Nature* (New York: Simon and Schuster, 1985).

7. *Understanding and Preventing Violence*, National Academy of Sciences Panel on the Understanding and Prevention of Violent Behavior, eds. Albert J. Reiss, Jr., and Jeffrey A. Roth (Washington, D.C.: National Academy Press, 1993), p. 118.

8. Terrie E. Moffitt, Sarnoff A. Mednick, and William F. Gabrielli, Jr., "Predicting careers of criminal violence: descriptive data and predispositional factors." In David A. Brizer and Martha Crowner, eds., *Current Approaches*

to the *Prediction of Violence* (Washington, D. C., American Psychiatric Press, 1989), pp. 13–34.

9. C. R. Cloninger and I. I. Gottesman, "Genetic and Environmental Factors in Antisocial Behavior Disorders." In S.A. Mednick, T. E. Moffitt, and S. A. Stack (eds.), *The Causes of Crime: New Biological Approaches* (Cambridge: Cambridge University Press, 1987); M. Bohman, C. R. Cloninger, S. Sigvardsson, and A.L. von Knorring, "Predisposition to petty criminality in Swedish adoptees: I. Genetic and Environmental Heterogeneity," *Archives of General Psychiatry*, 39:1233–1241, 1982.

10. Allan Siegel and Allan F. Mirsky, "The neurobiology of violence and aggression." Unpublished background research review prepared for the National Academy of Sciences Panel on the Understanding and Prevention of Violent Behavior, Washington, D.C., 1993, p. 59.

11. Reiss and Roth, op. cit., p. 118.

12. *Ibid.*, p. 12.

13. *Ibid.*, p. 122.

14. *Ibid.*, pp. 123–24.

15. *Ibid.*, p. 189.

16. *Ibid.*, p. 14.

17. *Ibid.*, p. 13.

18. *Ibid.*, p. 13.

19. *Ibid.*, p. 13.

Chapter 10 (pp. 225–239)

1. Wyatt-Brown, p. 35.

Epilogue (pp. 241–267)

1. Tolstoy, op. cit., p. 559 (emphasis added).

2. Violence is a part, usually a large part, of the history of all societies. As Gibbon put it, "History . . . is, indeed, little more than the register of the crimes, follies, and misfortunes of mankind" (*Decline and Fall of the Roman Empire*, Chap. 3). I refer to history in general here, because I want to make it clear that in focusing on the American character, and America's unsolved and rapidly worsening problem with violence, I do not mean to imply that America is unique with respect to having either a history of violence or

present problems with it. But we are unique among the democracies of the world, and among the economically developed nations of the world, and among all other nations that are counted as part of "Western civilization," with respect to the sheer magnitude of criminal violence in our society. No other nation in any of those groups even comes close to the level of individual or interpersonal violence that we inflict and suffer. And I do not know of any other nation or culture in the history of the world that has inflicted *more* collective violence on its victims than white (or European) Americans have inflicted on both native Americans and African-Americans over the past five centuries, although many others may well have killed, enslaved, and raped roughly *as many* people.

A C K N O W L E D G M E N T S

I HAVE BEEN WRITING THIS BOOK ALL MY LIFE, AND MANY PEOPLE HAVE CONTRIBUTED TO my thinking, more than I could possibly name or thank in this short space. The early development of my ideas about the emotions of shame, pride, guilt, and innocence was greatly facilitated by the insightful comments and wide learning of several inspiring teachers, mentors, and advisers who range across the whole spectrum of the human sciences—among them the sociologist David Riesman; the psychologists Daniel J. Levinson, Elliott Mishler, and Lawrence Kohlberg; the psychoanalysts Douglas Bond, J. Douglas Lenkoski, and Erik Erikson; the anthropologists Dorothy Lee and Cora DuBois; and two pioneers in the development of social, community, and preventive psychiatry, Milton Greenblatt and Gerald Caplan.

I was inspired by Elvin Semrad to work with the most deeply disturbed individuals, at a time when psychoanalytic attention was being restricted mostly to those at the healthier end of the spectrum of mental functioning. Gerald Adler introduced me to the possibility, and the importance, of extending that approach to those whose unsolved psychological and social problems had led to their imprisonment for violent or other antisocial behavior. Shervert Frazier later expanded my opportunity to work with this population in prisons and prison mental hospitals. And the person who first influenced me to approach violence as a problem in public health and preventive medicine was Bernard Lown, through his founding of two groups devoted to educating the public about the medical dimensions of collective violence: Physicians for Social Responsibility and International Physicians for the Prevention of Nuclear War.

Perhaps the single most direct catalyst for the writing of this book was the invitation to deliver the Erikson Lectures at Harvard University in 1991. For that opportunity I am deeply grateful to Dorothy Austin, the director of the Erikson Center. Further development of this material became possible when the Association of Child Psychotherapists, the Scholarship and Guidance Association, and the Chicago Institute for Psychoanalysis, through the kind offices of Irving B. Harris, president of the

Harris Foundation and the Erikson Institute, and William W. Harris, treasurer of KidsPac, invited me to give the eighteenth annual Esther Schour Zetland Lecture on the subject of violence in 1992.

I am thankful also to the Institute of Criminology and Clare Hall, of the University of Cambridge, England, for giving me the opportunity to write this book as a Visiting Fellow, from 1993 to 1994. I especially want to thank Dr. Adrian Grounds for his intellectual colleagueship and personal friendship, and his generosity in making it possible for me to gain access to the full range of British institutions in which I was interested. The acting director of the Institute of Criminology, David Farrington, and Lorraine Gelsthorpe were also very hospitable to me while I was writing this book in England, extending me every courtesy and convenience, for which I am deeply grateful. Drs. Nicholas Humphrey, Terri Apter, David Good, and Ian Goodyer all gave me further opportunities, which I deeply appreciate, to present my work in progress before diverse audiences at Cambridge University, and to benefit from the ensuing discussions. I benefited especially from the detailed and perceptive comments of Anthony Giddens, professor of sociology at Cambridge.

I am very grateful to Dr. Estela V. Welldon, who has become both a colleague and a friend, and who was most generous in facilitating the presentation and development of my work in progress, both at the Portman Clinic of the Tavistock Institute, London, and at the 1995 meeting of the International Association for Forensic Psychotherapy, of which she was president. Additional thanks are due to Dr. Welldon and to Anthony, Lord Lloyd, and his colleagues among the senior Law Lords of England, who invited me and a small group of British and American colleagues to participate in an intellectually challenging and stimulating weekend retreat in Windsor Great Park in 1994, during which we had a chance to engage in an intensive discussion of the psychiatric approach to understanding the causes and prevention of violent criminal behavior.

I also want to give special thanks to Dr. Murray Cox, my "new old friend," for inviting me to write a chapter for Volume II of *Forensic Psychotherapy: Crime, Psychodynamics and the Offender Patient* (London, England, and Bristol, Pennsylvania: Jessica Kingsley, 1995), of which he is co-editor, which stimulated me to develop further some of the ideas presented in this book. The publisher, Ms. Jessica Kingsley, was also most supportive in that endeavor. I think of Dr. Cox as my British "doppelganger," since he, more than almost anyone else I know, shares my deep interest in two kinds of tragedy and the many ways in which they illuminate each other: the tragedies of Shakespeare and the tragedies of everyday life, as exemplified by the violent individuals who come to inhabit our prisons and hospitals for the criminally insane. The only other person I know who shares those interests to the same degree—but with the emphasis on the former rather than the latter—is my close friend Tina Packer, founder and artistic director of Shakespeare and Company, of Lenox, Massachusetts, who has very kindly invited me to participate with her and her group in developing and expressing, intellectually, emotionally, and artistically, the reciprocity between art and life—Shakespearean tragedy and everyday tragedy. Ms. Packer's colleague and former student, Janet Land, also facilitated the development of my work by arranging for me to present and discuss it in Toronto in 1992 and 1993, with professionals in drama and forensic psychiatry.

One of my deepest debts, and certainly the most specific one, without which this book absolutely could not have been written, is to the many men, and the few women, who were incarcerated in the various prisons and prison mental hospitals of the United States, the United Kingdom, and Canada. They were my teachers in the subject of violence. Most of the perpetrators of violence whom I have come to know are also among the group to whom I have dedicated this book—the victims of violence. Their joining with me in this inquiry into the causes of violence has made this book possible. Where I have quoted, paraphrased, or summarized what they said, I have changed their names and all identifying information, in order to protect their privacy. I have often altered the geographical location in which they were incarcerated or in which they committed whatever violent acts that led to their incarceration. My therapeutic work and diagnostic, prognostic, and forensic psychiatric evaluations with violent individuals, and my consultations about group and collective violence (including prison riots, hostage-taking incidents, hunger strikes, terrorism, gang rapes, prison suicides and homicides, and numerous other examples of individual and collective violence), have taken place in maximum-security prisons and mental hospitals throughout the United States, Canada, and the United Kingdom. I want to emphasize here that the case material on which I have drawn in this book ranges across all those states and nations. The fact that I have worked most intensively in the prisons and mental hospitals of Massachusetts does not mean that the examples cited in this book necessarily come from that source; they are equally likely to come from other states in this country, and from corresponding institutions in Canada, England, Scotland, Ireland, and Wales.

Another group without which the work presented in this book could not have been accomplished, and to whom I am profoundly grateful, is the extraordinarily competent and dedicated staff of psychologists, social workers, and psychiatrists with whom I had the good fortune to be able to work during my years of directing the Prison Mental Health Service and the prison mental hospital in Massachusetts. I learned so much from so many people about the violent population with whom we were working that I cannot name everyone to whom I am indebted, but I particularly want to thank those with whom I worked especially closely at one time or another during the past twenty-five years, especially Marie King, Silvia Dominguez, Steven Caliri, Joan Eccleston, Cynthia Jeffers, Wesley Profit, Renate Wack, Pamela Graves, and Ebi Okara; and among consultants to our various programs, Drs. Robert Hopkins, Chester Pierce, and Thomas Gutheil. Of particular help to me was Dr. Cornelis Heijn. I was also fortunate to be able to work closely with numerous judges and attorneys throughout the criminal justice system whose dedication and competence were an inspiration to everyone who knew them. Also too many to mention, I name two judges with whom I worked frequently and closely, the Honorable Maurice Richardson and the late Edith Fine.

I would also like to express my gratitude to the administrators and corrections officers of the various prisons and prison mental hospitals in which I have worked. Without their presence, I could not have engaged in the clinical work I did. I emphasize this because the stereotype of the brutal prison guard or warden is so popular and widely believed, and also because in this book I cite examples of how prisons as they are presently structured, in the United States especially, show much higher levels of violence on the part of both inmates and officers than either of those groups would commit under other conditions. I want to thank those officers and officials who facilitated my work in the prisons and who were themselves models of humane and effective treatment, often despite the conditions under which they were forced to work.

Every author should be so lucky as to have agents as skilled and knowledgeable as John Brockman and Katinka Matson, who have also been models of understanding and support. My deepest thanks to them for their help and friendship.

Finally, I want to extend my deepest gratitude to three individuals who saw what I was trying to say, believed in it, and helped me to express it in as clear, succinct, and well-organized a way as possible. Without their encouragement, support, and energetic editorial help, this book would not be what it is. Dorothy Austin took a lengthy manuscript in hand and helped to shape it into a readable book. Jane Isay, my editor and publisher, brought her great editorial skill and experience to bear on my work, and devoted herself to the completion of the project.

Most of all, my wife, Carol Gilligan, encouraged me to draw on the whole range of my experiences with violence, to speak from my deepest self, and to write in my own voice. Her eye for clarity and organization and her ear for tone and nuance were invaluable. In addition, my three grown sons, Jonathan, Timothy, and Christopher, have each made deeply intelligent comments and suggestions that have improved the book beyond what I could have done without their help. My family, of course, was helpful in many more ways than just with respect to the manuscript. No one member of a family can spend long hours engaged in physically and emotionally draining work in the most stressful and dangerous institutions in our society without exposing the entire family to a degree of emotional strain and sacrifice, which comes at a high price to everyone. I could not have had the experiences or gained the knowledge that I have attempted to summarize in this book without the willingness of my whole family to make that sacrifice and to give me the moral support I needed in order to persevere in what I was attempting to do. To speak merely of gratitude for what they have given me is an understatement that is justifiable only because of the inadequacy of any words to express their generosity toward me, and my love for them.

It goes without saying that no one except myself is responsible for whatever errors of fact or interpretation are still to be found in this book. In writing it I have been reminded of the French poet who commented that one never finishes a poem, one merely abandons it. I have had to abandon this book, with all its shortcomings, in order to publish it at all. It is of course not the last word on the many subjects subsumed under the concept of violence; the most I can hope for is that it is the first word on some of them. I have written it in the hope that it might influence the public policy debate on the subject of violence in the direction of focusing more on answerable questions such as, What are the public policies and social conditions that stimulate or prevent violence? and less on unanswerable ones such as, How much punishment does any particular violent person, or category of crime, "deserve"? My final acknowledgment will be to those readers who respond to it in that spirit.

I N D E X

Abel, 109
Abrahamsen, David, 272n. 11
Acting out, 61–62, 212
Adams, John, 198–99
Adler, Gerald, 25
Adoption studies, 214–15
African-Americans
  high death rates, 193–95
  as objects of violence, 197
  as perpetrators of violence, 222
  and revolution of rising expectations, 202
  social shame felt by, 199–200, 203–5,
    206, 208
  structural violence and, 193–200, 203–8,
    222, 290n. 38
Aggressive violence, 16–27, 98–99, 211–14,
  221–23
Alcock, Norman, 195
Alcohol, violence and, 188, 219
American system, 145–48
Anabaptists, 226–27
Andersonville prison, 16
Anglicanism, 13
Angola (La.) State Penitentiary, 170–72,
  174–75, 178–79, 181
Animals
  aggression in, 211, 214, 221
  dominance and submission in, 151–52

Anti-Semitism, 67–69
Ann S. (case study), 124
Antisocial personality, 25, 113, 183, 215–16
Antony and Cleopatra (Shakespeare), 72
Arendt, Hannah, 68, 198–99
Aristotle, 4, 65
Arkansas state prisons, 285n. 10
Atmore (Ala.) state prison, 169–70
Auburn (N.Y.) prison, 146
Augustine, St., 273n. 3
Authoritarianism, 212–13

Badlands (movie), 37
Baroja, Julio Caro, 282n. 3
Bartollos, Clemens, 170, 176
Beaumont, Gustave de, 146
Beecher (Episcopal bishop), 13
Behavioral violence, 192, 195, 196
  etiology of, 200–208
  See also Structural violence; Warfare
Beloved (Morrison), 20
Berkowitz, David, 38–39, 53
Bible, 57, 70–71, 83, 109
Billy A. (case study), 107–9
Biological violence, 104–5, 209–23
  civilization and, 234–35
  two innate variables, 221–23
Black Rage (Grier and Cobbs), 203

Blacks. *See* African-Americans
Body language, 73–75
Bohannan, Paul, 291n. 38
Boone, Daniel, 15
Boston Brahmins, 245–46
Brain lesions, 217–18
Brandeis, Louis D., 272n. 12
Brenner, M. H., 194
Brown v. Board of Education (1954), 203
Bulhan, H. A., 194
Burke, Edmund, 250
Burke, Kenneth, 61
Burkert, Walter, 78

Cain, 109, 265
Capital punishment, 41–42, 95, 167, 272n.
    12
Cappannari, Stephen, 68
Carelessness, 100
Caste, 199–208. (*see also* Social class
    system; Racism)
Cather, Willa, 13
Charles B. (case study), 124–25
Chekhov, Anton, 32
Chesnut, Mary, 231
Chester T. (case study), 106–7
Child abuse, 43, 45–47, 49, 50, 189, 218,
    232
Childers, Thomas, 275n. 11
Christian communism, 226
Civilization, 233–35, 267
Clark, Kenneth, 203–4
Class. *See* Social class system
Classless societies, 226
Cobb, Jonathan, 200–201
Cobbs, Price M., 203
Collective violence, 66–69, 141, 275–76nn.
    10, 11
Colvin, John, 15–16
Communism, Christian, 226
Community, 119–20, 252–53, 260–61
Cotton, Donald, 176
Courts. *See* Legal process
Crime
    causes of, 89–102, 279n.1 (*see also*
        Theories)
    heredity and, 215
    incomprehensible, 132–35
    policies that increase, 187–90
    social class and "war on," 186, 187
    socioeconomic systems and, 226
    See also Murder; Punishment; Violence
Crime And Human Nature (Wilson and
    Herrnstein), 213
Criminals. *See* Perpetrators; Prison inmates
Criminology, 100

Culture
    gender roles and, 229–33
    personality and, 96–97
    punishment and, 140–41
    self-esteem and, 205–6
    and violence, 225–28, 233–35
    See also Civilization
Culture of guilt, 227
Culture of shame, 227–28
Cultures of honor, 230–33, 261–63
Cultures of violence, 15–16, 66–69, 112,
    227–28
Currie, Elliott, 22

Dante Alighieri, 29, 31, 32, 48, 143, 158
Darwin, Charles, 64, 73–74
Davis, Allan J., 170, 173
Death. *See* Capital punishment; Living
    death; Murder; Suicide
Death Comes for the Archbishop (Cather), 13
Death penalty. *See* Capital punishment
Death rates, 100–101, 192–96
Death of self, 36, 47–49, 52, 96–97, 153,
    154, 256, 271n. 5
Death of Tragedy, The (Steiner), 17
Defensive violence, 98–99, 235
Degradation ceremony, 152–54
Delilah, 70
Denmark, 215
Dennis X. (case study), 78–85
Dependency, 81–82, 117–19, 121–32, 213–
    14, 237–38
Deprivation, relative, 201–3, 239
Dickens, Charles, 146–47
Discrimination. *See* Racism; Social class
    system
Disease, violence as, 99–100, 103–4, 135–
    36, 272–73n. 12
Disrespect, 105–10
Domestic violence, 13–15, 45–47, 130–32,
    179, 280–81n. 6
Domination, 151–52
Donald C. (case study), 46–47
Dostoevsky, Feodor, 96, 213, 237, 273n. 2,
    281n. 7
Douglas R. (case study), 125–26
Drugs, 23, 187–88, 219–21, 245–46
Du Bois, W. E. B., 199
Dumond, Robert W., 284–85nn. 10, 16–17,
    20
Dunn, James, 178–79
Dusk of Dawn (Du Bois), 199

Ears, 83, 144
Edgerton, Samuel, 157–58, 159, 274–75n.
    9, 283nn. 17–21

Education, 188, 206
Einstein, Albert, vii, 110
Ellison, Ralph, 199
Empiricism, 19–20
Engel, George, 99–100
Environment, changing, 50–51
Envy, 68–69
Epilepsy, 217–18
Erikson, Erik, 64–65
Evil, 23, 91–92, 251–52, 258
Evil eye, 65–66, 68, 69, 70–75
Eyes, 58, 65, 65–66, 69, 70–75, 78, 142, 144, 147 (see also Evil eye)

Fame, pride and, 198
Families. See Domestic violence; Honor; Stories, family
Fanon, Frantz, 110, 203
Fantasies, 61–62
Faust (Goethe), 58
Fear, 77, 113, 156–57, 189
Federal Bureau of Investigation (FBI), 173, 280n. 6
Feelings, absence of, 35, 36, 47–49, 52
Forgiveness, 24–25, 93
Foucault, Michel, 145
Fox, James Alan, 271n. 4
Fra Angelico, 158
Franklin, Benjamin, 4, 269n. 1
Frazier, Shervert, 135
French Revolution, 145, 202
Freud, Sigmund, 21, 113, 118
    on cultural super ego, 140–41
    on instinctual violence, 210, 213, 234–35
    on Oedipus, 49–50
    on paranoia, 154–55
    on symbolism, 61, 62, 144
Friedman, Lawrence, 146, 282nn. 8–11

Gabrielli, William F., Jr., 215
Gaddi, Taddeo, 159
Gandhi, Mahatma, ix, 191
Gang rapes, 185n. 21
Garfinkel, Harold, 152–53
Garrity, W. Arthur, 41
Gender
    biological violence and, 221–23
    honor vs. shame, 228, 233
    socialization and violence, 16–17, 189, 229–33, 237
    of violence victims, 269–70n. 2, 280–81n. 6
    See also Maleness; Women
Genitalia
    punishment and, 143–44, 274n. 9
    as shaming organs, 83–84, 151, 152, 164

Genocide, 69, 196, 227, 235, 242–43
George T. (case study), 125
Germ theory, 103–4, 135–36
Gibbon, Edward, 293n. 2
Giotto di Bondone, 158
Goethe, Johann Wolfgang von, 58
Goffman, Erving, 152
Grier, William H., 203
Groth, Nicholas, 176
Guilt
    absence of, 35, 60, 77, 80, 113
    inhibiting love, 273n. 3
    morality and, 6, 8, 235–36
    pain and punishment relieving, 206–7
    shame of poverty vs., 198
    suicide and, 207, 227, 265–66
    syndromes caused by, 273–74n. 3
Guilt-ethics, 235–36

Harlem (N.Y.), 193–94
Harold R. (case study), 46
Harvard Medical School, 25, 26, 124
Hate, 53–54
Hawthorne, Nathaniel, 253
Hell
    absence of love and joy as, 273n. 3
    Dante on, 29, 31, 32, 48
    Dostoevsky on, 273n. 2
    prisons as, 29–33, 40–41, 157–61
Henry, Andrew F., 207, 290n. 38
Heritability (of violence), 214–17
Heroism, 30
Herrick, E., 284–85n. 10
Herrnstein, Richard, 213
Hitler, Adolf, 67–69, 242–43, 275n. 10, 277n. 15
Holocaust, 69, 196
Homicide. See Murder
Homophobia, 76, 81, 83–84, 156–57, 164, 171, 189
Homosexual panic, 79, 156–57, 164, 283n. 1
Homosexual rape, 154–57, 164–83, 189, 283n. 1, 284n. 2
Honor
    family, 261–65
    male violence and, 111–12, 189, 230–31, 233
    punishment and, 144
    shame vs., 228, 231–32, 233, 235
    See also Justice
"Horatio Alger" myth, 202–3
Human Rights Watch, 24
Humiliation. See Shame
Hutterites, 226–27
Huxley, Sir Julian, 74

Impulsivity, 58
Inadequacy feelings, 130, 131–35, 200–203, 214, 222
Incest, 47, 50, 61–62, 179, 232
Inferiority. *See* Inadequacy feelings
Innocence, 6, 8, 206–7, 257
Insanity, 250, 257, 258 (*see also* Antisocial personality)
Insanity defense, 6, 8–9, 101–2
Instinctual violence, 209–14, 223, 234–35
Intact cultures, 205–6
Integration, racial, 203–4
Invisible Man, The (Ellison), 199
Irrational acts, 59, 60

Jacobson, Edith, 197
Japan, 227–28, 235
Jeffrey L. (case study), 166–68
Jews, 67–69
Job (Old Testament), 7, 40–41
Jose L. (case study), 126
Joy, 273n. 3
Judas Iscariot, 265
Justice (emotional sense of), 11–12, 18–19
Justice (legal). *See* Legal system
Justice, William W., 173–74

Kane, Thomas, 176, 285n. 21, 286n. 24
Katz, Jack, 77, 277n. 19
Kelvin C. (case study), 120–23
King, Martin Luther, Jr., 197
King Lear (Shakespeare), 58, 72–73
Kohler, Gernot, 195

Laite, William, 177–78
Lamar, Lucius Quintus Cincinnatus, 231
Lambert, Lige, 170
Language. *See* Symbolism
Last Judgment, 158–59
Legal process
  discourse of, 6, 257
  goals of, 18–19
  as Last Judgment, 158–59
  and psychiatry, 6, 8, 101–2, 250
  See also Punishment
Levi, Primo, 57
Levin, Jack, 271n. 4
Leyton, Elliott, 272n. 11
Lipset, Seymour Martin, 67, 275n. 11
Literature. *See* Myth; Symbolism
Living death, 31–34, 36, 37–41, 43, 271n. 5
Lloyd A. (case study), 148–51
Lockwood, Daniel, 176
Lorenz, Konrad, 210
Louisiana prison system, 170–72, 174–75, 178–79, 180, 181–82

Love
  absence of, 47, 51–54, 113, 273nn. 2, 3
  guilt and shame inhibiting, 236, 273n. 3
  need for, 129–32, 236–37
  of self, 47–48, 51–52, 54
  tragedy and, 2
Luther, L. Bernard, 210–11
Lynd, Helen Merrell, 281n. 7

Macbeth (Shakespeare), 232
Macek, Richard, 271n. 5
Mafia, 262–63
Magical thinking, 144
Major, John, 150
Malcolm X, 203–5
Maleness
  aggression and, 16–17, 30, 111–12, 189, 221–23, 228
  prison rapes and, 173, 175, 180–81, 284n. 1
  socialization of, 229–33, 267
Marx, Karl, 67, 199, 201
Massachusetts state prison system, 26, 29, 31–33, 41
Matthew T. (case illustration), 247–67
Medea, 20, 58
Mednick, Sarnoff A., 215
Melville, Herman, 15, 23, 246–47
Men. *See* Maleness
Menninger, Karl, 139
Mental illness. *See* Insanity
Miller, Arthur, 103
Miller, S. J., 170
Mirsky, Allan F., 215
Moby-Dick (Melville), 15, 23, 246–47
Moffitt, Terrie E., 215
Molière, Jean Baptiste, 92, 279–80n. 4
Morality
  assumptions of, 18
  guilt-ethic, 235–36
  of shaming, 200
  simplification of, 8
  and violence, 9–10, 17, 18–19, 24, 93–94
Morality play, 7–8, 11
Morrison, Helen, 271n. 5
Morrison, Toni, 20
Mortality rate. *See* Death rates
Mortification, 49 (*see also* Shame)
Moss, Leonard, 68
Motivation 9–10, 18–19, 111 (*see also* Shame)
Murder
  male perpetrators and victims, 16–17, 269–70n. 2
  mate killings, 280–81n. 6
  paranoia and, 75–77

personality disorder correlates, 101, 102
race and gender correlates, 222
rate in United States, 95, 194, 291–92n. 38
righteousness and, 18, 77, 277n. 19
ritual and, 80, 85
social class and, 207, 290n. 38
suicides of perpetrators, 41–42
See also Prison inmates; Suicide
Mutilation, 39–40, 52, 58, 59, 64, 70–71
Myth
  origins of violence in, 49–50
  reflecting reality, 4, 23, 57
  symbolic language of, 57–58, 70–73
  See also Stories, family

Nacci, Peter L., 176, 285n. 21, 286n. 24
Narcissism, 183, 273n. 3
National Academy of Sciences, 90–91, 214, 215, 216, 217–19
National Commission on the Causes and Prevention of Violence, 280n. 6, 289n. 25
Native Americans, 241, 243–45
Nazi Germany, 66–69, 235, 242–43, 272n. 12, 275nn. 10, 11
New England, 245–46, 247, 253
Newton, Sir Isaac, 110
New York state prison system, 146, 176
New York Times, 182–83
Nonviolence, 197
Nuclear war, 196
Nussbaum, Hedda, 77

Obscurity, 198, 199
Oedipus, 49–50, 58, 266
Othello (Shakespeare), 58

Pain
  emotional responses and, 40, 50–53
  as guilt-feelings relief, 206–7
  punishment as, 184
  vulnerability to, 52–53
Palmer, Stuart, 273n. 1
Paranoia
  anti-Semitism and, 69
  murder and, 75–76
  of prison inmates, 107–8, 155–57
  sexuality and, 80, 154–55, 156–57
  shame and, 65, 75–76, 107, 273n. 3
Passivity. *See* Dependency
Pasteur, Louis, 135
Pathos, 6–7, 8, 234
Patriarchy. *See* Structural violence
Patterson, Haywood, 169

Penal system. *See* Prison inmates; Prison system
Penance, 207, 274n. 3
Pence, Walter, 181
Pennsylvania system, 145–48
Perpetrators
  as "living dead," 31–34
  motives of, 9–10, 18–19, 111
  ordinariness of, 33–34, 271n. 4
  personality of, 183
  symbolizing evil, 23
  tragedy and, 7
  as victims, 10–11, 45–47
  See also Prison inmates
Personality, culture and, 96–97
Personality disorders, 101–2, 183
Phelps, C. Paul, 171, 175, 182
Philadelphia prisons, 145–47, 170, 173
Pitt-Rivers, Julian, 109–10
Plato, 58, 61–62
Political violence, 196
"Pornography of violence," 30
Poverty
  death rates and, 192–96
  education and, 188
  and "insult of oblivion," 199
  as pain and punishment, 207
  relative deprivation feelings and, 201–2
  shame and, 197, 198, 201–2, 237–39
  as violence, ix, 191
  See also Social class system; Structural violence
Preventability (of violence), 21–22, 26, 211, 225–26, 233, 236–37, 267
Preventive medicine. *See* Public health
Pride. *See* Honor; Self-esteem
Prison inmates, 31–43
  booking process, 152–55
  case studies, 34–39, 115–23, 128–30, 148–51, 166–68
  as child abuse victims, 43, 45–47
  disrespect and, 105–10
  heterosexual deprivation of, 164–65
  need to be cared for, 121–28, 129–30
  paranoia of, 107–8, 155–57
  psychiatric understanding of, 25–26
  rape among, 165–82, 284n. 10, 285n. 21
  rates of, 23–24, 31, 95
  self-anesthetization of, 50–52
  suicides of, 41–42
  violence among, 163–87
Prison system
  guards, 159–61, 168–72, 178
  as hell, 29–33, 157–61
  punishment in, 145–51
  racism in, 172

shame and, 107–9
silence system in, 145–48
Psychiatry, 8–9, 17–18, 25–26, 101–2, 250
Psychoanalysis, tragedy and, 21, 258–59
Psychological deprivation, 201–2, 239
Psychopaths. *See* Antisocial personality
Public health, ix, 17, 19, 92–94, 97–98, 99,
    103–5, 192–95, 236, 239
Punishment
    crime intertwined with, 9, 18–19, 144,
        182–90
    guilt feelings and, 113, 206–7
    prisoner violence as, 163–66
    rational self-interest theory and, 95
    symbolism of, 70–71, 139–61, 182–84,
        274n. 9
    violence in context of, 24–25, 184–85
    See also Capital punishment; Prison
        inmates; Prison system

Racism
    as biological concept, 209
    in prison system, 172
    in social class system, 188–89, 199–200,
        205
Ralph W. (case study), 34–36
Randolph W. (case study), 46, 115–20
Rape
    FBI definition of, 173
    motives of, 84
    in prison system, 165–82, 284n. 10,
        285n. 21
    punishments for, 143–44, 274n. 9
    women and, 179, 232
Rationality (of violence), 9, 59–66, 85
Rational self-interest theory, 94–96, 102
Rejection, 48, 247–50
Relative deprivation, 201–3
Renaissance, Italian, 142–43, 157–59
Remorse. *See* Guilt
Respect. *See* Disrespect
Responsibility (acceptance of), 60–61
Resurrection (Tolstoy), 243–44
Revenge, 67, 273n. 3 (*see also* Honor)
Rideau, Wilbert, 170, 172, 176, 179, 180,
    181, 284nn. 3–4, 8–9, 285nn. 11–12,
    286nn. 26–33
Riedel, Marc, 291n. 38
"Rising expectations, revolution of," 202
Ritual, 77, 78, 80, 85, 152–55
Ross L. (case study), 59–66, 69–70, 75, 78,
    84
Rundle, Frank L., 172, 174
Russia, 23, 32, 95

Sadism, 183–84, 273n. 3
Samson, 58, 70
Saudi Arabia, 142
Scacco, Anthony M., Jr., 170, 174, 177–78
Scarlet Letter, The (Hawthorne), 253
Schoeck, Helmut, 277n. 13
Schumer, Charles, 186
Scott, J. P., 98, 211
Scottsboro Boy (Patterson), 169
Self-esteem
    guilt and, 207, 236
    intact cultures and, 205–6
    love and, 51–54, 273n. 3
    poverty and, 198–203
    shame as opposite of, 47–49, 198, 202,
        203
    violence and, 80–81, 111
    vulnerability and, 52–53
Self-love. *See* Self-esteem
Self-mutilation, 39–40, 52
Sennett, Richard, 200–201
Sensationalism, 30
Sex. *See* Gender
Sex hormones, 221–22
Sexism, 189
Sexuality
    child abuse and, 47, 50
    cultures of honor and, 230–31
    maturity and, 81, 82
    paranoia and, 80, 154–55, 156–57
    in prisons, 164–83, 283n. 1, 284nn. 2,
        10, 285n. 21
    shame and, 63–64, 79–84, 116–17, 151–
        52, 154–55, 164
Shakespeare, William, 12, 57, 58, 71–73
Shame
    as absence of self-love, 47–48
    civilization and, 234–35
    collective violence and, 67
    concealment underlying, 64–65
    culture of, 227–28
    dependency and, 81–82, 117–19, 128–32,
        213–14, 237–38
    disrespect and, 105–10
    ears and, 83
    envy and, 69
    eyes and, 65–66, 69, 70–75, 78, 142, 144
    fear of, 77
    genitalia and, 83–84, 151, 152, 164
    honor vs., 133, 228, 231–32, 235
    inadequacy feelings and, 130, 131–35,
        200–203, 214, 228
    innocence and, 207
    logic of, 64–66, 78
    love inhibited by, 236, 273n. 3
    Marx on, 201

mutilation and, 70–71, 85
mythic symbolism of, 70–73
paranoia and, 65, 69, 75–76, 107
poverty and, 197, 198, 201, 237–39
and preconditions leading to violence,
    110–15
as primary cause of violence, 110–11
prison system and, 107–9
punishment and, 144
rape and, 179–80
rejection and, 247–50
relative deprivation and, 201–3, 239
ritual and, 151–55
sexuality and, 63–64, 79–84, 116–17,
    151–52, 154–55, 164
social class system and, 197–208
social policies to reduce, 236–39
syndromes caused by, 273n. 3
tongues and, 65–66, 70–73, 142–43
triviality and, 112, 133–35, 281n. 7
violence as, 54–55, 276n. 11
Shame-ethics, 235
Short, James F., 207, 290n. 38
Sidney B. (case study), 53–54
Siegel, Allan, 215
Sieveides, Christopher, 176
Silberman, Charles, 127–28, 279n. 1
Sipes, R. G., 212
Slavery, 197, 199
Slighting, 198
Smart, Carol, 90
Social class system, 275–76n. 11, 287n. 9,
    289n. 25
    "divide and conquer" in, 185–87
    equitable systems/lower violence rate
        correlation, 226–27, 228
    and feelings of pride/guilt vs. shame/
        innocence, 207
    homicides vs. suicides in, 207
    intact cultures and, 205–6
    lower middle class in, 199–200, 275n. 11
    and policies that increase crime, 187–90
    racism and, 188–89, 199–200, 203–5
    shame stemming from, 197, 198
    as structural violence cause, 196–200,
        223
    See also Structural violence
Society. See Culture
Sociobiology, 210
Soledad Prison (Calif.), 174
"Son of Sam." See Berkowitz, David
South Africa, 23
Soviet Union. See Russia
Spain, 142
Speth, James, 287n. 9
Spinoza, Baruch, 273n. 3

Sports, 212
Staring eyes, 74, 77
Starkweather, Charles, 37–38
Status. See Social class system
Steinberg, Joel, 76–77
Steiner, George, 17
Stories, family, 1–2, 9–10, 12–14, 16–17,
    20
Street gangs, 235, 246, 262–63
Structural violence, 191–208
    behavioral violence caused by, 196
    behavioral violence vs., 192, 195
    biological violence and, 222
    class elements in, 196–200, 223
    death rates and, 100–101
    defined and described, 192, 194
    suicide and, 290n. 38
Submission, 151–52, 154–55
Suicide
    death rate and, 100
    guilt and, 207, 227, 265–66
    heritability of, 216–17
    mental illness and, 101
    of murderers, 41–42
    social class and, 207, 290–91n. 38
Sweden, 195, 215
Sykes, Gresham, 283n. 1
Symbolism
    of action, 57–58, 61–62, 70–78
    of collective violence, 66–69
    of punishment, 70–71, 139–61, 182–84,
        274n. 9
    of shame and violence, 70–73
    of thoughts and fantasies, 61

Testosterone, 221–22
Texas prisons, 173–74, 177–78
Theories (of violence), 89–102
    as disease, vii, 99–100, 103–4, 135–36
    rational self-interest, 94–96
    skepticism of, 89–91
    value judgments and, 91–94
Thomas Aquinas, St., 273n. 3
Thucydides, 57
Tinbergen, N., 210
Tinder, Glenn, ix
Tiresias, 58
Toch, Hans, 285n. 10
Tocqueville, Alexis de, 146, 202
Tofani, Loretta, 174
Tolstoy, Leo, 243, 281n. 7
Tongues, 65–66, 70–73, 142–43
Tragedy
    justice and, 11–12
    love and, 2
    pathos vs., 6–7, 8, 234

psychoanalysis and, 21
symbolic language of, 57–58, 70–73
violence as, 4–8, 11–12, 21, 245
Tragic flaw, 246
Tragic hero, 23
Tragic literature, 57–58
Triviality, 112, 132–36, 281n. 7
Troilus and Cressida (Shakespeare), 73
Twain, Mark, 152
Twin studies, 214, 215

Unconscious minds, 61–62
Unemployment, 189, 194
United Nations Standard Minimum Rules
    for the Treatment of Prisoners, 24
United States
    class system, 199–200
    death penalty, 42, 95
    dependency in, 237–38
    homicide rate, 95, 194
    southern honor code, 231
    tragic flaw of, 15, 246
    violence in, 21–24, 95, 246, 293n. 2

Vachss, Andrew, 183–84
Value judgments, 91–94, 258
Van Dulmen, Richard, 143
Vanggaard, Thorkil, 282n. 12
Versailles treaty, 67, 275n. 10
Victims
    male vs. female, 232, 280–81n. 6
    perpetrators as, 10–11, 45–47
    and victimizers, 7
Vietnam war, 196
Violence
    as acting out, 61–62, 212
    aggressive, 16–27, 98–99, 211–14, 221–
      23
    behavioral, 192, 195, 196, 200–208
    biological, 104–5, 209–23, 234–35
    as bio-psycho-social phenomenon, 99–100
    as civilization's problem child, 267
    collective, 66–69, 141, 275–76nn. 10, 11
    defensive, 98–99, 235
    as disease, 97–99
    gender roles and, 16–17, 189, 229–33,
      237
    guilt-ethics and, 235–36
    inherited, 214–17
    instinctual, 209–14, 223, 234–35
    as morality play, 7–8, 11
    mythic roots of, 49–50
    paranoia and, 75–77
    personal responses to, 30–31
    poverty as, ix, 191
    preventibility. *See* Preventability

within prisons, 163–87
psychological meaningfulness of, 9
punishment as form of, 184
against self. *See* Suicide
shame and preconditions of, 110–15
social policies that increase rate of, 187–
    90
theories of, 89–104, 135–36
trivial incidents precipitating, 112, 132–
    36
    as ultimate humiliation, 54–55
    universal cause of, 11–12
    See also Structural violence; Tragedy;
      specific aspects and related subjects
Virchow, Rudolph, 239
Vital statistics of the United States, 286n. 6
Vulnerability, 52–53

Walter T. (case study), 128–30
Warfare
    death rates, 196
    glorification of, 30
    Japan and, 227–28
    legality of, 100
    sports and, 212
War on drugs, 23, 187–88, 220–21
Wealth
    inequality of, 198–99, 201–3, 239
    shared collective, 226
    See also Poverty
Welfare dependency, 237
Welfare state democracies, 226, 227
Williams, Tennessee, 50
Wilson, E. O., 210, 279n. 1
Wilson, James Q., 89, 213
Wolfgang, Marvin E., 222, 280n. 6, 291n.
    38
Women
    honor and, 230–32
    as perpetrators of violence, 222, 228,
      280–81n. 6
    social roles and violence, 17, 189, 229–
      33, 237, 267
    as victims of violence, 13–14, 130–32,
      170, 232, 280–81n. 6
World Health Organization, 232
World War I, 223
World War II, 68, 196, 227, 235, 242–43
Wyatt-Brown, Bertram, 144, 231

X, Malcolm. *See* Malcolm X

Y chromosome, 215–16
Young men (violence correlate), 221–22

Zahn, Margaret, 291n. 38